DAY OUTINGS FROM SAN DIEGO

ON A TANK OF GAS

Where To Go...What To Do... And How To Get There

by

Rebecca A. Sanders

A Premier Publishing Book
San Diego, California

DAY OUTINGS FROM SAN DIEGO ON A TANK OF GAS

FOURTH EDITION

DISCLAIMER

Every attempt has been made to provide correct information on the destinations listed. However, the publisher does not guarantee the accuracy of the information. At press time, the information in this book was current; however, prices, area codes and certain other information is subject to change.

Cover Design: Chris Butscher & Rebecca A. Sanders

Map Design: Dana Southwood & Han Duong

Photos: Rebecca A. Sanders, Matt Gandall, Sayonna Martin

Editors: Rebecca A. Sanders, Susan M. Humason

ISBN: 1-928905-00-5

PUBLISHER:
Premier Publishing
Susan Humason
15721 Bernardo Heights Parkway
Suite B-17
San Diego, California 92128
Tel (858) 586-7692 • Msg: (858) 485-9596
Fax: (858) 586-7389
Email: dayoutings@earthlink.net • www.dayoutings.com

Printed in the United States of America

TRIBUTE TO MATT GANDALL

Without the dream, inspiration, effort and enthusiasm of Matt Gandall,the first author and originator of *Day Outings From San Diego On A Tank Of Gas*, our book series would not have been possible. I met Matt in 1993 when he interviewed me on Palomar Mountain for a travel article he was writing for a local paper. I told him I had a printing company, and he asked if I would publish his book. I had no idea of the responsibilities of a publisher. Upon receiving his manuscript the following week, I knew immediately I wanted to take on the challenge. Matt was 82 years old at the time when we published his first edition of the San Diego book. In the three years that he and I worked together I always looked forward to our weekly meetings discussing new destinations, updates, and sales strategies. I miss seeing him shuffle into my office on Monday mornings wearing his old fishing hat. Our entire goal was to sell 500 books...we did that in a few short months. To date the San Diego edition has sold in excess of 20,000 copies.

Matt Gandall lived and traveled throughout Southern California since 1928. He had written for every major newspaper in the San Diego County area, and had articles in many magazines, including <u>Westways, Ford, Times</u>, the <u>Fedco Reporter</u> and others. In 1996, Matt Gandall passed away at the age of 85. He is missed.

Susan M. Humason
Publisher

ACKNOWLEDGEMENTS

The publisher wishes to thank the following people:

Matt Gandall, the originator of the Day Outings book, for his vision, dream and work he contributed to make the first day outings book a reality. His daughter, Ann Kelly, for allowing me to continue her father's wish in the continuation of the book after his death. Dana Southwood for creating all of the well-detailed and useful maps, Chris Butscher for his creative ideas regarding the cover design and layout.

And lastly, Rebecca Sanders for taking on the huge task of revising, updating, photographing, remapping and rewriting the entire book. Working with her has always been enjoyable. I don't believe she or I had realized the extent of work that was necessary to complete the project. I can say that I am more than pleased with the outcome, and I know that Matt would be, too.

The author wishes to thank the following people:

Michael and Deborah Sanders, for their unconditional love and endless support as my parents, for their example as extraordinary people, for their unceasing confidence as my true believers, and, *of course* for their extra bedroom, home-cooked meals and keen dog-sitting abilities while writing this book; Susan Humason, for being the brave soul to give me my very first ISBN number, for being a patient mentor and for being a generous publishing partner; the family and friends of the Sanders, Depew and Humason families for whom we could not write and publish books without the patience, support and enthusiasm of; and to all the teachers who taught me how to read and write.

DEDICATION

To the tender memory of
Marcus Joseph Brown
with all my love.

The only thing missing in America's Finest City is you.

Quincy —

To one of the most genuine + generous persons I know. Thanks for your endless support + friendship over the years.

Hope you find a little inspiration in these pages + enjoy all sunny San Diego has to offer.

Love,
Rebecca

v

Table of Contents

- SAN DIEGO COUNTY -

2) COASTAL (From South to North)   2-1

ix

3) NORTH COUNTY   3-1

6) BACKCOUNTRY 6-1

San Diego County

DOWNTOWN & CENTRAL

- Balboa Park
- Downtown
- Embarcadero
- Gaslamp Quarter
- Harbor Island & Shelter Island
- Little Italy
- Mission Valley
- Old Town
- Point Loma
- Sports Arena
- Uptown

BALBOA PARK

Any city in the world would be eager to boast this magical place of ambiance and culture. Twelve-hundred beautifully manicured acres grace the city with this centrally located park, America's largest of its kind. A sublime wooded landscape with endless floral gardens is accented by Spanish-revival buildings which house dozens of museums and attractions. The ornamental Spanish architecture was originally designed for the 1915-16 Panama-California Exposition, including the glorious Cabrillo Bridge entrance to the park. A walk westward across the bridge leads to some wonderful uptown neighborhoods with cafes, antique shops and eclectic boutiques.

Locals and tourists alike enjoy Balboa Park's lush gardens, first-rate art galleries, world-class museums and theaters. The park is a favorite choice for unlimited athletic activities, education and entertainment. It is also home to the world-famous San Diego Zoo. The best way to explore the urban cultural park is by foot. There is ample parking and a free tram shuttles visitors to and from key locations. Cafes, food carts and picnic locations abound.

For significant savings, purchase a "Passport To Balboa Park" ticket for $30.00 at the Visitors Center or any of the thirteen participating venues. The book notes the thirteen "Passport" participants with a ☆. The pass is valid for seven days from the date of purchase.

Balboa Park Visitors Center

Location:	1549 El Prado, Hospitality House
Hours:	Daily 9am-4pm
Phone:	619-239-0512 Press "0" to reach an operator
Website:	www.balboapark.org

Balboa Park Attractions

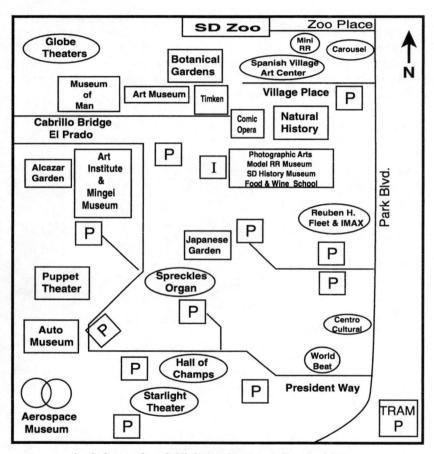

I = Information & Visitors Center   P = Parking

Balboa Park Museums

Several major museums are free one Tuesday of every month. The book lists which museums are free on which Tuesdays. Also note most museum gift shops are worth the visit.

Mingei International Museum ☆

Mingei comes from the Japanese words MIN "all people" and GEI "art". As its name suggests, the museum designs and presents intriguing, eclectic and creative exhibitions from all world cultures. Traditional and contemporary folk art is the focus. There is also a North County Mingei Museum in Escondido.

Location: 1439 El Prado, Balboa Park
Hours: Tues-Sun 10am-4pm. Closed national holidays
Admission: General-$5; Students (with ID)-$2;
                Youth(6-17)-$2; Under 6-Free
                Free 3rd Tuesday of the month
Phone: 619-239-0003
Website: www.mingei.org

Museum of Photographic Arts ☆

Contemporary and historic still photography displays enrich MoPA's outstanding permanent collection of mostly 20th century documentary work. The museum also screens unique films in a traditional-style movie theater.

Location: 1649 El Prado, Balboa Park
Hours: Daily 10am-5pm, Open until 9pm Thursdays
                Closed Thanksgiving, Dec 25, Jan 1 & July 4
Admission: General-$6, Films-$5;
                Seniors(65+)-$4, Films-$4.50;
                Military & Students (with ID)-$4, Films-$4.50;
                Youth(12-18)-$4; Under 12-Free
                Add $2 for double features
                Museum free 2nd Tuesday of the month
Phone: 619-238-7559
Website: www.mopa.org

Reuben H. Fleet Science Center
& IMAX Dome Theater ☆

This science museum embraces all ages with over a hundred interactive exhibits and three virtual reality attractions in the Virtual Zone. The displays and attractions change often, making this a favored destination for locals. The museum is designed in an entertaining hands-on manner to create a fun learning environment.

The Science Center is also home to San Diego's only IMAX theater where various films play on a giant 76-foot screen. The films tend to have an educational spin, while the screen is intended to give visitors the sensation of being in the film, similar to a simulator or virtual reality experience. Planetarium shows are also screened at the IMAX Dome Theater. Stars and animation effects are projected onto the dome, simulating the night sky anywhere in the world at any given time. Call for show times.

Location:	1875 El Prado, Balboa Park
Hours:	Daily 9:30am. Closing times vary
Admission:	General-$6.75; Seniors(65+)-$6;
	Youth(3-12)-$5.50; Under 3-Free
	Show prices vary. Expect $5.50-$15/Person
	Show price includes museum entrance
	Museum free 1st Tuesday of the month
Phone:	619-238-1233
Website:	www.rhfleet.org

San Diego Aerospace Museum ☆

Over a hundred aircraft and space vehicles, as well as endless flight-related artifacts, are on display chronicling the history and science of aviation and space flight. In addition to the "Spirit of St. Louis", highlights include an International Aerospace Hall of Fame and a covered outdoor garden and aircraft gallery called Pavilion of Flight.

Location:	2001 Pan American Plaza, Balboa Park
Hours:	Daily 10am-4pm
	Open until 5pm Memorial-Labor Day
	Closed Thanksgiving, Dec 25 & Jan 1
Admission:	General-$8; Seniors(65+)-$6;
	Youth(6-17)-$3; Under 6-Free
	Free 4th Tuesday of the month
Phone:	619-234-8291
Website:	www.aerospacemuseum.org

San Diego Automotive Museum ☆

Automotive chronology unfolds with an impressive permanent display of over eighty historically significant antique cars and vintage motorcycles. Along with special exhibitions, treasures include rare repair manuals, vintage auto publications, photos and films, as well as one of the West Coast's largest motorcycle collections.

Location:	2080 Pan American Plaza, Balboa Park
Hours:	Daily 10am-5pm
Admission:	General-$7; Youth-$3
	Free 4th Tuesday of the month
Phone:	619-231-2886
Website:	www.sdautomuseum.org

San Diego Hall of Champions Sports Museum ☆

Dedicated to the regions best athletes in more than forty sports, the museum showcases memorabilia representing thousands of hometown heroes. Photos and trophies relate the successes of people such as Ted Williams, Marcus Allen and Dan Fouts.

In addition to the displays that pay tribute to these local greats, other popular features are the hands-on "sportsability" exhibits, the multi-sport sculptures and the sports bloopers movies that are sometimes screened.

Location:	2132 Pan American Plaza, Balboa Park
Hours:	Daily 10am-4:30pm
	Closed Thanksgiving, Dec 25 & Jan 1
Admission:	General-$6; Seniors & Military (with ID)-$4;
	Youth(7-17)-$3; Under 7-Free
	Free 4th Tuesday of the month
Phone:	619-234-2544
Website:	www.sdhoc.com

San Diego Historical Society Museum ☆

Even those lackluster about history will enjoy this museum's interesting and entertaining exhibits. The society's well preserved photos, costumes and artifacts pay tribute to the city's history in fantastic permanent and rotating displays. A lesser-known gem of this museum is the Research Archive where yesteryears are accessible via banked maps, documents, nostalgia and a 2.5-million image photograph collection.

Location:	1649 El Prado, Balboa Park
Hours:	Museum: Tues-Sun 10am-4:30pm
	Archives: Thurs-Sat 10am-4pm
	Closed national holidays
	Archives closed the month of August
Admission:	General-$5; Seniors & Students (with ID)-$4;
	Youth(6-17)-$2; Under 6-Free
	Free 2nd Tuesday of the month
Phone:	619-232-6203
Website:	www.sandiegohistory.org

San Diego Model Railroad Museum ☆

The largest operating model railroad exhibit in North America permanently resides in this museum, which displays over 24,000 square feet of model railroad layouts, trains and related equipment. Visitors can play engineer in the Interactive Toy Train Gallery.

Location:	1649 El Prado, Balboa Park
Hours:	Tues-Fri 11am-4pm. Open until 5pm Sat-Sun
Admission:	General-$4; Seniors-$3;
	Military (with ID)-$2.50; Under 15-Free
	Free 1st Tuesday of the month
Phone:	619-696-0199
Website:	www.sdmodelrailroadm.com

San Diego Museum of Art ☆

San Diego's oldest and largest art museum leverages its prestige to host major traveling shows. The permanent collection contains works from American, Asian and European artists, including contemporary art and impressive Old Masters. There is also a nice outdoor sculpture garden.

Location:	1450 El Prado, Balboa Park
Hours:	Tues-Sun 10am-6pm. Open until 9pm Thursdays
Admission:	General(25+)-$8; Young Adults(18-24)-$6;
	Seniors(65+)-$6;
	Military & Students (with ID)-$6;
	Youth(6-17)-$3; Under 6-Free
	Free 3rd Tuesday of the month
Phone:	619-232-7931
Website:	www.sdmart.org

San Diego Museum of Man ☆

Human physical and cultural history over the millenniums is superbly detailed in San Diego's only anthropology museum. Of popular interest are mummies and artifacts from ancient Egypt and around the world. Compelling special exhibits complement the hallmark permanent collection. This museum is a locals favorite and often recognized with awards.

Location:	1350 El Prado, Balboa Park
Hours:	Daily 10am-4:30pm
	Closed Thanksgiving, Dec 25 & Jan 1
Admission:	General-$6; Students (with ID)-$5;
	Youth(6-17)-$3; Under 6-Free
	Free 3rd Tuesday of the month
Phone:	619-239-2001
Website:	www.museumofman.org

San Diego Natural History Museum ☆

This museum spotlights the significant geological history and the biodiversity of the southwest United States and northern Mexico region. Films and exhibits focus on the rare and endangered plants and animals of this territory. The museum also hosts a free Canyoneer Guided Nature Walk series across several locations throughout the county.

Location:	1788 El Prado, Balboa Park
Hours:	Daily 9:30am-4:30pm
	Open until 5:30 Memorial-Labor Day
	Closed Thanksgiving, Dec 25 & Jan 1
Admission:	General-$8; Seniors-$6;
	Military & Students (with ID)-$6;
	Youth(3-17)-$5; Under 3-Free
	Free 1st Tuesday of the month
Phone:	619-232-3821 Museum
	619-255-0203 Canyoneer Walks
Website:	www.sdnhm.org

Timken Museum

Coined the "jewel box of Balboa Park," this museum houses a highly praised and important collection of European Old Masters, American paintings and Russian icons that started as a privately owned treasure of the Putnam sisters during the 1940s.

Location:	1500 El Prado, Balboa Park
Hours:	Tues-Sat 10am-4:30pm. Open at 1:30pm Sundays
	Closed the month of September
Admission:	Free
Phone:	619-239-5548
Website:	http://gort.ucsd.edu/sj/timken/

Balboa Park Galleries

Within the park, there are two destinations dedicated to local artists. Everything from watercolors to hand blown glass, oil paintings to pottery is on display and for sale by the artisans or the galleries. Some artists may even be on site working in the studio galleries.

San Diego Art Institute Gallery ☆

Below a street level gift shop is 10,000 square feet of lucid studio space showcasing artwork for sale by local artists. The gallery is distinctive in that it displays work in inventive categories, such as One Foot, which spotlights pieces one square foot or less in size, next to more traditional categories, such as Youth Art. A launch pad for emerging talent, the institute coins itself "a museum for the living artist". It hosts a new show each month and one international show yearly.

Location:	1439 El Prado, House of Charm, Balboa Park
Hours:	Tues-Sat 11am-4pm. Opens at 12pm Sundays
	Closed major holidays
Admission:	General-$3; Seniors-$2;
	Military & Students (with ID)-$2;Under 13-Free
	Free 3rd Tuesday of the month
Phone:	619-236-0011
Website:	www.sandiego-art.org

Spanish Village Art Center

Over three hundred artists share thirty-seven historically-significant studios to create, show and sell their pieces in this village of working art galleries. The public is welcome to browse the studios as the painters, potters, jewelers, sculptors and other various medium artisans work. Several completed pieces are available for one-of-a-kind purchases.

Location:	Between Village Place & Zoo Place, Balboa Park
Hours:	Daily 11am-4pm
Admission:	Free
Phone:	619-233-9050
Website:	www.spanishvillageartcenter.com

Balboa Park Gardens

Balboa Park is a horticulturist's Mecca. The Visitors Center provides brochures for five self-guided garden walks, including the all-encompassing "Gardens of Balboa Park". Free one-hour walking tours are offered on Tuesdays, Saturdays and Sundays. Call for details. Enthusiasts will appreciate that San Diego's Floral Association (619-234-8901) and Botanical Foundation (619-234-8901) are located in the Casa del Prado and occasionally host botanical shows at the park.

The following gardens are all free and open 365 days a year.

Alcazar Garden is adorned with colorful tiled fountains, flawlessly trimmed hedges and perfectly rowed flower beds.

Desert Garden is known for colorful succulents, various cacti and bizarre trees. The garden features plants from America, Africa and Baja, Mexico.

Inez Grant Parker Memorial Garden is an award-winning garden with more than 1,850 aromatic rose bushes.

Marston House Garden is a fully matured formal English Romantic-style garden with California influences.

Morton Bay Fig Tree stands out among more than 7,600 trees of four hundred different species in the park with its 60-foot trunk, wild surface roots and 150 feet of sprawling limbs.

Old Cactus Garden contains exotic African and Australian protea plants in addition to its large cactus.

Palm Canyon is filled with more than fifty species of tropical palms along wood footbridges and stairways.

Zoro Garden is in a sunken stone grotto filled with colorful perennials, ficus trees and various butterflies.

Botanical Building & Lily Pond

The 1915 lattice-structured building and 193-foot reflecting pool are an architectural and floral favorite.

Location:	El Prado, just east of Museum of Art, Balboa Park
Hours:	Daily 10am-4pm
	Closed Thursdays & City Holidays
Admission:	Free

Japanese Friendship Garden ☆

This traditional Japanese, yet distinctly San Diego, garden has a tea house, sushi bar, activity center and gift shop set against decorated koi ponds, an impressive bonsai collection, strolling paths and a remarkable 60-foot wisteria arbor.

Location:	Plaza de Panama, Balboa Park
Hours:	Tues-Sun 10am-4pm. Tea Pavilion until 6pm
Admission:	General-$3; Seniors-$2.50;
	Military & Students (with ID)-$2;
	Youth(6 to18)-$2; Under 6-Free
	Free 3rd Tuesday of the month
Phone:	619-232-2721
Website:	www.niwa.org

Balboa Park Theaters

Everything from comic operas to puppet shows, from alfresco plays in a Shakespearean setting to outdoor musicals in an amphitheater with grassy hillside seating is performed at beautiful venues within the park.

Marie Hitchcock Puppet Theater

Puppet shows for children are performed weekly by a variety of troupes and resident puppeteers using marionette, hand, rod and shadow puppets.

Location:	Pan American Plaza, Balboa Park
Shows:	Wed-Fri 10am & 11:30am
	Sat & Sun 11am, 1pm & 2:30pm
	June-Aug: Wed-Sun 11am, 1pm & 2:30pm
Admission:	General-$3;Youth(2-14)-$2; Under 2-Free
Phone:	619-685-5990

San Diego Comic Opera

Fully-mounted productions of vintage musicals, operettas and Gilbert & Sullivan favorites by talented casts and a live professional orchestra make this a memorable experience. Productions are staged in the Casa Del Prado Theater.

Location:	Village Place, off Park Boulevard, Balboa Park
Hours:	Friday-Sunday. Call for show times
Admission:	General-$19-$26; Seniors-$2 discount;
	Military & Students (with ID)-$2 discount;
	Youth(5-12)-$10; Under 5-Not admitted
Phone:	619-239-8836
Website:	www.sdcomicopera.com

Starlight Theater

The 4,300+ capacity theater offers a unique cultural experience as playgoers enjoy large-scale, Broadway-quality musicals performed under the stars. Picnicking on the lush green lawns pre-show is a long held tradition. The season begins as early as June and typically ends during September.

Location:	Pan American Plaza, Balboa Park
Hours:	Thurs-Sun 8pm Curtain
	Box Office: Mon-Fri 10am-4pm,
	Sat & Sun 12pm-4pm
Admission:	General-$16.50-$44.50/Person; Discounts for Seniors(60+), Military & Students (with ID); Youth(Under13)-$10.50-$23/Person; Two youth per paid adult are free Thursdays & Sundays; each additional youth is half price
Phone:	619-544-7800 Information
	619-544-7827 Box Office
Website:	www.starlighttheatre.org

The Globe Theaters

The Globe Theaters are three separate and equally charming stages centered around the spectacular Copley Plaza, worth a visit even without performance tickets. Various classic, contemporary and musical productions are staged at The Old Globe Theater, Cassius Carter Center Stage and the outdoor Lowell Davies Festival Theater. Call for show information.

Location:	El Prado, behind Museum of Man, Balboa Park
Hours:	Backstage Tours: Sat & Sun 10:30am
	Shows: Tues-Sun. Call for show times
Admission:	Tours: General-$3; Seniors-$1; Students & Military (with ID)-$1; Youth-$1
Phone:	619-239-2255 Box Office
	619-231-1941 Tours & Information
Website:	www.theglobetheatres.com

Balboa Park Attractions

While the famous San Diego Zoo is the most visited attraction in the park, some lesser-known treasures add ambiance and lure to any visit. Be it an antique carousel or a cooking class, there are hidden treasures around every corner of this large park.

Balboa Park Carousel

This 1910 carousel has been so well preserved that all but two pairs of animals are original hand-carved pieces. The hand painted murals are also original as is the military band music that plays during the five minute ride. It has been operating in the park since 1922 and is one of the few in the world to still offer the brass ring game where a few lucky persons win a free ride.

Location:	Zoo Place, Balboa Park
Hours:	Sat, Sun & school holidays 11am-5:30pm
	Late June-Labor Day: Daily 1pm-5pm
Admission:	$1.50/Ride
Phone:	619-460-9000

Balboa Park Food & Wine School

Visiting professional chefs and vintners bring the culinary arts to life in a casual, more fun than technical, atmosphere at this cooking school. Daytime and evening classes are offered for a onetime adventure in either food or wine. Intimate cooking classes of sixteen people cover fun topics, such as *Dats Some Dim Sum!* or *Let's Get Saucy!* Wine courses are slightly larger at twenty-five to thirty people and focus both on variety, such as *Chardonnay Revolt*, and on region, such as *European Treasures*.

Location:	House of Hospitality, Balboa Park
Hours:	Cooking Classes: Mon & Wed 6pm
	Wine Courses: Wed 7pm
	Occasional Fri & Sat classes at 11am
Admission:	Prices vary. Expect $39-$49/Person
Phone:	619-557-9441 x210
Website:	www.balboafoodwine.com

Balboa Park Miniature Railroad

This 48-passenger train is scaled to one-fifth the size of the real General Motors F-3 diesels and is a rare antique model. There are as few as fifty remaining in the world. The three minute ride is operated by an on-train conductor suited in traditional navy-striped railroad cap and overalls. Since 1948, the miniature train has carried more than five million passengers across four acres of the park along 2,200 feet of track.

Location:	Zoo Place, Balboa Park
Hours:	Sat, Sun & holidays 11am-5pm
Admission:	$1.25/Ride
Phone:	619-239-4748

Spreckles Organ Pavilion

On New Year's Eve, 1914, the Spreckles family donated the world's largest outdoor organ to the City of San Diego for the opening of the Panama-California Exposition. The organ has been in almost continuous use since and is designed so that the 4,518 individual pipes are at the full command of a skilled organist. Free concerts operate on a regular schedule. Call for upcoming concert details.

Location:	1549 El Prado, Pan American Plaza, Balboa Park
Hours:	Sun 2pm-3pm
	Summer concerts Mon 7:30pm-9pm
Admission:	Free
Phone:	619-702-8138
Website:	www.serve.com/sosorgan

The San Diego Zoo

The world-famous San Diego Zoo and its sister facility, the San Diego Wild Animal Park, are both operated by the non-profit Zoological Society of San Diego. The 100-acre zoo is home to one of the world's most exotic and unusual animal collections. The 4,000-plus birds, mammals and reptiles are housed in natural, beautifully landscaped habitats. The ever-popular giant pandas are a visitor favorite with less than a thousand of these rare and endangered species in the world today. Beyond the hippos, tigers, polar bears, gorillas and koalas, favorite features include the double-decker guided bus tours and the Skyfari aerial tramway. Also known as a botanical garden, the zoo has over six thousand varieties of rare plants.

The first Monday in the month of October is Founder's Day and general admission is free to everyone. A two-park pass called the "Accommodation Ticket" grants one admission to the Zoo and one admission to the Wild Animal Park within five days for $46.80 per adult and $31.40 per child.

Location:	Zoo Place, off Park Boulevard, Balboa Park
Hours:	Daily 9am. Closing times vary
Admission:	General-$19.50; Youth(3-11)-$11.75
	Deluxe Ticket (includes admission, bus tour & aerial tram):
	Adults-$32; Seniors(60+)-$29; Youth-$19.75
Phone:	619-234-3153 Recorded Information
	619-231-1515 Press "0" to reach an operator
Website:	www.sandiegozoo.org

HOW TO GET THERE

From points north, exit 163 South at Park Boulevard and follow signs to the park or exit I-5 South at Airport/Sassafras and proceed to Laurel Street. Turn left at Laurel Street and stay in the right lane. Continue east on Laurel Street as it becomes El Prado. Cross the Cabrillo Bridge to the park entrance.

From points south, exit 163 North at Richmond Street and follow Zoo/ Museums signs. The ramp becomes Upas Street. Continue on Upas Street to Park Boulevard. Follow directional signs to the park. Another option is to take 94 West to the end of the freeway, which becomes F Street. Proceed on F Street and turn right at 12ᵗʰ Street, which becomes Park Boulevard. Follow directional signs to the park.

Balboa Park

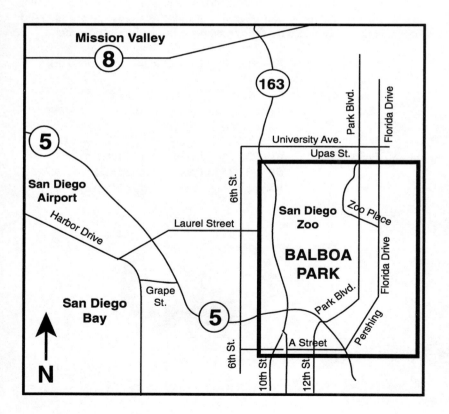

DOWNTOWN

Set against the sparkling bay, San Diego's urban core and downtown borders have sprawled with ongoing development, creating a safe and vibrant pedestrian environment catering to all tastes. Centrally located just outside downtown, are the popular areas of Point Loma, Harbor Island, Shelter Island, Old Town, Balboa Park and Uptown.

Several distinct areas, including the Gaslamp Quarter, Embarcadero, Horton Plaza and Little Italy are popular destinations. On game days, the up and coming East Village is sure to buzz with baseball fans flocking to the new downtown ballpark. Scattered throughout the neighborhoods are museums, theatre houses and music venues, including the city's opera and symphony. Restaurants, cafes, coffee houses, shopping districts, bars, nightclubs and movie theaters abound throughout the area, notable for its architecture and ambiance. A weekly Farmer's Market takes place in Horton Square at 225 Broadway on Thursdays 11am-3pm.

Downtown Information Center

Location:	111st Avenue at F Street, Downtown
Hours:	Mon-Sat 8:30am-5pm
	June-Aug: Open 11am-5pm Sundays
Phone:	619-236-1212
Website:	www.sandiego.org

ARTS TIX & Downtown Theatres

ARTS TIX is a half-price ticket booth that sells theater and event tickets the day of the show. Same day, half-price tickets are cash only and cover music, dance, theatre and art shows for several city-area theatres. Tickets for Monday shows are sold on Sunday. Regular price tickets for future shows, museums, concerts, sporting events and tours are also available.

Location:	Horton Plaza at Broadway Circle, Downtown
Hours:	Tues-Thurs 11am-6pm,
	Fri-Sat 10am-6pm, Sun 10am-5pm
Phone:	619-497-5000
Website:	www.sandiegoperforms.com

Call or visit ARTS TIX or the following downtown theatres for current performances, show times and ticket prices.

Civic Theatre – Broadway/San Diego

This prestigious theatre is San Diego's largest and best equipped stage for large-scale productions with nearly three thousand seats. It is home to Broadway/San Diego and the San Diego Opera, among other performance companies. Broadway/San Diego primarily performs blockbuster musicals, but also presents other productions.

Location:	Theater - 202 C Street, Downtown
	Box Office - 3rd Avenue at B Street, Downtown
Hours:	Box Office: Mon-Fri 10am-6pm
Phone:	619-570-1100 Box Office
Website:	www.broadwaysd.com

Culy Theatre

This lower Gaslamp Quarter theatre hosts wildly popular and humorous dinner theatre shows on weekends. It has been home to the popular *Soprano's Last Supper* and *Joey & Maria's Comedy Italian Wedding*.

Location:	338 7th Avenue, Downtown
Hours:	Box Office: Mon-Fri 6am-6pm, Sat 8am-5pm
Phone:	619-338-0526 Information
	800-944-5639 Box Office

Downtown & Central
1 - 22

Horton Grand Theatre

Near the historic Horton Grand Hotel, in a Gaslamp area steeped in history, this theatre presents shows with long runs, such as the runaway hit *Triple Espresso*.

Location:	444 4th Avenue, Downtown
Hours:	Box Office opens daily at 10am
	Closing times vary. Mon–Thurs 6pm,
	Fri 7pm, Sat 4pm, Sun 2pm
Phone:	619-234-9583 Box Office

Lyceum Theatre – San Diego Repertory Theatre

This intimate Horton Plaza theater is home to the adventurous "Rep" and their consistently promising and award-winning avant-garde productions. Some claim The Rep launched actress Whoopi Goldberg's career.

Location:	79 Horton Plaza, Downtown
Hours:	Box Office opens daily at 12pm
	Closing times vary. Sun & Tues 7pm,
	Wed-Sat 8pm, non-performance days 6pm
Phone:	619-544-1000
Website:	www.sandiegorep.com

Spreckels Theatre

One of the city's most historic theatres, this downtown stage has hosted everyone from Abbott & Costello to Ray Charles. A broad range of shows and performers still grace this 1912 theatre with plays, monologues, music and more.

Location:	121 Broadway, Downtown
Hours:	Box Office: Tues-Fri 11am-6pm, Sat 12pm-5pm
Phone:	619-234-8397 Theatre
	619-235-9500 Box Office
Website:	www.spreckelstheatre.com

Downtown & Central

Children's Museum/Museo de los Ninos

Children of various ages learn from hands-on experiences at this museum. Adventures include anything from a close-up examination of dinosaur replicas, to painting a derelict automobile, to taking an imaginary ride through San Diego and Tijuana. Educational displays are changed monthly and the dedicated staff does everything imaginable to prove children learn better by active participation.

Location:	200 W. Island Avenue, Downtown
Hours:	Tues-Sat 10am-4pm
Admission:	General-$5; Seniors-$3;
	Youth-$5; Under 2-Free
Phone:	619-233-5437
Website:	www.sdchildrensmuseum.org

Computer Museum of America

Unique artifacts and working displays, as well as interactive exhibits showcase major milestones in the development of the computer industry at this museum. Highlights include an analog vacuum tube computer, a 27" diameter hard disk, PONG, Atari games and a Hall of Fame, all of which showcase the rapid evolution of computers.

Location:	640 C Street at 7th Avenue, Downtown
Hours:	Tues-Sun 10am-5pm. Closed national holidays
Admission:	General-$2; Seniors-$1;
	Military & Students (with ID)-$1;
	Youth-$1; Under 3-Free
Phone:	619-235-8222
Website:	www.computer-museum.org

Horton Plaza

Downtown's redefinition began with Horton Plaza, named after San Diego's founder Alonzo Horton. The plaza houses an architecturally-stunning, multi-level, open air mall with unique specialty shops, boutiques and national retailers. The one-of-a-kind outdoor entertainment complex is also home to restaurants, a movie theater, and the award-winning San Diego Repertory Theater at the Lyceum.

Location:	From 1st Avenue to 4th Avenue between Broadway & G Street, Downtown
Hours:	Stores open 10am-9pm weekdays; 10am-8pm Saturday; 11am-7pm Sunday Restaurants and theaters open later
Admission:	Free
Phone:	619-238-1596 or 619-239-8180
Website:	www.hortonplaza.shoppingtown.com

Museum of Contemporary Art San Diego

This museum is a downtown satellite location to the highly-acclaimed La Jolla flagship facility. It presents thought-provoking exhibitions, including painting, sculpture, installation, drawings, prints, photography, video and multi-media works.

Location:	1001 Kettner Boulevard at Broadway, Downtown
Hours:	Daily 11am-5pm. Closed Wednesdays
Admission:	Free
Phone:	619-234-1001
Website:	www.mcasandiego.org

San Diego Opera

January through May, five works as well as recital and concert events are staged at the Civic Theatre. Each season is a mix of contemporary and classical operas featuring top U.S. and international stars along with rising artists.

Location: Theatre - 202 C Street, Downtown
           Box Office - 3rd Avenue at B Street, Downtown
Admission: Prices vary. Expect roughly $50/Person
Hours: San Diego Opera Ticket Office:
           Mon-Fri 8:30am-4:30pm
Phone: 619-232-7636 San Diego Opera
           619-570-1100 Civic Box Office
Website: www.sdopera.com

San Diego Symphony

Historic Copley Symphony Hall is home to the symphony musicians who perform over a hundred concerts each season, some with world-renown guest performers. Each year, from July through September, the symphony presents an outdoor Summer Pops season at Navy Pier on downtown's waterfront.

Location: 750 B Street at 7th Avenue, Downtown
Admission: Prices vary. Expect $8.50-$70/Person
Hours: Symphony Box Office:
           Mon-Thurs 10am-6pm, Fri 10am-5pm,
           Performance days 12pm-Intermission
Phone: 619-235-0804 Box Office
Website: www.sandiegosymphony.com

Villa Montezuma

The San Diego Historical Society operates this Victorian house, which was built in 1887 for Jesse Shepard, an eccentric pianist-writer. Considered a treasured relic of old San Diego, its ornate interior features authentic furniture, artifacts and outstanding stained glass windows.

Location:	1925 K Street at 20th Street, Downtown
Hours:	Fri-Sun 10am-4:30pm
	Tours hourly 10am-3pm & at 3:45pm
Admission:	General-$5; Youth-$2; Under7-Free
Phone:	619-239-2211 Recorded Message
Website:	www.sandiegohistory.org

HOW TO GET THERE

To reach downtown, connect to I-5.

Exit I-5 South at Front Street and proceed south to Broadway. Turn left at Broadway and proceed east a few blocks to find a central downtown location for parking.

Exit I-5 North at 4th Avenue and proceed south to Broadway. This is a central downtown area with several parking options.

Downtown San Diego

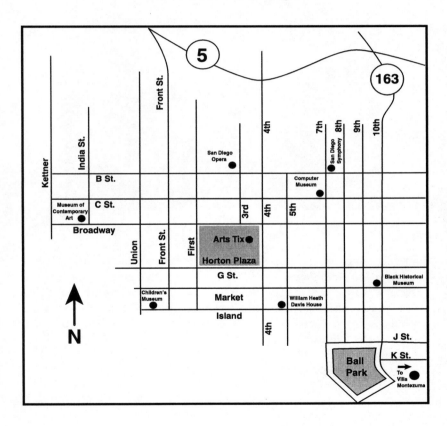

EMBARCADERO

The Embarcadero area of San Diego's 27-mile scenic waterfront lies closest to downtown and offers a vast range of activities along the bay. Fine restaurants with fresh seafood, fun eateries, attractions and shops line the Embarcadero. The bike-pedestrian ferry to Coronado provides exceptional views of the bay. During December, the San Diego Bay Parade of Lights showcases dozens of sailboats as they slowly sail across the bay lit up with Christmas lights. A resource for events and attractions specific to the bay is www.thebigbay.com.

Bay Tours & Cruises

Two companies offer tours and cruises in the San Diego Bay, Harbor Excursion and Hornblower Cruises & Events. Both companies operate out of Broadway Pier. One- and two-hour harbor tours run daily, starting at 10am. Call for a full schedule. There are discount rates for seniors fifty-five years and older as well as for military. Children rates are for youth ages four through twelve. Reservations are not accepted.

Admission:		1-Hr.	2-Hr.
General:	Harbor:	$13	$18
	Hornblower:	$15	$20
Discount:	Harbor:	$11	$16
	Hornblower:	$13	$18
Youth:	Harbor:	$6.50	$9
	Hornblower:	$7.50	$10

Dinner and dance cruises depart nightly. Hornblower Cruises departs at 7pm and runs three hours, while Harbor Excursion departs at 7:30pm for a two and a half hour cruise. Saturday night cruises costs an extra $5. Two-hour champagne brunch cruises depart on Sundays at 11am. Both companies board all cruises thirty minutes before departure and offer cruise enhancements such as guaranteed window tables, open bar packages and additional courses at an extra costs. There are discount rates for seniors fifty-five years and older as well as for military. Youth rates are for children ages four through twelve. Reservations are highly recommended, but not required.

Admission:		Dinner	Brunch
General:	Harbor:	$50	$39.50
	Hornblower:	$54.50	$37.50
Discount:	Harbor:	$50	$39.50
	Hornblower	$52.50	$35.50
Youth:	Harbor:	$29.95	$29.50
	Hornblower:	$33	$22.50

Harbor Excursion

Harbor Excursion also operates a Coronado ferry ride. Prices are $2 per person and 50¢ per bicycle. The ferry departs Broadway Pier daily on the hour 9am-9pm. It departs Coronado's Ferry Landing Marketplace daily on the half hour 9:30am-9:30pm. The ferry operates one hour later on Friday and Saturday nights with departures at 10pm and 10:30pm.

Location:	1050 N. Harbor Drive, Embarcadero
Hours:	Daily 8am-7:30pm
Phone:	619-234-4111 or 800-442-7847
Website:	www.harborexcursion.com

Hornblower Cruises & Events

Hornblower Cruises & Events also operates Whale Watching Tours from mid-December through March. Prices are $25 per person. Seniors and military get a $2 discount and children ages 4-12 are half price. The 3.5 hour tour operates twice daily, usually departing at 9:30am and 1:30pm.

Location:	1066 N. Harbor Drive, Embarcadero
Hours:	Mon-Sat 8:30am-7:30pm, Sun until 6pm
Phone:	619-725-8888 Harbor Tours
	619-686-8715 Dining Cruises
Website:	www.hornblower.com

Cinderella Carriage Company

Nostalgic horse drawn carriage rides are a unique way to see the city and waterfront. Rides depart from Seaport Village and last anywhere from ten minutes to an hour. On Friday and Saturday nights, a Gaslamp Quarter departure is available from 6pm-midnight at the corner of 5th Avenue and F Street.

Location:	801 W. Market Street, Embarcadero
Hours:	Daily 11am-11pm
Admission:	Prices vary. Expect $25-$95/Carriage
Phone:	619-239-8080
Website:	www.cinderella-carriage.com

San Diego Maritime Museum

The famous "Star of India" draws visitors to this museum. Built in 1863, the "Star of India" is the world's oldest iron sailing vessel still afloat. It boasts twenty-one circumnavigations of the globe via the longest regular sailing route in history. That route included rounding the roughest known sea conditions at Cape Horn.

The museum also features two more ships, the 1898 ferry boat "Berkeley" and the 1904 Scottish built steam yacht "Medea". The three ships have onboard exhibits.

Location:	1492 N. Harbor Drive, Embarcadero
Hours:	Daily 9am-8pm. Open until 9pm during Summer
Admission:	General-$6; Seniors-$4;
	Youth(6-12)-$3; Under 6-Free
Phone:	619-234-9153
Website:	www.sdmaritime.com

SEAL Tours

"Seal Tours" allows you to see San Diego from both land and sea aboard a unique, amphibious boat with wheels. The narrated tour winds through San Diego's streets before cruising the waters of Mission Bay and San Diego Bay. Call for a schedule. The last tour usually departs at 3pm or 4pm.

Location:	Central Plaza at Seaport Village, across from Harbor House Restaurant, Embarcadero
Hours:	Daily 9am. Closing times vary
Admission:	General-$24; Youth(4-12)-$12
Phone:	619-298-8687
Website:	www.sealtours.com

Seaport Village

This 14-acre waterfront extravaganza consists of an East, Central and West Plaza. One plaza depicts early California, another a Victorian-era, while the third is reminiscent of a New England fishing village. Dozens of shops and galleries, sidewalk eateries and four bay view restaurants draw in locals and visitors to this quaint bayside setting. Spectacular views of the cityscape and Coronado Bridge, along with an 1890s Looff carousel add extra charm to the already existing ambiance.

Location:	849 W. Harbor Drive at Kettner Boulevard, Embarcadero
Hours:	Daily 10am-9pm. Open until 10pm June-August Restaurants have extended hours
Admission:	Free. Parking: 2 Hours Free with validation; $3/Additional Hour
Phone:	619-235-4014 Information 619-235-4013 Events Hotline
Website:	www.seaportvillage.com

Summer Pops at Navy Pier

The San Diego Symphony hosts an outdoor summer pops series with the bay as their backdrop. The series runs late June through September at Navy Pier. The musicians play with visiting guests and celebrate summer with firework spectaculars. If interested, ask the box office about seats with table service, where you can order gourmet boxed dinners and beverages throughout the concerts. Glass, alcoholic beverages, chairs and strollers are not permitted.

Location:	960 N. Harbor Drive, Navy Pier, Embarcadero
Admission:	Prices vary. Expect $15-$59/Person
Hours:	Gates 6pm, Performances 7:30 pm
	Box Office: Mon-Thurs 10am-6pm,
	Fri 10am-5pm, Sat 12pm-3pm,
	Performance days 12pm-Intermission
Phone:	619-235-0804
Website:	www.sandiegosymphony.com

HOW TO GET THERE

To reach the waterfront Embarcadero area, connect to I-5.

Exit I-5 South at Front Street and proceed south for three blocks. Turn right at Ash Street and continue to Harbor Drive. Most attractions are to the left, heading south on Harbor Drive.

Exit I-5 North at Hawthorn Street and proceed west towards the water to Harbor Drive. Most attractions are to the left, heading south on Harbor Drive.

Downtown Embarcadero

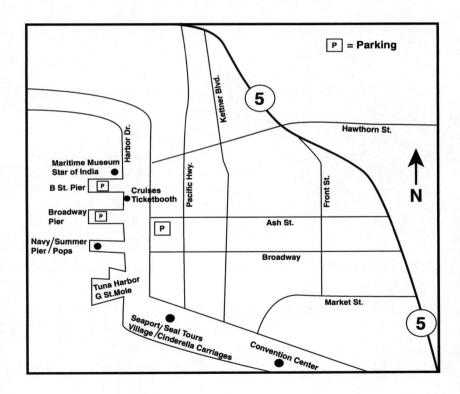

GASLAMP QUARTER

Sixteen blocks of Victorian-style buildings constructed between 1880 and 1910 define the Gaslamp Quarter. Shopping, dining and entertainment are the reasons most people visit this neighborhood. The Gaslamp's electric nightlife is balanced by first rate shopping and endless ambiance by day. Everything from vintage rare finds to modern utilitarian treasures can be

found in bookstores, art galleries, clothing boutiques, jewelry stores and specialty shops. Candlelit restaurants, umbrella-lined sidewalk cafes, pubs, clubs, bistros and breweries serve foods from around the world. A movie theater on 5th Avenue can accommodate a "dinner and a movie" evening. Live music, stand-up comedy, DJs and dancing are additions to an already-thriving club and bar scene. Art walks and street festivals are common to this area. Every year, festive celebrations erupt for Mardi Gras in February or March, ShamRock on March 17th, Cinco in the Gaslamp on May 5th, Taste of Gaslamp in June and Street Scene, California's largest music festival, in early September.

The Gaslamp Quarter runs from 4th Avenue to 6th Avenue between Broadway and Harbor Drive.

Gaslamp Quarter Association

Location:	614 5th Avenue, Suite E
Hours:	Mon-Fri 9am-5pm
Phone:	619-233-5227
Website:	www.gaslamp.org

William Heath Davis House/
Gaslamp Quarter Historical Foundation

The William Heath Davis House is the oldest surviving structure in the area and serves as home to the Gaslamp Historical Foundation, a museum and information center. A quaint park surrounds the pre-framed lumber "salt box" house, which was built in 1850 as part of Davis's effort to establish a town on San Diego's waterfront.

The foundation promotes the historical, cultural and architectural significance of the Gaslamp Quarter, a lively part of what was known as New Town during the 1800s. Docents lead vivid walking tours through the Quarter, relating a more richly textured past than one would expect. The walking tour includes a thorough walk-through and detailed history of the Davis House. A professionally produced, self-guided audio tour is also available during museum hours. Beyond the interesting tours, the foundation hosts ShamRock and two Victorian-era themed festivals, A Walk Through Time in May and Fall Back Festival in October. The festivals fall in relation to Standard Time and Daylight Savings.

Location:	410 Island Avenue, Gaslamp Quarter
Hours:	Call for museum hours
	Davis House Tours: Tues-Sun 11am-3pm
	2-Hour Walking Tours: Sat at 11am
Admission:	Davis House Tours: $3 Donation
	Walking Tours: General-$8; Seniors-$6;
	Military & Students (with ID)-$6
Phone:	619-233-4692
Website:	www.gaslampquarter.org

Ghosts & Gravestones Tour

"Ghosts & Gravestones" is a night tour that reveals San Diego's darker side through local tales and legends. This trolley ride incorporates a walking tour through the Gaslamp Quarter and includes entrance into three historically-significant buildings, the William Heath Davis House, the Victorian Mansion and Villa Montezuma. It also includes a visit to one of the city's oldest graveyards and the famous haunted Whaley House.

Location:	311 Island Avenue, Horton Grand Hotel, Gaslamp Quarter
Admission:	General-$28; Under 8-Not admitted
Hours:	Nightly 6:30pm. Call to confirm
Phone:	619-298-8687
Websites:	www.ghostsandgravestones.com

Harlem West Museum/ Gaslamp Black Historical Society

The Gaslamp Black Historical Society conducts tours of the Gaslamp and adjacent areas that relate downtown's black history. The society seeks to preserve and restore designated black historic properties, such as the downtown Clermont Coast Hotel, Ideal Hotel and Harlem Locker Club, in an effort to create an African-American thematic district within the thirteen blocks once known as Harlem of the West.

The historic Harlem of the West area is defined by the blocks between Market Street and Island Street from 3rd Avenue to 16th Avenue.

Location:	906 Market Street, Gaslamp Quarter
Hours:	Saturday Tours 10am-2pm
Admission:	Free. Donations welcome
Phone:	619-685-7215
Website:	www.harlemofthewest.com

Gaslamp Quarter Historic Districts

The Gaslamp Quarter is downtown San Diego's historic district. However, within this historic district lie two other historic districts, one paying tribute to the African-American community and the other paying tribute to the Asian-American community.

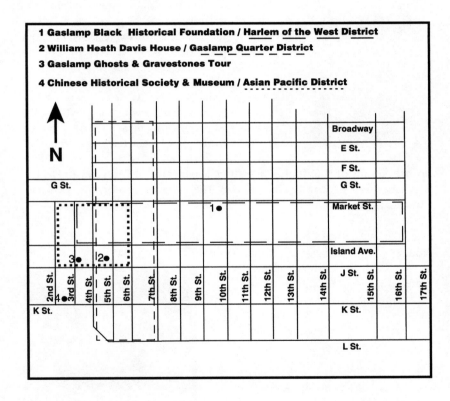

1 Gaslamp Black Historical Foundation / Harlem of the West District

2 William Heath Davis House / Gaslamp Quarter District

3 Gaslamp Ghosts & Gravestones Tour

4 Chinese Historical Society & Museum / Asian Pacific District

San Diego Chinese Historical Museum/ Asian-Pacific Historic District

Early structures of Asian-style architecture lie within parts of the Gaslamp Quarter and Marina Area. These buildings were once part of old Chinatown and now house several associations, clubs and the San Diego Chinese Historical Museum. The museum recognizes the contributions of San Diego's Asian community and features exhibits which have included Chinese New Year prints, opera costumes, paintings and calligraphy.

The museum building was originally located on 1st Avenue and built as a Chinese Mission. Beside the museum is a beautiful Asian garden with a small waterfall and stream that leads to a koi pond. A stone path leads to a bronze statue of Confucius, creating a peaceful and serene place for meditation among downtown's bustle. The entrance gate to the garden is dedicated to the memory or Dr. Sun Yat-sen.

Location:	404 3rd Avenue, Gaslamp Quarter
Hours:	Tues-Sat 10:30am-4pm
	Opens at 12pm Sundays
Admission:	Free. Donations
	welcome
Phone:	619-338-9888
Website:	www.sdchm.org

The eight-block Asian-Pacific Historic District runs from 2nd Avenue to 6th Avenue between Market Street and J Street.

HOW TO GET THERE

The corner of Broadway and 4th Avenue marks the northwest corner of this 16-block historic district. This is a central downtown area with several parking options.

To reach the Gaslamp Quarter in downtown, connect to I-5.

Exit I-5 South at Front Street and proceed south to Broadway. Turn left at Broadway and proceed east a few blocks to 4th Avenue.

Exit I-5 North at 4th Avenue. Turn left at 4th Avenue and proceed south to Broadway.

Gaslamp Quarter

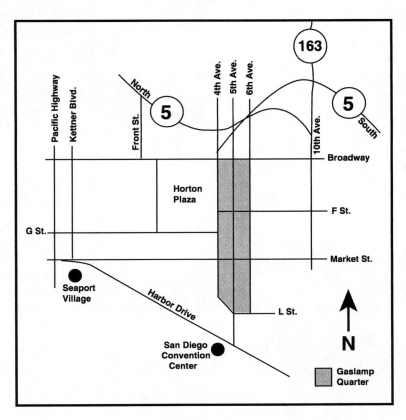

HARBOR ISLAND &
SHELTER ISLAND

Northwest of the Embarcadero, Harbor Island and Shelter Island hug the waterfront. Beautifully manicured parks and pristine promenades allow for prime picnic spots, walking, jogging, cycling or catching a cityscape view.

These areas are renowned for San Diego's world-famous sportfishing fleet, explaining why most charters reside in this area. It is also a great area to buy fresh seafood or immediately indulge at any of several restaurants with patio seating and fantastic views.

Harbor Island offers the best opportunity for sailing lessons and charters, while Shelter Island is a better choice for sportfishing. Shelter Island runs at a more lively pace with its active marina and busy docks, public fishing pier at 1776 Shelter Island Drive and boat launching ramp at 2210 Shelter Island Drive. Every year, fishing and boating is celebrated with the Day at the Docks Festival in April and the Wooden Boat Festival in May.

Long paved walkways runs the length of both islands hugging the bay with

unobstructed views of downtown, the San Diego-Coronado Bridge and bay activity. Near the end of Shelter Island, the Japanese Friendship Memorial provides a scenic place to picnic, throw a Frisbee or simply rest.

Humphrey's By The Bay

Humphrey's Concerts by the Bay is an experience not to be missed. With an ideal location on San Diego Bay, concert-goers bask in waterfront ambiance while enjoying first rate entertainment in an intimate outdoor theater with less than 1,300 seats. Rock, jazz, folk music, comedy and other events run May through October. Front row seats are reserved for those that dine at Humphrey's Restaurant before the show at an additional $45 per person. All other reserved seats start in row ten. Call for a schedule and prices.

Location:	2241 Shelter Island Drive, Shelter Island
Hours:	Box Office: Tues-Sat 11:30am-6:30pm
Admission:	Prices vary
Phone:	619-224-3577 Restaurant & Lounge
	619-523-1010 Concert Info Line
Website:	www.humphreysbythebay.com

Sailboat Charters

Several sailing options abound for passengers, beginner sailors and experienced yachtsmen, from sailing inside the bay and around local harbors to venturing as far as Catalina Island or Mexico. Sailing instructions and certification are also available. Contact the following outfitters for details.

Classic Sailing Adventures

This company offers a first-rate, intimate sailing experience with a maximum of six passengers per cruise and complimentary beverages and hors d' oeuvres aboard their 38-foot yacht "Soul Diversion". Guests are welcome to participate in the sport of sailing or simply relax as a passenger. Reservations are required.

Location:	2051 Shelter Island Drive, Shelter Island
Hours:	Reservations: Daily 9am-8pm
	Summer Sailing Trips: Daily at 1pm & 5pm
	Whale Watching Expeditions:
	Dec-Mar Daily 8:30am & 1pm
Admission:	$60/Person
Phone:	619-224-0800 or 800-659-0141
Website:	www.classicsailingadventures.com

Harbor Sailboats

This company, which has been operating since 1969, offers charters and rents sailing yachts ranging in size from 22 to 46 feet to certified sailors. It also has an instructional facility for people seeking to learn how to sail.

Location:	2040 Harbor Island Drive, Harbor Island
Hours:	Daily 9am-5pm
Phone:	619-291-9568 or 800-854-6625
Website:	www.harborsailboats.com

S.D. Yacht Charters

Chartered or unchartered sailing yachts and power boats, ranging in size from 31 to 42 feet, are available for bay tours, day sails or vacations through this outfitter.

Location:	1880 Harbor Island Drive, Harbor Island
Hours:	Mon-Sat 8am-5pm, Sun 9am-3pm
Phone:	619-297-4555
Website:	www.sdyc.com

Sportfishing Charters

Captains with years of experience guide you to waters where, depending on the season and length of your trip, catches typically include Albacore, Bass, Baracuda, Bonito, Bluefin, Bigeye Tuna, Rockfish, Dorado, Yellowtail, Wahoo and Marlin. There are several outfitters that both first time sailors or seasoned fisherman can choose from. Considerations for your trip should include skill level, tackle and equipment, boat size and trip length. Charters start as basic as half days around the bay and along coastal hot spots and get as intricate as two week trips past the southern tip of Baja, Mexico. Call the following outfitters for trip options, sailing times and prices.

Fisherman's Landing

Several trip options are available, from a family day of fishing to 19-day trips deep into Mexico, aboard any one of several boats, ranging in size from 57 to 124 feet. A favorite day trip is Mexico's Coronado Islands. Natural History Adventures are multi-day cruises to remote islands and secluded lagoons along the Baja California coast. Seasonally, Whale Encounter excursions are offered.

Location:	2838 Garrison Street, Shelter Island
Hours:	Daily 7am-7pm
Phone:	619-221-8500
Website:	www.fishermanslanding.com

H&M Landing

Since 1935, this outfitter has offered half-, full- and multi-day sportfishing trips, whale watching and nature expeditions, as well as dive trips and private charters. A large fleet of boats can accommodate as few as four and as many as a hundred passengers.

Location:	2803 Emerson Street, Shelter Island
Hours:	Daily 6am-7pm
Phone:	619-222-1144
Website:	www.hmlanding.com

Interpac Yachts

While Interpac offers sportfishing charters and harbor cruises, they specialize in private charter vacations to places including the Bahamas, Caribbean, Florida, Mediterranean, South Pacific, Mexico, Pacific Northwest and Alaska. Both power and sailboat crewed charters are available.

Location: 1050 Anchorage Lane, Shelter Island
Hours: Mon-Fri 8am-6pm
Phone: 619-222-0327
Website: www.interpacyachts.com

Lee Palm Sportfishers/Red Rooster III

Lee Palm Sportfishers offers a variety of long-range fishing expeditions aboard Red Rooster III, a 30-passenger, 105-foot sportfishing yacht. This outfitter is for the more serious fisherman as trips are a minimum of three days.

Location: 2801 Emerson Street, Shelter Island
Hours: Mon-Sat 9am-5pm
Phone: 619-224-3857
Website: www.redrooster3.com

Point Loma Sportfishing

This company offers a large selection of boats ranging from 45 to 105 feet and a wide variety of trips from half-, full- and multi-day bay and ocean fishing expeditions. Twilight bay fishing trips are a great option for families. May through September, a twilight ocean trip is offered by private charter.

Location: 1403 Scott Street, Shelter Island
Hours: Daily 6am-10pm
Phone: 619-223-1627
Website: www.pointlomasportfishing.com

HOW TO GET THERE
To reach these two bay areas, connect to I-5.

Exit I-5 South at Sassafras Street and continue towards the airport along Kettner Boulevard. Turn right at W. Laurel Street and continue onto N. Harbor Drive towards the airport.

Exit I-5 North at Hawthorn Street and proceed west towards the water. Turn right at N. Harbor Drive and proceed towards the airport.

Harbor Island will be on the left across from the airport. Turn left off N. Harbor Drive at Harbor Island Drive. Most of the attractions and boat docks are to the right.

Shelter Island is further west. Continue west along N. Harbor Drive past the airport and past Harbor Island. Turn left at Scott Street and proceed west. Turn left at Shelter Island Drive. Note that most of the sportfishing charters are located along Scott Street.

Harbor Island & Shelter Island

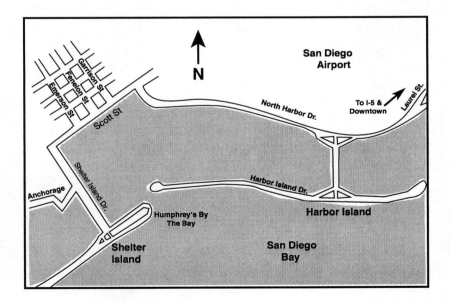

LITTLE ITALY

The irresistible location of this charming neighborhood between downtown

and the waterfront is due to the thousands of Italian families who lived in this area working to make San Diego the center of the world tuna industry. Today the Italian heritage remains, but the streets are quite different.

The heart of Little Italy is at Date Street and India Street. The neighborhood entices with wonderful family-owned Italian restaurants, pizzerias, specialty food shops, gelato and espresso cafes. Amici Park at the corner of Date Street and State Street is worth a visit just to see one of four permanent recipes bronzed on red and white checkered mosaic tables or to play Bocce. Colorful wall murals decorate the streets. The brightly painted eccentric shops known as Fir Street Cottages, at Fir Street and Columbia Street, were home to the DeLuga, Giolzetti and Cresci families, who immigrated during the 1900s.

Among a handful of art supply, antique and gift shops is The Studio Arts Complex, an art gallery haven at 2400 Kettner Boulevard. Each year, Festa graces the streets as the largest Italian street festival of its kind on the west coast. It falls during autumn in conjunction with Chalk La Strada, a traditional street chalk painting festival. The events include food, entertainment, raffles, Bocce and stickball tournaments. ArtWalk brings Little Italy to life in the spring with an outdoor artist showcase involving painting, sculpture, dance, music and more.

Little Italy Association

Location: 1830 Columbia Street, Little Italy
Phone: 619-233-3898
Website: www.littleitalysd.com

Firehouse Museum

This once operating firehouse now traces San Diego's significant fire-fighting history dating back to the 1800s. It houses a large variety of fire-fighting vehicles and vintage equipment, including an 1841 Rumsey hand pumper.

Location: 1572 Columbia Street at Cedar Street, Little Italy
Hours: Thurs-Fri 10am-2pm, Sat & Sun until 4pm
Admission: General-$2; Seniors-$1; Military (with ID)-$1; Youth-$1; Under 12-Free; Firefighters-Free
Phone: 619-232-3473

HOW TO GET THERE

To reach Little Italy, connect to I-5.

Exit I-5 South at Sassafras Street and continue southbound along Kettner Boulevard. Turn left at Date Street and proceed one block to India Street. This is the heart of Little Italy.

Exit I-5 North at Hawthorn Street and proceed west towards the water. Make a quick left at Columbia Street. Turn right at Date Street and proceed one block to India Street. This is the heart of Little Italy.

Little Italy

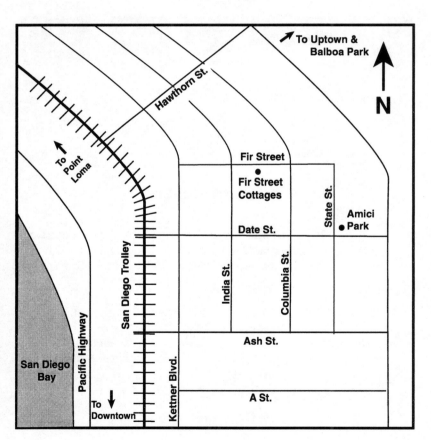

Downtown & Central

MISSION VALLEY

Most people visit Mission Valley for one of two reasons. Either they are heading to a football game at Qualcomm Stadium or San Diego State University, or they are seeking some serious shopping at any or all of the malls in this area. However, it is worth noting that two of San Diego's most important treasures lie near the eastern end of Mission Valley. The first of California's twenty-one missions, Mission San Diego de Alcala, remains preserved in the valley as does one of the city's most prized outdoor recreational destinations, Mission Trails Regional Park.

Mission Trails Regional Park

Less than ten miles from the city lies this gigantic rural wonderland of nearly six thousand acres. There are over forty miles of hiking, mountain biking and equestrian trails that cross over mountains, valleys and lakes. Picnic tables for day use are scattered throughout the park and well-maintained campsites are available for overnight use. The Visitors Center can provide details on seasonal boating and fishing activities.

The Visitor and Interpretive Center offers information and audiotape tours of park highlights. Daily films are shown in a 94-seat theater. A gift shop features quality crafts made by Kumeyaay Indians.

Location:	1 Junipero Serra Trail, Mission Valley
Hours:	Daily Dawn-Dusk, Visitor Center: 9am-5pm
Admission:	Free
Phone:	619-668-3275 Visitor Center
	619-668-2748 Camping Reservations
Website:	www.mtrp.org

HOW TO GET THERE

From points north, exit Highway 52 at Mast Boulevard and proceed north to West Hills Parkway. Turn right at West Hills Parkway and proceed to Mission Gorge Road. Turn right at Mission Gorge Road. Turn right at Junipero Serra Trail.

From points south, exit I-8 at Mission Gorge Road/Fairmount and proceed north on Mission Gorge Road for several miles. Turn left at Junipero Serra Trail.

Mission San Diego de Alcala

Throughout California, twenty-one missions were founded by Franciscan Missionaries from Spain. Mission San Diego de Alcala was the first of these missions. Enjoy the church, beautifully landscaped grounds and archaeological ruins free of charge. The popular Festival of the Bells is celebrated the weekend closest to July 16th to honor the day Junipero Serra founded this church, California's first, in 1769.

There is also a historically-significant museum and gift shop to enjoy. The museum was originally founded on Presidio Hill by Junipero Serra but moved to this location in 1774. Today Presidio Hill is graced by The Serra Museum.

Location:	10818 San Diego Mission Road, Mission Valley
Hours:	Museum: Daily 9am-4:45pm
	Masses: Saturday 5:30pm,
	Sunday hourly 7am-12pm & 5:30pm
Admission:	Museum: General-$3; Youth-$2; Under 12-Free
Phone:	619-281-8449 Visitor Info
	619-283-7319 Parish
Website:	www.misionsandiego.com

HOW TO GET THERE
Exit I-8 at Mission Gorge Road and proceed north. Turn left at Twain Avenue which becomes San Diego Mission Road after 1 block. The mission is on the right.

OLD TOWN

Old Town represents the largest area of the city's original settlement, which is meticulously preserved at Old Town State Historical Park. Not only is the park the most visited attraction in the city, but it is the most visited state park in California. The area surrounding the state park is loosely considered the Old Town neighborhood.

Bazaar Del Mundo

This highly-spirited, colorful village is a cultural destination of international restaurants and shops. It is loaded with furnishings and housewares, garden accessories and fountains, folk art and crafts, hand-woven textiles and ethnic clothing, art and jewelry. Occasionally, Hispanic dancers, mariachis and festive markets called mercados set up among the colorful and decorative gardens, fountains and courtyards.

The Mexican food is some of the city's best and at times a small tortilla stand sets up outside churning out irresistible fresh hand-made corn tortillas.

Celebrations take place for Cinco de Mayo, Dias de los Muertos, the annual Festival of Lights and Latin American Festival.

Location:	Wallace Street at Juan Street, Old Town
Admission:	Free
Hours:	Daily 10am-9pm
Phone:	619-296-3161
Website:	www.bazaardelmundo.com

Heritage Park

Six Victorian houses, which were threatened to be demolished with the post-WWII downtown expansion, have been preserved on this eight-acre hillside county park. The buildings, each one representing a different style of Victorian architecture, are used for art, craft and antique shops. One of the building is a charming bed and breakfast inn. Temple Beth Israel, San Diego's first synagogue from 1889, is also one of Heritage Park's treasures.

Location:	Harney Street at Juan Street, Old Town
Admission:	Free
Hours:	Daily 8am-5pm
Phone:	619-565-3600
Website:	www.co.san-diego.ca.us/parks/

Old Town San Diego State Historic Park

This area has been preserved to capture San Diego's history from 1821 to 1872 at the site of the first permanent settlement in California. The park surrounds a central plaza called Washington Square and is bound by Wallace Street, Juan Street, Twiggs Street and Congress Street. Some of the buildings along the plaza are originals from the 1820s. Historic places are free to the public and many contain museums relating their significant past. There is an admission charge for the Whaley House. The buildings open at 10am daily and are closed on January 1st, Thanksgiving and December 25th.

The Visitor Center, in the northwest corner of the plaza at the Robinson-Rose house, provides free self-guided tour brochures and offers historic walking tours daily at 2pm. Highlights include Blacksmith Shop, Seeley Stables, Dentist Shop, the Mason Street School House, the first San Diego Courthouse, the 1868 birthplace of the San Diego Union newspaper, El Campo Santo Cemetery and the popular, historically-rich 1856 Whaley House.

Whaley House is best known as the most haunted house in California, perhaps even in America, and is one of only two Certified Haunted Houses in the State of California. The still "active" house has served as a residence, a granary, a theater, a billiard hall, a ballroom, a courthouse and the Hall of Records. The house is open Wednesday through Sunday 10am-4:30pm and remains open until 7pm on Friday and Saturday nights. General admission is $5. Seniors fifty-five years and older pay $4 and children ages three through twelve are $3. For further information, visit www.whaleyhouse.org or call 619-297-7511.

In addition to the historical buildings, restored adobes and museums fill the plaza. Active artisans sell their goods and demonstrate their crafts, including glass blowing, diamond cutting, soap making, wood carving and pottery. Most restaurants, cafes and specialty shops are along San Diego Avenue. There is a Farmer's Market at the corner of Twiggs Street and Juan Street on Saturdays 8am-12pm.

Location: Visitors Center: 4002 Wallace Street, Old Town
Admission: Free
Hours: Museums daily 10am-5pm
               Restaurants and shops open later
Phone: 619-220-5422
Website: www.ot-boot.com

Old Town Trolley Tours

This award-winning city trolley tour is a comprehensive, fast-paced, educational and entertaining two hour narrated ride that covers over a hundred points of interest. The trolley stops at eight major locations where passengers are free to hop on and off throughout the day to explore different areas. This flexible tour allows you to pay for, begin at or stop at any of the eight designated city Trolley Tour locations. Residents should ask about the San Diego Hometown Pass.

On Tuesday mornings, a 2-hour 40-minute land-and-sea "Tour of Patriotism" is offered via an amphibious vehicle that winds through Old Town, drops into the bay and arrives at Harbor Island's Marine Corps Recruit Depot. San Diego's military history unfolds with a behind-the-scenes look at the base and a narrated walking tour of the museum. Departures from the Twiggs Street Old Town kiosk start at 9am.

Location:	Twiggs Street, near Theatre in Old Town
Admission:	General-$24; Youth(4-12)-$12; Under 4-Free
Hours:	Daily 9am-5pm
Phone:	619-298-8687
Website:	www.trolleytours.com

Presidio Park & The Serra Museum

The lush grounds of Presidio Park offer stunning views of the bay and provide several places to picnic. From the corner of Juan Street and Mason Street in Old Town, you can hike the Old Presidio Historic Trail uphill to reach the park and museum. The park and museum rest on the first European settlement in Alta California established in 1769 by Father Junipero Serra. The museum, which was built in mission-style architecture in 1929, features San Diego's Native American, Spanish and Mexican heritage through 1850.

Location:	Presidio Park, above Old Town
Hours:	Fri-Sun 10am-4:30pm. Call to confirm
Admission:	Park: Free
	General-$5; Seniors-$4;
	Military & Students (with ID)-$4;
	Youth(6-17)-$2; Under 6-Free
Phone:	619-297-3258
Website:	www.sandiegohistory.org

The Theatre in Old Town

This 244-seat theatre located in the Sate Historic Park is operated by Miracle Theatre Productions, an award-winning professional theatre company that produces Broadway and off-Broadway shows for audiences of all ages. Shows run Thursday through Sunday.

Location:	4040 Twiggs Street, Old Town
Admission:	Prices vary. Starting at $25/Person
Hours:	Box Office: Mon-Wed 10am-6pm,
	Thurs-Sat 10am-8pm, Sun 12pm-7pm
Phone:	619-688-2494 Box Office
Website:	www.theatreinoldtown.com

HOW TO GET THERE

To reach Old Town:

Exit I-5 at Old Town Avenue and proceed east. Turn left at San Diego Avenue and proceed into Old Town.

Exit I-8 at Taylor Street and proceed west. Turn left at Juan Street or Congress Street and proceed a few blocks to Old Town.

To reach Presidio Park:

Exit I-5 at Old Town Avenue and proceed east. Turn left at San Diego Avenue. Turn right at Taylor Street. Turn right at Presidio Drive and wind up the hill.

Exit I-8 at Taylor Street and proceed west. Turn left at Presidio Drive and wind up the hill.

Old Town

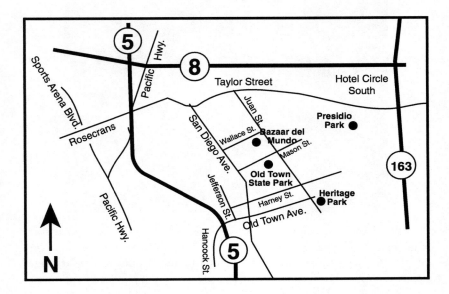

POINT LOMA

The Point Loma peninsula is a favorite destination for incredible views of downtown, the bay and Coronado. During winter months, it is a prime viewing point for the gray whale migration. To one side of the peninsula is the bay and to the other side are steep bluffs perched above beaches.

Cabrillo National Monument & Old Point Loma Lighthouse

At the farthest edge of Point Loma, the monument occupies one of the most inspiring pieces of real estate in California. In 1913, President Woodrow Wilson set aside these priceless 144 acres in honor of Captain Juan Cabrillo, who landed here on September 28, 1542. Cabrillo named the site San Miguel. Spanish explorer Sebastian Viscaino later called it San Diego.

The Old Point Loma Lighthouse, which was built in 1854, is a popular point of interest. For 36 years the lighthouse stood watch over the entrance to San Diego Bay, providing a beacon twenty-five miles out on a clear night. However, fog and low clouds often obscured the light and a new lighthouse was built in 1891 at the water's edge. The new lighthouse is still used today and the old one has been refurbished to its historic 1880s appearance. Ranger led talks, displays and brochures explain the lighthouse's interesting past.

From the park's western overlooks, you can view the new Point Loma

lighthouse and, on a clear day, see the Coronado Islands off the coast of Mexico. From late Dec to mid-March, this is a prime location to watch the Pacific gray whale migration. Although the whales measure over forty feet long and weigh more than forty tons each, binoculars are helpful.

Bayside Trail is a two-mile round trip trail that descends three hundred feet through native coastal sage scrub. It provides views of the bay, but no beach access. During low tides, the coastal tidepool area exposes hundreds of sea plants and animals which survive the harsh environment of pounding surf and jagged rocks. Winter months, full and new moons are the best times to view anemones, shore crabs, darting sculpin, limpets and octopi. Expect to get wet and wear good shoes.

Location:	1800 Cabrillo Memorial Drive, Point Loma
Hours:	Daily 9am-5:15pm
	Open until Sunset during Summer
Admission:	$5/Vehicle; $3/Pedestrian
Phone:	619-222-4797
Website:	www.nps.gov/cabr/home.html

HOW TO GET THERE

Exit I-5 at Rosecrans and proceed southwest to Canon Street. Turn right at Canon Street. Turn left at Catalina Boulevard and proceed through the Naval Ocean Systems Center gate, past the military cemetery to the monument.

Sunset Cliffs Natural Park

Bordering the western edge of Point Loma, this 68-acre park is an ideal place to catch a sunset, hence its name. The walking paths above the ocean reveal the rugged coastline, intricate bluffs, naturally carved arches, sea caves and panoramic views. Watch for migrating whales during the winter months. The beaches below are accessible at low tide, but it can be treacherous and unsafe reaching them. There are no lifeguards. The park's hillside is a designated conservation area linking to the 640-acre Point Loma Ecological Reserve.

HOW TO GET THERE

I-8 West turns into Sunset Cliffs Boulevard. Continue west along Sunset Cliffs Boulevard to the park. Parking lots are located at the north and south ends of Sunset Cliffs Boulevard.

SPORTS ARENA

The San Diego Sports Arena names this centrally located neighborhood between Old Town and Mission Bay. Seasonally, the San Diego Gulls play hockey at the arena and each weekend the age-old swap meet takes place just outside the circular mainstay, featured in the movie *Almost Famous*.

Kobey's Swap Meet

Thousands of people visit this gigantic open-air market searching for bargains on everything from new and used furniture and computers to jewelry, toys and clothes. Food vendors and entertainment, as well as fresh flower and produce stands add a county fair touch to the shopping event.

Location:	3500 Sports Arena Boulevard, Sports Arena
Hours:	Fri-Sun 7am-3pm
Admission:	Fri-50¢; Sat & Sun-$1; Under 12-Free
Phone:	619-226-0650
Website:	www.kobeyswap.com

HOW TO GET THERE
Exit I-8 at Rosecrans and continue on Camino Del Rio West. Turn right at Sports Arena Boulevard and proceed to the arena parking lot.

UltraZone - The Ultimate Laser Adventure

Up to thirty-six players at a time compete in a multilevel, blacklit laser-tag arena designed as an underground city of the future with foggy mazes and passageways. The interactive sport is a fifteen minute adrenaline-filled experience.

Location:	3146 Sports Arena Boulevard, #21, Sports Arena
Admission:	General-$7; Under 7-Not admitted
Hours:	Mon-Thurs 4pm-11pm, Fri 2pm-2am, Sat 10am-2am, Sun 10am-11pm
Phone:	619-221-0100
Website:	www.ultrazonesandiego.com

HOW TO GET THERE
Exit I-8 at Rosecrans and continue on Camino Del Rio West. Turn right at Sports Arena Boulevard. Turn right into the first driveway.

UPTOWN

Uptown is graced with several historic quaint neighborhoods. Hillcrest is among the most popular of these. The heart of this urban neighborhood and

its bohemian spirit is at 5th Avenue and University. One-of-a-kind boutiques and specialty shops are scattered among excellent restaurants, sidewalk cafes and local bars. A movie theatre is located in the Hillcrest Village complex along 5th Avenue.

Slightly northeast of Hillcrest, "antique row" crosses the University Heights and Normal Heights neighborhoods. Along Adams Avenue, from Park Avenue to 40th Street, vintage clothing, records and books are matched by antiques, art and collectibles. Pubs, restaurants and teahouses offer respite to exhausted shoppers.

Bankers Hill holds a secret treasure, Palm Canyon Bridge. Hidden among the urban environment is San Diego's one true suspension bridge at the corner of Front Street and Spruce Street. Crossing the 375-foot swaying bridge over the tree-filled Kate Sessions Canyon floor seventy feet below is amusing. City engineer Edwin Capps built the pedestrian bridge in 1912, a few years before he became mayor. Nearby, on Quince Street between Third Avenue and Fourth Avenue, and on First Avenue between Palm Street and Nutmeg Street are two other neighborhood bridges which cross over Maple Canyon.

Comedy Sportz

Improvisational comedy is performed by the National Comedy Theatre who has been performing for more than twenty years. The family-friendly comedy is a competition between two teams of professional comedians who perform a series of scenes based on audience suggestions.

Location:	3717 India Street, Uptown
Hours:	Fridays & Saturdays 7:30pm & 9:45pm
Admission:	General-$12; Seniors-$10;
	Students & Military (with ID)-$10
Phone:	619-295-4999
Website:	www.nationalcomedy.com

HOW TO GET THERE

Exit I-5 at Washington Street. If northbound, simply continue on India Street. If southbound, continue on Hancock Street and veer left at W. Washington Street. Turn right at India Street.

Mystery Café Dinner Theatre

On weekends, this campy, yet entertaining murder mystery show unfolds in four acts as guests indulge in a four course meal at The Imperial House Restaurant between laughs. During the final act, the audience attempts to solve the mystery.

Location:	505 Kalmia Street, Uptown
Hours:	Fridays & Saturdays 8pm
	Reservations required
Admission:	$42.50-$49.50/Person
Phone:	619-544-1600
Website:	www.mysterycafe.net

HOW TO GET THERE

Exit I-5 North at 6th Avenue and continue on Elm Street. Turn right at 5th Avenue. Turn right at Kalmia Street.

Exit I-5 South at Front Street and proceed east onto Cedar Street. Turn left at 5th Avenue. Turn right at Kalmia Street.

Theatre Sports

In the spirit of "Who's Line Is It Anyway?", a group of improv actors create comedic scenes, skits and songs on the spot, based on audience suggestions. The show is family friendly and appropriate for all ages.

Location:	1531 Tyler Street, Uptown
Hours:	Fridays 8pm
Admission:	General-$15; Seniors-$12
	Military & Students (with ID)-$12
Phone:	619-465-7469
Website:	www.improvise.net

HOW TO GET THERE

Exit 163 at Washington Street and proceed east. Turn left at Cleveland Avenue. Turn right at Tyler Avenue.

Uptown

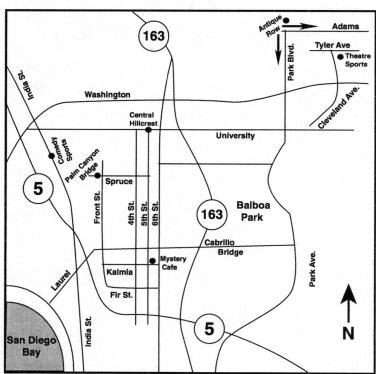

Downtown & Central

San Diego County

COASTAL AREAS

- Coronado Island
- Mission Bay & Mission Beach
- Ocean Beach
- Pacific Beach
- La Jolla
- Torrey Pines
- Del Mar
- Encinitas
- Solana Beach
- Carlsbad
- Oceanside

Coastal San Diego

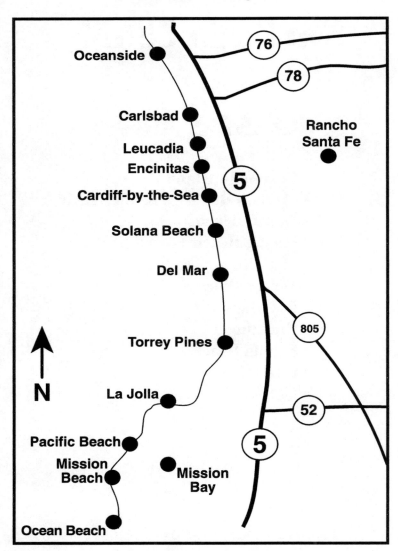

COASTAL SAN DIEGO

For over a hundred miles, the Pacific Ocean breaks on the white sand shores of San Diego. The beautiful coastline stretches from Imperial Beach, near the Mexico border, north to San Onofre which lies just past Camp Pendleton. Between these two points are dozens of destinations for swimming, sun bathing, pier fishing, tide pool exploration, beach bonfires, sand volleyball and, of course, surfing.

San Diego's surfing culture is felt at every beach town up and down the coast. There are surf festivals and competitions, surf-speak, surf clothes and endless surf shops. For those wanting to try the sport, surf lessons are offered by numerous outfitters:

Eli Howard Surf School	760-809-3069 / www.elihoward.com
Kahuna Bob's Surf School	760-721-7700 / www.kahunabob.com
San Diego Surfing Academy	760-230-1474 / www.surfsdsa.com
Surf Sessions Surf Lessons	858-481-1450 www.surfsessions.com
Surfari Surf School	858-337-3287 / www.surfarisurf.com

Encinitas boasts the famed Swami's, where surfers seem to permanently decorate the water waiting for the perfect wave. To watch the surfers at this

world-renowned break, visit Sea Cliff Park, just off Highway 101. Locals often gather here to watch the sun set, check the waves and observe the surfers. A staircase leads from the small park to the beach below. At low tide, this is a prime area for tide pool exploration. Further south, San Elijo State Beach and Seaside Day Use Area also provide good reefs for tide pool exploration. At the lowest tides of the year, one can walk the coastline for nearly fifteen miles from La Jolla Shores north to the beaches of Encinitas. Tide charts are available at most local surf shops.

A drive along San Diego's waterfront can be accomplished in a day, but with so much to see, one might not get too far. Each

coastal community is easily accessed from Interstate 5, but for waterfront views one should hug coastal frontage streets. Start in Imperial Beach, where a walk less than four miles south along the sand can lead to Mexico and a walk along the pier can lead to lunch over the ocean.

From Imperial Beach, exit Seacoast Drive at Palm Avenue and proceed east to connect with Silver Strand Boulevard. Continue north along Silver Strand Boulevard which doubles as Highway 75 to reach Coronado Island. Between these two communities, a sunken gambling ship has remained in the waters along Silver Strand Boulevard since 1936. At low tide, the hull of the SS Monte Carlo can be seen from shore. Coronado is well worth exploring. Most attractions are along palm-lined Orange Avenue.

Take Orange Avenue to the San Diego-Coronado Bay Bridge to reach downtown San Diego. The waterfront Embarcadero runs along Harbor Drive. Harbor Drive leads to marinas, waterfront parks and the Shelter Island, Harbor Island and Point Loma communities. From Harbor Drive, connect with Nimitz Boulevard in Point Loma and proceed north along Nimitz Boulevard to reach Sunset Cliffs Boulevard. The community of Ocean Beach hugs Sunset Cliffs Boulevard. Newport Avenue in Ocean Beach offers some of the best vintage shopping in the county.

Follow Sunset Cliffs Boulevard north as it becomes Mission Bay Drive to reach the Mission Beach, Mission Bay and Pacific Beach communities. Mission Bay Drive crosses over the bay and becomes Mission Boulevard. The beach runs along Mission Boulevard. This area boasts the seaside Giant Dipper Roller Coaster and adjoining amusement park, Historic Crystal Pier and endless eateries, bars and specialty shops. The area is loaded with twenty-somethings, creating a contagious youthful energy. This is also one of the last beach communities to allow beach bonfires in designated fire rings.

Follow Mission Boulevard north to La Jolla Boulevard to reach upscale La Jolla. A seawall perfect for walking or jogging follows La Jolla's breathetaking coastline. Above the bluffs, Prospect Avenue offers boutique shopping and several restaurants. Take Prospect Avenue to Torrey Pines Road and proceed north to reach beautiful Torrey Pines. The ocean views from the Torrey Pines Glider Port and Torrey Pines State Reserve are worth the stop.

Proceeding north along Torrey Pines Road it becomes Camino Del Mar in Del Mar. Turn west on 15th Street to access the beach and connect to the famed Pacific Coast Highway 101. Proceeding north along this road will lead visitors to all the north county beach communities. The road changes names throughout the communities, but is technically S21, also known as Highway 101.

North of Del Mar is Solana Beach. Turn west on Lomas Santa Fe to reach Fletcher Cove Park and Tide City Beach. Turn east on Lomas Santa Fe to reach the popular boutique-filled Cedros Design District.

Proceeding north along S21/Highway 101 leads to Cardiff-by-the-Sea with sand day-use beaches, a Restaurant Row with ocean views, San Elijo State Beach with ocean bluff campsites and a lagoon with nature trails.

Just north of Cardiff-by-the-Sea, the famed Swami's Beach at First Street welcomes visitors to Encinitas. Moonlight Beach at B Street is a popular beach with easy parking and access. Between Swami's and Moonlight is Boneyards Beach and D Street Beach. Stonesteps Beach is north of Moonlight off El Portal Street. Further north, Beacon's Beach off Neptune Avenue and Grandview Beach off Grandview Avenue stretch into the Leucadia neighborhood. From D Street south to Swami's, an Underwater Marine Life Refuge provides incredible scuba opportunities. S21/Highway 101 in Encinitas is lined with shops, restaurants and local pubs.

En route north to Carlsbad, La Costa State Beach hugs S21/Highway 101. Three coastal lagoons, Batiquitos, Agua Hedionda and Buena Vista, are within the Carlsbad area. Carlsbad has two beaches, South Carlsbad State Beach and Carlsbad State Beach. South Carlsbad State Beach allows camping. A lengthy seawall follows the coastline along Carlsbad's ocean bluff providing a nice breeze and views of the water and beach activity. Just east of S21/Highway 101, which doubles as Carlsbad Boulevard in this area, is Carlsbad-Village-by-the-Sea. The "Village" is loaded with beach shops, antiques, coffee shops, bars and restaurants.

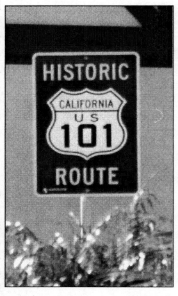

Continuing north along S21/Highway 101 leads to Oceanside. West on Oceanside Boulevard leads to Oceanside City Beach. This is another area that allows beach bonfires in designated fire rings. At the north end of the beach is Oceanside Pier and Harbor Beach. Harbor Beach lies adjacent to Oceanside Harbor's scenic marina. The harbor has everything from specialty stores and nice restaurants to souvenir shops and fish-and-chips shacks.

North of Oceanside lies Camp Pendleton, which is closed to the public. By connecting to Interstate 5 and proceeding north, one can reach San Onofre Surf Beach and San Onofre State Beach Campground at the northern edge of the county line. Exit Basilone Road and proceed west for beach access. Anything north of this point lies within Orange County.

The Coaster is a regional train that runs along the coast between downtown San Diego and Oceanside with stops at eight train station between the two destinations. Before boarding a train, passengers simply buy a ticket from vending machines located on station platforms. The Coaster and Amtrak share the railway at the depots in downtown San Diego, Solana Beach and Oceanside, but a ticket for the Coaster is not valid on Amtrak and vice versa. The service operates continuously on weekdays and makes four roundtrips on Saturdays. It does not operate on Sundays or holidays. For further details, contact Coaster Information at 760-722-6283 or 800-262-7837.

CORONADO

With beaches, parks, marinas, theatres, a golf course, fifteen miles of dedicated bike and rollerblading paths and one very famous hotel, one wouldn't mind being stranded on this island.

Coronado, meaning "the crowned one" in Spanish, can be reached via the beautiful 2-mile San Diego-Coronado Bridge or via a ferry boat that runs between downtown San Diego and Ferry Marketplace. The ferry ride offers spectacular views of the bay and city skyline. Prices are $2 per person and 50¢ per bicycle. The ferry departs Broadway Pier daily on the hour 9am-9pm and Coronado's Ferry Landing Marketplace daily on the half hour 9:30am-9:30pm. On Friday and Saturday nights, an extra run operates at 10pm and 10:30pm.

Beyond the popular Silver Strand State Beach, Coronado has two other public beaches. Coronado Central Beach, which runs along Ocean Boulevard, has lifeguards, showers and restrooms. It also features tide pools and fishing in front of the Hotel del Coronado. Fire rings and a dedicated dog beach are at the north end. Beaches to the north and south of this area are reserved for the US Navy. To the south, the Naval Amphibious Base and USN Training Beach is where Navy SEALS are trained under realistic conditions. The small Glorietta Bay Beach is south of the Hotel Del Coronado and offers views of the bay and of the San Diego-Coronado Bridge.

Glorietta Bay Marina offers boat rentals ranging from paddleboats and jet skis to deep sea fishing boats and sailboats. Fishing is allowed on the pier at Ferry Landing Marketplace and off the Hotel del Coronado breakwater.

Old Ferry Landing hosts a weekly Farmer's Market on Tuesdays 2:30pm-6pm at First and B Streets. On Sundays during the summer, Spreckles Park located on Orange Avenue between 6th Street and 7th Street, hosts concerts at the gazebo bandstand. Art-in-the-Park is held at Spreckles Park the first and third Sundays of every month 9am-4pm. In April, the longheld Annual Flower Show is held. Visit www.coronadoflowershow.com for dates and information. Each fall, the annual Do The Bridge Run/Walk covers a scenic five mile journey from Seaport Village to Coronado's Tidelands Park. Visit www.strideamerica.com for dates and further information.

HOW TO GET THERE
Take I-5 South to Crosby Street and cross the San Diego-Coronado Bridge.

Ferry Landing Marketplace

Beyond being the ferry station, the marketplace houses a collection of shops, art galleries, eateries and fine restaurants. It is also a good place to rent bikes, which provide the perfect way to explore the island. Coronado has continuous flat riding paths and endless scenery. Bikes & Beyond is located at the marketplace and can be reached at 619-435-7180. A sandy beach and grassy lawns with great city views are adjacent to the fishing pier.

Location:	1201 1st Street at B Avenue, Coronado
Hours:	Open daily at 10am. Closing times vary
Admission:	Free
Phone:	619-435-8895
Website:	www.coronado.ca.us/sd_ferry.html

HOW TO GET THERE
Follow the bridge west and turn right at B Avenue. Turn left at 1st Street.

The Gondola Company

This lesser-known attraction provides guests with a one-hour guided tour of Coronado via a ride on a 36-foot Venetian gondola through the Coronado Cays canals. Hors d'oeuvres or dessert are served and guests are welcome to bring their own beverages. A warm blanket, wine glasses and an ice bucket are provided. Special champagne, dinner and brunch packages are available.

Location:	4000 Coronado Bay Road, Coronado
Hours:	Daily 11am-12am
Admission:	Prices vary. Expect roughly $60-$95/Couple
Phone:	619-429-6317
Website:	www.gondolacompany.com

HOW TO GET THERE
Follow the bridge west and turn left at Orange Avenue. Continue along Orange Avenue and proceed nearly 5 miles past the Hotel Del Coronado as it becomes Highway 75. Turn left at Coronado Bay Road and enter the Loews Coronado Bay Resort. The Gondola Company is at the Marina Office on the right side.

Hotel Del Coronado

One of the most celebrated structures in the world, this National Historic Landmark is one of the largest wooden structures in existence. The stunning 1888 Victorian has been graced by several celebrities and is quite famous for

being the location where *Some Like It Hot* starring Marilyn Monroe, Tony Curtis and Jack Lemmon was shot.

The hotel has a fascinating history. Numerous presidents, royalty and heads of state have stayed here. Legends including Charles Lindbergh, Frank Sinatra and the ghost of Kate Morgan adorn the hotel walls via photos and memorabilia. Visitors are welcome to wander through the impressive hotel and visit the shops and restaurants.

Live entertainment is offered most evenings in one of the bars and a formal afternoon tea is served on Sundays 12pm-4pm in the Palm Court. In early December, the Annual Lighting of the Del ceremony is held on the Windsor lawn. With the flick of a switch the Victorian is outlined in thousands of lights and a fifty foot Christmas tree is lit for the season.

Location:	1500 Orange Avenue, Coronado
Hours:	Daily 24 Hours
	Shops and restaurants hold regular hours
Admission:	Free
Phone:	619-435-6611 or 800-468-3533
Website:	www.hoteldel.com

HOW TO GET THERE

Follow the bridge west and turn left at Orange Avenue. Hotel Del Coronado is on the right.

Day Outings From San Diego

Coronado Playhouse

This "Theatre on the Bay" has been operating a year round schedule for nearly sixty years. The Playhouse has cabaret seating for just over a hundred and a full service bar. Productions tend to be classic choices, everything from *Cinderella* to Neil Simon.

Location:	1775 Strand Way, Coronado
Hours:	Show times vary
	Box Office: Tues-Fri 11am-4pm
Admission:	Ticket prices vary
Phone:	619-435-4856
Website:	www.coronadoplayhouse.com

HOW TO GET THERE
Follow the bridge west and turn left at Orange Avenue. Follow Orange Avenue about 3 miles. The playhouse is on the left just past the Hotel Del Coronado.

Lamb's Players Theatre

Lamb's Players Theatre, which is run by the artists, maintains a year-round schedule. An acclaimed resident ensemble cast is supplemented by outside actors. Playbills run the gamut. Everything from musicals and timeless classics to original plays and adaptions have been performed by this award-winning performing arts group. All 350 seats are within seven rows of the performers in this European-style thrust stage theatre. Shops and restaurants are within walking distance.

Location:	1142 Orange Avenue, Coronado
Hours:	Show times vary
	Box Office: Tue-Sat 12pm-7pm, Sun 12pm-5pm
Admission:	Ticket prices vary
Phone:	619-437-0600
Website:	www.lambsplayers.org

HOW TO GET THERE
Follow the bridge west and turn left at Orange Avenue.

Coastal Areas
2 - 10

Museum of History and Art

There are four galleries in this museum. Special exhibits change quarterly while permanent galleries focus on Coronado's early history, including Tent City, the Hotel del Coronado and the island's Army and Navy military history.

Location:	1100 Orange Avenue, Coronado
Hours:	Mon-Fri 9am-5pm, Sat 10am-5pm
	Sun 11am-4pm
Admission:	$4 Voluntary Donation
Phone:	619-437-8788
Website:	www.coronadohistory.org

HOW TO GET THERE

Follow the bridge west and turn left at Orange Avenue. The museum is on the right at 10th Street.

Silver Strand State Beach

Four and a half miles south of downtown Coronado, this sandy beach offers camping, swimming, surfing, boating, fishing, water-skiing, volleyball, and picnicking. Sandy strips line both the Pacific Ocean and the San Diego Bay. A pedestrian tunnel under Silver Strand Boulevard connects the bayside beach to the ocean beach. A paved path allows one to bike, rollerblade or jog nearly eight miles to Imperial Beach. South of designated formal areas is a mile and a half of ocean and natural preserve.

Location:	5000 Highway 75, Coronado
Hours:	Daily 8am-7pm
Admission:	Day-Use: $4/Vehicle
	Camping: General-$14/Night;
	Seniors-$12/Night; Dogs-$1/Night
Phone:	619-435-5184
Website:	www.parks.ca.gov

HOW TO GET THERE

Follow the bridge west and turn left at Orange Avenue. Follow Orange Avenue south to Silver Strand Boulevard/Highway 75. The beach is located on the sand strip between Coronado and Imperial Beach. The entrance is from Highway 75, which divides the ocean side of the park and the bay side.

Coronado Island

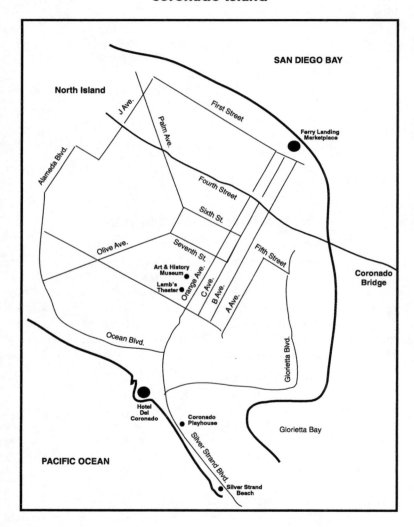

MISSION BAY & MISSION BEACH

Mission Bay was created when the city carved out a river marsh to create roughly nine square miles of beaches, parks, bicycle paths and marinas. It is one of San Diego's most popular outdoor recreation and vacation areas with several hotels and the popular Sea World.

Mission Beach at the south end of Mission Boulevard is favored for its boardwalk and beach combination. Biking, roller blading, outdoor basketball, sand volleyball, swimming, surfing and endless people watching are favorite pasttimes along the Boulevard. The historic Giant Dipper rollercoaster is just steps from the boardwalk and the beach. A lively energy continues at night with packed local clubs and bars.

Near Belmont Park, a Farmer's Market is held Saturday mornings 9am-1pm at 3146 Mission Boulevard. A nice scenic drive from Mission Bay to Ocean Beach can be made by following Mission Boulevard south and turning left onto West Mission Bay Drive.

Connect to Sunset Cliffs Boulevard and proceed south for spectacular views of the cliffs, Newbreak Beach and Abe Reef. A right turn on West Point Loma Boulevard leads to the low key community of Ocean Beach.

Bahia Belle Bay Cruise

For more than 30 years, this Victorian-style sternwheeler has provided one hour tours of the bay with music and entertainment on two spacious interior decks and a wide observation deck for night sky views. Departures are from the Bahia Hotel.

Location:	998 W. Mission Bay Drive, Mission Bay
Hours:	Hours vary. Call for sailing schedule
Admission:	General-$6
Phone:	858-539-7779
Website:	www.bahiahotel.com

HOW TO GET THERE
Exit I-5 at Garnet Avenue and proceed west. Merge left to Grand Avenue. Turn left at Mission Boulevard and proceed south. Turn left at W. Mission Bay Drive. The hotel is on the left.

Belmont Park & Giant Dipper Roller Coaster

Belmont Park is an oceanfront amusement park featuring the historic Giant Dipper Roller Coaster. The coaster was wildly popular during the 1930s and 40s, but closed after major disrepair during the 70s. A multi-million dollar restoration project re-opened the upgraded wooden coaster while retaining its same nostalgic look. There is also a carrousel, an arcade, rides and an indoor children's play center.

Location:	W. Mission Bay Drive at Mission Boulevard, Mission Beach
Hours:	Opens daily at 11am. Closing times vary
Admission:	Free. Giant Dipper- $4/Ride
Phone:	858-488-1549
Website:	www.belmontpark.com

HOW TO GET THERE
Exit I-5 at Garnet Avenue and proceed west. Merge left to Grand Avenue. Turn left at Mission Boulevard and proceed south to W. Mission Bay Drive.

Mission Bay Park

This 4,000+ acre park is more water than land, making it the largest aquatic park on the west coast. Everything from sailboats and sportfishing charters, to wave runners and wind surfers, to kayaks, paddle boats and swimmers fill the bay waters.

Nearly twenty miles of sandy beaches accommodate volleyball, sunbathing and picnicking. Campsites and fire rings are offered as well. Twenty-seven miles of shoreline make for incredible scenery and nice breezes for those that choose to cycle, jog or rollerblade the waterfront paved walkways. The nature reserve at the north end near Crown Point attracts several rare bird and animal species.

Fiesta Island hosts a wildly popular annual Over-The-Line tournament, which is a three-person softball game, every July. The team names alone make it worth attending. Be forewarned the names are sometimes salty. Hotels, restaurants, cafes, markets and shopping are plentiful. There are numerous rental companies that can outfit visitors for any sport or recreational activity:

Action Sports Beach & Bay Rentals	619-581-5939
Bahia Resort Hotel Marina	619-488-0551
CP Watersports	619-275-8945
Islandia Sportfishing	619-222-1164
Mission Bay Sportcenter	619-488-1004
Seaforth Boat Rentals/Sportfishing	619-223-1681

Location:	Accessed from Mission Bay Drive, Mission Bay
Hours:	Daily Sunrise-Sunset
Admission:	Free
Phone:	619-221-8900 General Info
	858-581-7879 Park Rangers
Website:	www.sannet.gov/park-and-recreation

HOW TO GET THERE

Exit I-5 at Clairemont Drive and proceed west one block to reach the east side of Mission Bay Park.

SeaWorld Adventure Park

Home of world-famous Shamu, this popular theme park is frequented by locals and tourists alike. While most visitors map out their visits independently, a guided 90-minute behind-the-scenes walking tours is offered. Proximity to the animals is one of this park's bragging rights, whether its rubbing a bottlenose dolphins melon or riding *Wild Arctic* to get close up

with polar bears, beluga whales and walruses or feeding seals and sea lions.

Stingray filled aquariums and special exhibits such as *Shark Encounter* and *Penguin Encounter* are other favorites.

The animals are often featured in inventive and entertaining shows and thematic performances. Special programs like Breakfast with Shamu, Trainer For a Day and Adventure Camps are other unique highlights for visitors. The park hosts annual Halloween spectaculars and is particularly festive at Christmas.

Location:	500 Sea World Drive, Mission Bay
Hours:	Opens daily at 10am. Closing times vary
	Summer: Opens daily at 9am
Admission:	General-$45, 2-Day Pass-$49;
	Youth(3-9)-$36, 2-Day Pass-$40; Under 3-Free
	Parking: $4-$9/Vehicle
Phone:	619-226-3901
Website:	www.seaworld.com

HOW TO GET THERE
Exit I-5 at Sea World Drive and proceed west towards the entrance.

OCEAN BEACH

This area, affectionately known as "OB", is the southernmost public beach on the Point Loma peninsula. The sandy beach is complemented by a 1960s municipal pier that allows free fishing and boasts a restaurant with great views. Good surf, fire pits and one of the few no-leash dog beaches in the county are all favorite reasons locals enjoy Ocean Beach.

The community enjoys a large antique district, surf shops, numerous restaurants and a weekly Farmer's Market every Wednesday afternoon 4pm-7pm at the 4900 block of Newport Avenue off of Sunset Cliffs Boulevard. During the summer there are free concerts at the outdoor market and llama rides have been offered to children ages four through eight in the past.

Ocean Beach Main Street Association

Location:	4993 Niagra, Suite 105, Ocean Beach
Hours:	Mon-Fri 9am-5pm
Phone:	619-224-4906
Website:	www.oceanbeachsandiego.com

HOW TO GET THERE
Take I-8 West to its end and continue onto Sunset Cliffs Boulevard.

PACIFIC BEACH

Affectionately known as "PB", Pacific Beach buzzes with a young energy around the clock. During the day, the Pacific Beach Boardwalk and aligning soft sand fill up with surfers, swimmers, sunbathers, Boogie boarders, bikers, joggers, rollerbladers and people watchers. At night, the streets come alive with people hopping from one bar, club, music venue, coffeehouse or restaurant to the next. PB is also one of the last communities to allow evening bonfires on the beach.

Attractions along the beach include Historic Crystal Pier and the Grand and Garnet Avenue Shopping District, just a few blocks in from the boardwalk. Further inland, off of Soledad Road, Kate Sessions Park offers views of the Pacific Ocean, Mission Bay and downtown San Diego.

The PB Farmer's Market is held Saturdays 8am-12pm at Mission Boulevard and Pacific Beach Drive. Annually, Pacific Beach hosts the PB Block Party in May, Pacific BeachFest in October and PB Restaurant Walks in May and September.

Discover Pacific Beach - Information

Location:	1503 Garnet Avenue, Pacific Beach
Hours:	Mon-Fri 9:30am-4:30pm
Phone:	858-273-3303
Website:	www.pacificbeach.org

HOW TO GET THERE

Exit I-5 at Balboa/Garnet Avenue from points north or Grand/Garnet Avenue from points south. Proceed west towards the ocean.

Historic Crystal Pier

Built in 1927, Crystal Pier once had a ballroom perched at its end, which now affords fantastic views of Mission Beach to the south. In 1936, Crystal Cottages were built on the pier and remain there today. With some planning, one can sleep over the ocean on the pier and listen to the waves roll in. Crystal Pier Hotel & Cottages suggests 6-8 weeks advance for reservations. Pier fishing is allowed with a license 8am until sunset daily.

Crystal Pier Hotel & Cottages

Location:	4500 Ocean Boulevard, Pacific Beach
Hours:	Daily 8am-Sunset
	Hotel Office: Daily 8am-8pm
Admission:	Free. Hotel & Cottage prices vary,
	Expect $125-$300/Night
Phone:	858-483-6983 Hotel Office
	800-748-5894 Reservations

HOW TO GET THERE

Exit I-5 at Balboa/Garnet Avenue from points north or Grand/Garnet Avenue from points south. Proceed west towards the ocean.

Great News Cooking School

This cooking school provides several class options. The mega-kitchen, which is full with classes eight to ten times each week, features television monitors and seats 45 people. Most classes are demonstration, but smaller, technical classes such as knife skills and sushi classes are hands-on. Guests always sample the food and take home the recipes from each class. Classes cover everything from Asian, Thai and Italian meals to Vegan and Tofu cooking.

Location:	1788 Garnet Avenue, Pacific Beach
Hours:	Times vary; classes likely Mon-Fri 6pm, Sat 1pm
Admission:	Prices vary. Expect roughly $30-$60/Person
Phone:	858-270-1582
Website:	www.great-news.com

HOW TO GET THERE

Exit I-5 at Balboa/Garnet Avenue from points north or Grand/Garnet Avenue from points south and proceed west along Garnet Avenue.

Mission Bay, Mission Beach, Pacific Beach & Ocean Beach

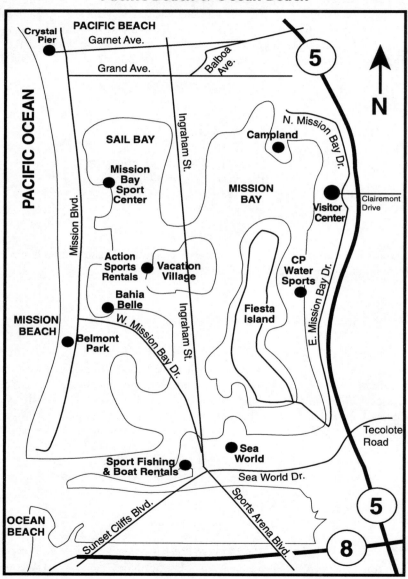

LA JOLLA

La Jolla, meaning "the jewel", is an exclusive coastal community that balances its beach spirit with rich arts and culture. With the prestigious Museum of Contemporary Art and the award-winning La Jolla Playhouse, as well as one of the country's finest art festivals, there is much more than soft sand and quality scuba and snorkeling in La Jolla. The annual Festival of the Arts and Food Faire is held in June at the La Jolla Country Day School campus. Visit www.lajollaartfestival.org for details.

Picturesque La Jolla is best absorbed by strolling the paved ocean front promenade that hugs the dramatic coastline. The Cove is an ideal area for walking and picnicking with ocean views or partaking in beach activity. The Shores is usually packed with sunbathers and has the only city beach  with a public boat launch. La Jolla has some premiere scuba and snorkeling waters. Caves that have been naturally carved out of the sandstone cliffs make for great scuba and kayaking adventures. The Sunny Jim Cave can be accessed by land through a staircase at a curio shop at 1325 Coast Boulevard.

Shopping along Prospect Avenue and Girard Avenue will delight those who appreciate specialties from small boutiques and upscale shops. Art galleries and gourmet restaurants surround this area. The Upper Girard Design District, surrounding the Pearl Street and Girard Avenue intersection, offers inspiring home décor ideas with a plethora of furniture, art and design stores.

Soledad Mountain, accessible via Torrey Pines Road or Ardath Road, and Torrey Pines Glider Port off of North Torrey Pines Road offer spectacular panoramic views of the area. Famous Blacks Beach can be viewed from the glider port looking north.

HOW TO GET THERE
Exit I-5 at La Jolla Village Drive from points south and at Ardath Road from points north. Proceed west to La Jolla.

Birch Aquarium at Scripps

With spectacular views overlooking the Pacific Ocean, this stunning oceanographic museum and marine life collection is well worth a visit. It is the largest of its kind with over 3,000 colorful fish in more than 30 aquarium tanks, including a two-story kelp forest. Most fish are native to the Pacific Ocean, Mexico's Sea of Cortez and the Indio-Pacific.

The hands-on tide pool exhibit is an opportunity to examine marine life in a natural environment without getting wet feet. Although the tide pool is manmade and does not depend on the ocean's natural tides, it does adapt to nature's ebb and flow of weather between seasons. The creatures survive because each is uniquely equipped with instincts and physical apparatus that allow them to adapt in dangerous environments. A gift shop focused on ocean sciences offers educational books, gifts and souvenirs.

Location:	2300 Expedition Way, La Jolla
Hours:	Daily 9am-5pm
	Closed Thanksgiving, Dec 25 & Jan 1
Admission:	General-$9.50; Seniors(60+)-$8;
	Students (with ID)-$6.50;
	Youth(3-17)-$6; Under 3-Free
	Parking-$3/Vehicle
Phone:	858-534-3474
Website:	www.aquarium.ucsd.edu

HOW TO GET THERE

Exit I-5 at Genessee Avenue or La Jolla Village Drive and proceed west. Connect to North Torrey Pines Road (south of Genesee Avenue and north of La Jolla Village Drive). Turn onto Expedition Way.

La Jolla Cove

This small beach is tucked between sandstone cliffs and lies below the popular

grassy Scripps Park with views of the shores. The area lies within an underwater ecological reserve where water visibility can exceed 30 feet, making it a scuba and snorkeling mecca.

Further south along the cove, the Casa a.k.a. the Children's Pool, is a small beach sheltered by a seawall. The concept of creating a fully protected swimming area was never fully realized as sand slipped inside the wall. Nevertheless, the beach is a favorite with its panoramic view and

frequent visits by seals and sea lions. These mammals typically sunbathe on the nearby Seal Rock, but at times come right up on the beach. Between late December and early to mid March, Pacific gray whales can sometimes be spotted from the cove as they migrate south. It is helpful to have binoculars.

Location:	The Cove: 850 Coast Boulevard, La Jolla
	Children's Pool: 1100 Coast Boulevard, La Jolla
Hours:	Daily Sunrise-Sunset
Admission:	Free

HOW TO GET THERE

Exit I-5 at La Jolla Village Drive from points south and at Ardath Road from points north. Proceed west to Torrey Pines Road. Follow Torrey Pines Road west and turn right at Prospect Street. Bear right on Coast Boulevard and follow signs to the cove.

La Jolla Cove Snorkel & Kayak Adventures/ Scuba San Diego

Scuba San Diego offers guided tours to the world famous La Jolla Cove Underwater Park, highlighting the large variety of sea life, the sea cliffs and the sea caves. After an orientation, a naturalist guides guests into the waters in their kayaks or snorkel gear for a 2-3 hour water adventure. Solo, tandem and triple ocean kayaks are available. It is common to have close encounters with sea lions and harbor seals. Equipment and lunch is included in the tours. Reservations are required at least one day in advance. The company also offers scuba experiences and certification for non-divers and excursions for certified divers.

Location:	2132 Avenida de la Playa, La Jolla
Hours:	Daily 8am-5pm
	Kayak Tours at 8am and 11am
	Snorkel Tours at 10am
Admission:	Snorkel: $55/person; Kayak: $65/Person
Phone:	619-260-1880 or 619-341-1900
Website:	www.scubasandiego.com
	www.sandiegokayakadventure.com

HOW TO GET THERE

Exit I-5 at La Jolla Village Drive from points south and at Ardath Road from points north. Proceed west to Torrey Pines Road. Follow Torrey Pines Road west and turn right at La Jolla Shores Drive. Turn left at Avenida de la Playa. Meet the guide on the beach at the Boat Launch area.

La Jolla Shores

This sandy stretch of beach is about a mile long and usually attracts crowds during the summer months. A paved boardwalk connects part of the beach to Kellogg Park, a grassy area ideal for picnicking. Scripps Institute of Oceanography and Scripps Pier lie at the north end of the beach but are closed to the public. The only beachfront boat launch within city limits accommodates small vessels seeking to launch directly into the ocean.

Location: 8200 Camino del Oro, La Jolla
Hours: Daily Sunrise-Sunset
Admission: Free

HOW TO GET THERE
Exit I-5 at La Jolla Village Drive from points south and at Ardath Road from points north. Proceed west to Torrey Pines Road. Follow Torrey Pines Road west and turn right at La Jolla Shores Drive. Turn left at Avenida de la Playa. Turn right at Camino del Oro.

La Jolla Playhouse

This playhouse, founded in 1947 by Gregory Peck, Dorothy McGuire and Mel Ferrer, has built its strong reputation on Tony-award winning presentations of classics, musicals and original plays. Several productions have enjoyed stints on Broadway and world tours. Shows are staged in the Mandell Weiss Theatre and Mandell Weiss Forum May through November.

Location: 2910 La Jolla Village Drive, UCSD, La Jolla
Hours: Shows: Tues-Sat 8pm Curtain, Sun 7pm Curtain
Sat & Sun 2pm Matinee Curtain
Box Office: Mon 12pm-6pm, Tues-Sat 12pm-8pm, Sun 12pm-7pm
Non-Performance Weeks: Mon-Fri 12pm-6pm
Admission: Ticket prices vary
Phone: 858-550-1010
Website: www.lajollaplayhouse.com

HOW TO GET THERE
Exit I-5 at La Jolla Village Drive and proceed west. Continue along La Jolla Village Drive. Turn right at Revelle College Drive onto the UCSD campus. The two playhouse theaters are on the right. Parking is on the left.

Museum of Contemporary Art

This 60,000 square-foot internationally renowned museum is located on a slope overlooking the Pacific. MCA's permanent collection is one of the best of its kind reflecting the most important artists and movements of the past fifty years. The 3,000+ artworks show examples of minimalism, pop, conceptual art, Installment art, Latin American art and works by artists from San Diego and the Tijuana region.

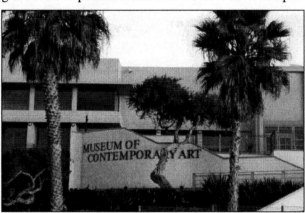

Location:	700 Prospect Street, La Jolla
Hours:	Labor Day-Memorial Day:
	Thurs-Tues 11am-5pm
	Open until 8pm Thursdays
	Memorial Day-Labor Day:
	Mon-Tues & Thurs-Fri 11am-8pm
	Sat-Sun 11am-5pm
Admission:	General-$6; Seniors(65+)-$2;
	Students & Military (with ID)-$2;
	Youth(12-18)-$2; Under 12-Free
	Free 1st Sun and 3rd Tues every month
Phone:	858-454-3541
Website:	www.moca.org / www.mcasandiego.org

HOW TO GET THERE

Exit I-5 at La Jolla Village Drive from points south and at Ardath Road from points north. Proceed west to Torrey Pines Road. Follow Torrey Pines Road west and turn right at Prospect Street. Follow Prospect Street to downtown La Jolla and MoCA.

TORREY PINES

Torrey Pines Glider Port

The off-shore air currents allow for quality paragliding and hangliding conditions along the Torrey Pines cliffs, a world-famous soaring site since 1928. For those anxious to try the sport, tandem flights and instruction are offered. For those uncertain, the views make it a worthwhile stop for watching the gliders, catching a glimpse of the famous Blacks Beach and Pacific coastline or enjoying a casual meal at the cliff-top cafe. There is a flight sport shop and several friendly specialists and enthusiasts for expert advice at the glider port.

Location:	2800 Torrey Pines Scenic Drive, Torrey Pines
Hours:	Daily 9am-Sunset
Admission:	Free. Flights roughly $150/Person
Phone:	858-452-9858
Website:	www.flytorrey.com

HOW TO GET THERE
Exit I-5 at Genesee Avenue and proceed west. Turn left at Torrey Pines Road. Turn right at Torrey Pines Scenic Drive (before Salk Institute Drive) and proceed to the gliderport.

Torrey Pines State Reserve

This unique day-use park features chaparral plants and rare Torrey Pine trees leading to miles of pristine beaches. The torrey pine is the country's rarest pine tree and only grows in this area. A similar subspecies grows on Santa Rosa Island near Santa Barbara.

The Visitor Center building was once called Torrey Pines Lodge. The lodge had a character all its own with a restaurant filled with stubby tables, lampshades made of Torrey Pine needles, chintz curtains and a jukebox. Today it houses a museum with historical exhibits. On weekends and holidays guided nature walks are offered at 10am and 2pm. During winter months, gray whales and bottlenose dolphins are occasionally spotted and during Spring, wildflowers bloom.

There are eight miles of trails to choose from. The short High Point Trail near the Visitor's Center gives one a great overview of the area with panoramic views of the reserve, the ocean and inland. Another easy trail is Guy Fleming Trail, a forested 2/3-mile loop with changing scenery, ocean views and sandstone formations. The secluded Parry Grove Trail is a short 1/2-mile loop, with a steep beginning and end. There is a native plant garden at the trailhead. The Razor Point Trail offers dramatic views of gorges, wilderness and some incredible trees. The popular Beach Trail is the least scenic, but provides access to the beach and Flat Rock. The trail becomes steep and narrows near the beach. It is important to check the tides to ensure the beach is sandy enough for walking or picnicking. The more demanding Broken Hill Trail also provides beach access via a north fork and south fork. This is the longest trail passing chaparral, a few trees and a scenic overlook of the "broken hill." Hikers can combine this trail with Razor Point and Beach Trails for a 3-mile loop.

Location:	1221 Camino Del Mar, Torrey Pines
Hours:	Daily 8am-Sunset
Admission:	General-$4/Vehicle; Seniors(62+)-$3/Vehicle; Pedestrians & Bicycles-Free
Phone:	858-755-2063
Website:	www.torreypine.org

HOW TO GET THERE
Exit I-5 at Carmel Valley Road and proceed west for about 1.5 miles. Turn left at Coast Highway 101 and proceed along the beach for about a mile. The park entrance is on the right just before the highway begins to climb the Torrey Pines grade.

Coastal Areas

La Jolla & Torrey Pines

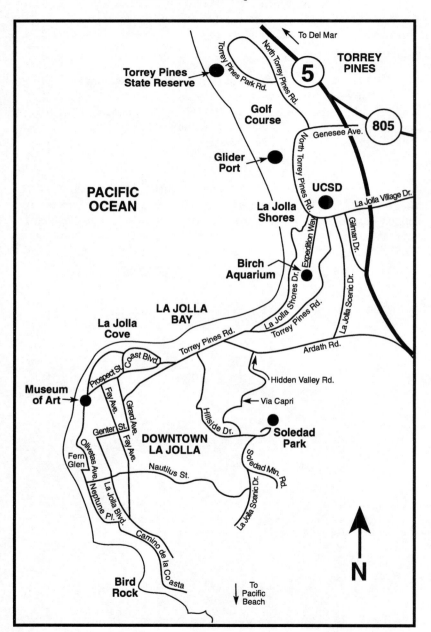

Torrey Pines State Reserve

Golf Course

Glider Port

PACIFIC OCEAN

La Jolla Shores

Birch Aquarium

LA JOLLA BAY

La Jolla Cove

Museum of Art

DOWNTOWN LA JOLLA

Soledad Park

Fern Glen

Bird Rock

To Del Mar

TORREY PINES

5

805

Genesee Ave.

UCSD

La Jolla Village Dr.

Torrey Pines Park Rd.

North Torrey Pines Rd.

North Torrey Pines Rd.

Expedition Way

Gilman Dr.

La Jolla Shores Dr.

Torrey Pines Rd.

La Jolla Scenic Dr.

Ardath Rd.

Hidden Valley Rd.

Via Capri

Hillside Dr.

Soledad Mtn. Rd.

La Jolla Scenic Dr.

Coast Blvd.

Prospect St.

Fay Ave.

Girard Ave.

Genter St.

Fay Ave.

Torrey Pines Rd.

Olivetas Ave.

La Jolla Blvd.

Neptune Pl.

Nautilus St.

Camino de la Costa

To Pacific Beach

N

DEL MAR

Del Mar, meaning "by the sea", is a two square mile seaside city with beautiful bluffs perched above long sandy beaches. Desirable homes decorate the hillside overlooking the Pacific Ocean and a lucky few rest square on the sand of Del Mar's most popular beach area.

Seagrove Park and Del Mar's trademark Powerhouse Building provide a nice setting for a grassy picnic with ocean views. This area offers oceanfront restaurants as well.

A walk on the beach north of Seagrove Park leads to the most common sunbathing and swimming locations and ends at a dog beach. A walk south leads to locations frequented mostly by surfers, and eventually becomes Torrey Pines State Beach.

The city holds a weekly Farmer's Market on Saturdays 1pm-4pm at City Hall on Camino Del Mar and 10th Street. Del Mar Plaza on Camino Del Mar

offers shopping, galleries, a wine bar and fine restaurants with stunning views. A lesser-known Del Mar gem is the Parisi Gallery & Sculpture Garden at 2002 Jimmy Durante Boulevard. In April 2003, the gallery began hosting a monthly Chef & Art Series. The series features lectures on art and food followed by a gourmet meal prepared by a visiting celebrity chef. The cost is roughly $45 per person. Call 858-259-0490 for upcoming dates and details.

HOW TO GET THERE
Exit I-5 at Via de la Valle and proceed west to the ocean. Del Mar is just south of Via de la Valle.

Del Mar Fairgrounds

On opening day in 1937, Bing Crosby personally collected the ticket from the fairground's very first customer. Since that day, the world-famous race track has become known as the place "where the surf meets the turf."

The ocean front facility hosts several events year-round, but the main draws are the San Diego County Fair in late June and early July followed by the Del-Mar Thoroughbred Race Meet from mid-July to September. Several horse races are followed by free concerts in an open-air plaza and in the off-season, thoroughbred racing diehards may wager at the Surfside Race Place off-track betting facility. The beautiful setting makes for a nice day at the track. In December, the Holiday of Lights display draws a crowd.

Location:	2260 Jimmy Durante Boulevard, Del Mar
Hours:	Hours vary by event
Admission:	Prices vary by event
Phone:	858-755-1141
	858-793-5533 Information Line
Website:	www.delmarfair.com/www.dmtc.com

HOW TO GET THERE

Exit I-5 at Via de la Valle and proceed west. Turn left at Jimmy Durante Boulevard. The fairgrounds are on the right.

Skysurfer Balloon Company

This family owned and operated company offers sunrise flights from Temecula and sunset flights from Del Mar. The balloons carry six to fourteen passengers for a 45- to 60- minute ride. The company prides itself on safety and customer satisfaction.

Location:	1221 Camino Del Mar, Del Mar
Hours:	Daily 9am-9pm. Reservations required
Admission:	Weekdays: Starting at $135/Person
	Weekends & holidays: $145/Person
Phone:	858-481-6800 or 800-660-6809
Website:	www.skysurferballoon.com

HOW TO GET THERE

Exit I-5 at Via de la Valle and proceed west. Turn left at Jimmy Durante Boulevard and continue past the Del Mar Racetrack. Turn left at Camino Del Mar.

ENCINITAS

Sandwiched between the San Elijo Lagoon to the south and the Batiquitos

Lagoon to the north, Encinitas encompasses the communities of Leucadia, Cardiff-by-the-Sea, Olivenhain and old and new Encinitas.

The six coastline miles are the coveted of the twenty-two square mile city. Historic downtown, lined with sidewalk cafes, shops, bars and restaurants, runs along both sides of Coast Highway 101. Notable among the several charming stops is the vintage La Paloma Theatre built in 1928, possibly the first "talking" theatre in the rural United States. Today, it screens contemporary favorites.

While this community evokes a sense of the eclectic and diverse, the beaches attract people from all over the county. Swami's Beach is world-renown for great surf and San Elijo State Beach has a campground that sells out immediately each year with prime sites perched on the bluffs above the ocean.

San Elijo and Seaside Beach are great for tide pool exploration one or two hours before extremely low tides. Moonlight Beach to the north is a favorite with sunbathers and swimmers. During July and August, Moonlight Beach hosts a Sunday concert series. Cardiff State Beach to the south attracts board and body surfers, swimmers and Boogie boarders. Scuba divers and snorkelers appreciate the Encinitas Underwater California State Marine-Life Refuge.

The area has several first-rate nurseries and is home of the popular poinsettia. A Farmer's Market is held on Fridays 2pm-5pm in the Old Encinitas Lumberyard Shopping Center. In April, Encinitas

Street Fair draws a crowd. Other festive events are held throughout the year, including the Encinitas Soccer Cup in August and the Rob Machado Surf Classic & Cardiff Beach Fair in the fall at Seaside Beach.

HOW TO GET THERE
Exit I-5 at Encinitas Boulevard and proceed west to the ocean.

California Dreamin'

This hot air balloon operator offers coastal sunset flights out of Encinitas. Via an inland departure point, flights over the Temecula wine country and east county mountains are offered in either a balloon or a thrilling open cockpit biplane.

Location:	3615 Manchester Avenue, Encinitas
Hours:	Daily
Admission:	Prices vary. Starting at $128/Person
Phone:	800-373-3359
Web:	www.californiadreamin.com

HOW TO GET THERE
Exit I-5 at Manchester Avenue and proceed west. Proceed on Manchester Avenue three quarters of a mile to the second stop light. Turn right onto the Manchester Avenue extension (large metal sculptures will be on the left). Pull into the Encinitas Art Ranch.

Kitchen Witch Gourmet Shop

For over fifteen years this cooking school has been teaching as many as ten classes per week to small groups of twenty or less per class. Some classes are hands-on, some are demonstration. Students always sample food, receive wine and coffe and take home recipes. Classes usually last three hours. Special classes include Friday Night Dinner Parties tailored to couples and the one-hour Learn-A-Lunch tailored to friends or co-workers.

Location:	127 North El Camino Real, Suite D, Encinitas
Hours:	Times vary; classes likely Mon-Sat 11am & 6pm
	Gourmet Shop: Mon-Sat 10am-5:30pm
Admission:	Prices vary. Expect roughly $40-50/Person
Phone:	760-942-3228
Website:	www.kitchenwitchonline.com

HOW TO GET THERE
Exit I-5 at Manchester Avenue and proceed east. Continue straight as Manchester becomes S. El Camino Real and eventually N. El Camino Real. The school is at N. El Camino Real and Encinitas Boulevard.

San Elijo Lagoon Ecological Reserve

Hiking trails wind through this rare coastal wetland between Cardiff Beach and Solana Beach. The trails east of I-5 allow for equestrians. More than 300 species of birds live in this natural wonderland, as well as different mammals, fish, reptiles and invertebrates. Plants and vegetation include coastal strand, salt marsh, freshwater marsh, riparian scrub, coastal sage scrub and mixed chaparral. The Nature Center provides details on the various plants and animals, as well as hiking trail details.

Location:	2710 Manchester Avenue, Encinitas
Hours:	Daily Sunrise-Sunset
Admission:	Free
Phone:	619-694-3049 Dept. of Parks & Rec
Website:	www.sanelijo.org

HOW TO GET THERE
Exit I-5 at Manchester Avenue and proceed west. The lagoon and Nature Center are on the left. Longer trails can be accessed from the Solana Beach and Rancho Santa Fe trailheads.

Quail Botanical Gardens

This 30-acre natural oasis is San Diego's only formal botanical garden. Nature trails and scenic walkways take visitors to 20 unique gardens, a 60-foot waterfall in a tropical rain forest and to the largest display of bamboo in North America. Cork oaks from North Africa, Dragon trees from the Canary Islands, MacPherson Waterfall and Palm Canyon are highlights. Several rare fruit trees, including cherimoya, feijoa, white sapote and macadamia nut, create a subtropical fruit forest. The tremendous plant variety is possible due to the areas several mini-climates and topographies, from sunny hillsides to deep canyons and ocean mists. A gift shop and nursery are open 10am-4pm. Free tours are offered Saturdays at 10am and a botanical library is on site.

Location:	230 Quail Gardens Drive, Encinitas
Hours:	Daily 9am-5pm
	Closed Thanksgiving, Dec 25 & Jan1
Admission:	General-$8; Seniors(60+)-$5;
	Students & Military (with ID)-$5
	Youth(3-12)-$3; Under 3-Free
	Free 1st Tues of every month
Phone:	760-436-3036
Website:	www.qbgardens.org

HOW TO GET THERE

Exit I-5 at Encinitas Boulevard and proceed east. Turn left at Quail Gardens Drive. The garden is on the left.

Self-Realization Fellowship Center

In 1937, Paramahansa Yogananda, a renowned meditation teacher who dedicated his life to promoting Eastern and Western spiritual understanding, established the Self-Realization Fellowship Center. He lived at the Hermitage and wrote his *Autobiography of a Yogi*, which today is widely regarded as a modern spiritual classic.

World travelers flock here to reflect over the Pacific Ocean at the bluff-top Meditation Garden. The garden, which includes a small waterfall and koi pond, is open to the public. The Temple and bookroom are open for meditation and prayer. A book and gift shop offers arts, crafts and musical instruments from India.

Location:	Temple: 939 2nd Street, Encinitas
	Garden: 215 K Street, Encinitas
Hours:	Hours vary
	Temple: Tues-Sun 12pm-4pm
	Garden: Tues-Sat 9am-5pm & Sun 11am-5pm
	Gift Shop: Tues-Sun 10am-5pm
Admission:	Free
Phone:	760-436-7220
Website:	www.yogananda-orf.org/temples/encinitas/

HOW TO GET THERE

Exit I-5 at Encinitas Boulevard and proceed west. Turn left at Highway 101/ 1st Street and proceed south. Turn right at I Street and proceed to 2nd Street. The temple is to the right and the garden is to the left.

"The ideal of love for God and service to humanity found full expression in the life of Paramahansa Yagananda. Though the major part of his life was spent outside India, still he takes his place among our great saints. His work continues to grow and shine ever more brightly, drawing people everywhere on the path of the pilgrimage of the Spirit."

- Government of India

SOLANA BEACH

This small beach community of four square miles is home to many active artists and the town evokes the spirit of these residents. City Hall, which is located on Old Highway 101, features an intimate gallery that hosts new art exhibits each month. The shows have included everything from watercolors

and photos to recycled metal sculpture, surfboards and children's art. The gallery is open during regular business hours and hosts evening receptions to launch new exhibits and introduce featured artists.

A few blocks in from the beach, the Cedros Design District is loaded with several charming boutiques, artisan stores, an incredibly well-stocked antique warehouse and one of San Diego's best night spots, The Belly Up Tavern. National acts visit this intimate venue, which has an attached restaurant called Wild Note Cafe.

Solana Beach's oldest building, the 1890 Stevens Ranch House, is permanently located in La Colonia Park and acts as a historical museum for the area. The collection includes 1890's furniture, photographs, antiques and writings. The wood-burning kitchen stove and

1880 reed organ are treasured pieces, but it is the period photographs that fascinate visitors.

A weekly Farmers' Market takes place every Sunday 2pm-5pm across from the Solana Beach train station at Lomas Santa Fe and Cedros Avenue. Each June, the popular annual Fiesta del Sol serves up top-rate entertainment with two full days of free live music, arts and crafts, food booths and children's activities.

HOW TO GET THERE
Exit I-5 at Lomas Santa Fe Road and proceed west to the ocean.

Del Mar, Encinitas & Solana Beach

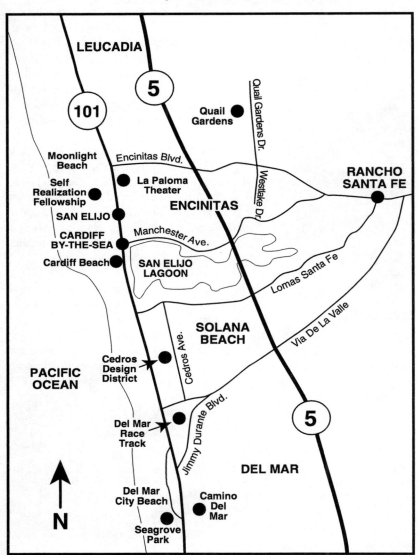

CARLSBAD

Carlsbad is a thriving beach community with a sizeable town, seven miles of beautiful beaches and endless attractions.

Carlsbad State Beach, located at 100 Tamarack Avenue, has a nice sandy strip for sunbathing and is good for swimming, surfing, skin diving and fishing. Further south, at Carlsbad Boulevard and Poinsettia Lane, South Carlsbad State Beach has 222 beachside camping sites and offers decent surfing. The popular Carlsbad Seawall accommodates a walk, jog or bike ride along a path that follows the ocean from Carlsbad Village Drive south to Tamarack Avenue.

In 1929, the Alt Karlsbad Hanse House was built as a place for visitors to soak in the local mineral springs. Today, the Carlsbad Mineral Water Spa pumps roughly 40,000 gallons of the curative water for guests who indulge in mineral baths and spa treatments at 2802 Carlsbad Boulevard. Call the historic spa at 760-434-1887 for further details.

At Carlsbad Village Drive and Elm Street, the historic 1887 Carlsbad Santa Fe Depot doubles as the Visitor's Information Center at 400 Carlsbad Village Drive. Visit their website at www.carlsbadca.org or call them at 760-434-6093 or 800-227-5722 for further area information.

A local Farmer's Market is held on Wednesday and Saturday afternoons 2pm-5pm on Roosevelt Street between Grand Avenue and Carlsbad Village Drive. During summer months, free jazz concerts are offered at community parks. Call 760-434-2920 for concert details. Annually, the Carlsbad Village Faire occurs the first Sundays of May and November. With over 850 exhibitors and more than 90,000 attendees, it is the largest one-day street fair in California.

HOW TO GET THERE
Exit I-5 at Carlsbad Village Drive and proceed west to the ocean.

Barnstorming Adventures

This thrill-seeking adventure gives visitors a bird's eye view of San Diego. Passengers sit in front of the pilot in open cockpit biplanes. Rides can be as gentle or exhilarating as requested. The company also offers WWII Warbird plane flights or interactive Air Combat flights where a 30-minute briefing prepares customers to bank, dive and climb in real aerial dogfights. Rides accommodate one or two passengers.

Location:	2160 Palomar Airport Road, Carlsbad
Hours:	Daily 9am-6pm
Admission:	Starting at $59/Person
Phone:	760-438-7680 or 800-759-5667
Website:	www.barnstorming.com

HOW TO GET THERE
Exit I-5 at Palomar Airport Road and proceed east 3 miles. Turn left at Yarrow Road and proceed to McClellan-Palomar Airport.

Batiquitos Lagoon Ecological Reserve

This coastal wetland, between Carlsbad and Encinitas, is one of the few remaining tidal wetlands along the southern California coast. The saltwater lagoon is fed by ocean tides and two fresh water streams. Several permanent and fly-through birds, including the Great Blue Heron, can be seen while hiking nearly three miles of trails that hug the north shore.

Location:	7380 Gabbiano Drive, Carlsbad
Hours:	Daily Sunrise-Sunset
Admission:	Free
Phone:	760-845-3501 or 760-943-7583
Website:	www.batiquitosfoundation.org

HOW TO GET THERE
Exit I-5 at Aviara Parkway and proceed towards Poinsettia Lane. Proceed east on Poinsettia Lane. Turn right at Batiquitos Drive. Turn right at Gabbiano Lane.

Carlsbad Village By-The-Sea & Historic Downtown District

"The Village" is a quaint part of downtown Carlsbad with restaurants, sidewalk eateries, coffee houses, ice cream shops, specialty stores and clothing boutiques. Along Ocean Avenue, surf shops with equipment rentals, a popular boardwalk and beach access provide the area with beach city charm. A few blocks in, State Street offers eclectic window shopping for antiques and other one-of-a-kind finds. The main thoroughfare, Carlsbad Boulevard, doubles as part of historic Highway 101.

Perched above the ocean, the small but picturesque Magee Park is a welcome area for picnics and barbecues at the corner of Beech Street and Garfield Street. At 200 Beach Street, the 1926 vintage town meeting hall called Heritage Hall, and the Magee House are open for tours Saturdays and Sundays 1pm-5pm.

HOW TO GET THERE
Exit I-5 at Carlsbad Village Drive and proceed west to Carlsbad Boulevard.

Children's Discovery Museum

Educational hands-on exhibits allow children to be creative and imaginative at this discovery center. *World of Sound* focuses on exploring music and sound with multi-cultural instruments. *Kids' Marketplace* introduces the concept of recycling in a child-sized grocery store and allows kids to work a real cash register. *Solar Energy* is an opportunity to power a toy train or plasma sphere and *Fishin' Boat* offers a chance to catch fish. *Creative Corner* allows visitors to create arts and crafts and medieval-themed *Castle Play* outfits kids in princess gowns, king robes and knight's armor.

Location:	300 S. Carlsbad Village Drive, Suite #103, Carlsbad
Hours:	Tues-Thurs & Sun 12pm-5pm
	Fri & Sat 10am-5pm
	Closed Thanksgiving, Dec 25 & Jan 1
Admission:	General-$5; Under 2-Free
Phone:	760-720-0737
Website:	www.museumforchildren.org

HOW TO GET THERE

Exit I-5 at Carlsbad Village Drive and proceed west. Turn right into Village Faire Shopping Center one half mile west of the freeway.

Snug Harbor Marina & California Water Sports

California Water Sports operates and maintains Snug Harbor and Agua Hedionda Lagoon. Weather permitting, the harbor is open year-round for water skiing, boardsailing, kayaking, canoeing, rowing and fishing. The water sport outfitter rents ski boats, wave runners, canoes and kayaks.

Location:	4215 Harrison Street, Carlsbad
Hours:	Daily 9am-5pm
	Call ahead. Open based on weather conditions
Admission:	$3/Vehicle. Rental prices vary
Phone:	760-434-3089
Website:	www.californiawatersports.net

HOW TO GET THERE

Exit I-5 at the Tamarack Avenue and proceed east. Turn right at Adams Street. Turn right at Harrison Street.

Legoland California

This 128-acre family theme park has over fifty rides, shows and attractions geared towards children ages two through twelve. Children are encouraged to play, explore and create in a LEGO world.

The attractions are themed to provide children with several different adventures. The *Dragon Coaster* takes kids by King's Castle on Castle Hill. Youngsters can joust while riding LEGO horses in this medieval land with enchanted forests. In *Village Green*, a jeep ride on Safari Trek winds visitors through Africa to see life size LEGO wildlife. *Miniland USA* showcases detailed and animated replicas of American landmarks built with millions of LEGO bricks by on-site LEGO Master Builders. Children can build their own LEGO creations in *Imagination Zone*.

Kids are empowered in *Fun Town* where they can drive electric LEGO cars and earn an official Legoland driver's license at Driving School. LEGO planes, helicopters and boats, along with pedal-powered Sky Cruisers and Aquazone Wave Racers are other favorite vehicles.

There are eateries, restaurants and shops filled with everything LEGO, especially The Big Shop which has the country's largest selection of LEGO products.

Location:	1 Legoland Drive, Carlsbad
Hours:	Call to confirm the seasonal schedule
	Spring/Summer: Daily 10am-5pm
	Fall/Winter: Thurs-Mon 10am-5pm
	Open until 8pm on select days
Admission:	Prices vary by season
	General-$42; Seniors(60+)-$35;
	Youth(3-12)-$35; Under 3-Free
	2-Day Passes & Annual Passes available
	Parking: $4-$8
Phone:	760-918-5346
Website:	www.legoland.com

HOW TO GET THERE

Exit I-5 at Cannon Road in Carlsbad and proceed east. Turn right at Legoland Drive and follow signs to the parking lot.

Museum of Making Music

This audio-filled interactive journey showcases music history with over 450 vintage instruments on display. Visitors can make their own music by testing out a digital piano, guitar, drum set or electric violin. Interactive listening stations highlight memorable tunes from over a hundred years. Guided tours are available by reservation. The museum store sells everything pertaining to music, including jewelry, books, stationary, CDs and small instruments such as harmonicas. Major musical instruments are not sold at the museum.

Location:	5790 Armada Drive, Carlsbad
Hours:	Tues-Sun 10am-5pm
	Closed holidays
Admission:	General-$5; Seniors(60+)-$3;
	Military & Students(with ID)-$3
	Youth(4-18)-$3; Under 4-Free
Phone:	760-438-5996 or 877-551-9976
Website:	www.museumofmakingmusic.org

HOW TO GET THERE

Exit I-5 at Palomar Airport Road and proceed east. Turn left at Armada Drive. The museum is on the right.

The Flower Fields at Carlsbad Ranch

International visitors flock here each spring for a spectacular display of blooming ranunculus during the peak March and April season. In May, over 20,000 sunflowers bloom to recognize the coming summer and in early winter a 166-foot star is shaped with poinsettias. Nature products including bulbs, flowers and plants are sold in the gift shop.

Location:	5704 Paseo Del Norte, Carlsbad
Hours:	Mar-April: Daily 9am-5pm
	Hours vary rest of year
Admission:	General-$7; Seniors(60+)-$6;
	Youth(3-10)-$4; Under 3-Free
Phone:	760-431-0352
Website:	www.theflowerfields.com

HOW TO GET THERE
Exit I-5 at Palomar Airport Road and proceed east one block. Turn left at Paseo Del Norte. Parking is on the right.

Wineries

Bellefleur

This vintner no longer operates an onsite winery, but still produces Chardonnay, Sauvignon Blanc, Merlot, Cabernet Sauvignon and Pinot Noir wines, which are bottled by a private Fallbrook vintner. Tastings are available at Bellefleur Restaurant, which is located in the Carlsbad Company Stores mall complex. Wine flights are comprised of two ounces each of your choice of three different wines.

Location:	5610 Paseo Del Norte, Carlsbad
Hours:	Daily 11am-9pm
Admission:	Free. Tastings: $8.50-$10/Wine Flight
Phone:	760-603-1919
Website:	www.bellefleur.com

HOW TO GET THERE
Exit I-5 at Palomar Airport Road and proceed east one block. Turn left at Paseo Del Norte. Bellefleur is on the right.

Witch Creek Winery

This winery has been using grapes from all over the state to press their own wines in Carlsbad since 1996. The Tasting Room offers a generous sampling of Chardonnays, several reds and a few dessert wines in a keepsake glass for $3. Wines, vinegars, oils and gifts are sold in the tasting room. The winery also has a Julian tasting room at 2000 Main Street, which is open daily during the fall season but only on weekends the rest of the year.

Location:	2906 Carlsbad Boulevard, Carlsbad
Hours:	Daily 11am-5pm
Admission:	Free. Tastings: $3/Person
Phone:	760-720-7499
Website:	www.witchcreekwinery.com

HOW TO GET THERE
Exit I-5 at Carlsbad Village Drive and proceed west. Turn right Carlsbad Boulevard and proceed one block. The tasting room is on the right.

OCEANSIDE

This city lies at San Diego County's most northern coastline with nearly four miles of white sandy beaches and a prized pier. The historic Oceanside Pier measures 1,942 feet in length and remains one of the longest wooden recreational piers on the West Coast. Visitors can fish off the pier without a license for free. However, a  fishing license is required for surf fishing on the beach.

The Harbor attracts many visitors with its restaurants, picnic tables, lighthouse and Harbor Village shopping center. Helgren's Sportfishing offers daily charters and seasonal whale watching tours December through  March. Harbor Days is held the third weekend in September annually. A Farmer's Market is held Thursdays 9am-12:30pm at North Coast Highway and Pier View Way.

Several historic original buildings are preserved at Heritage Park Village & Museum, including Oceanside's first General Store, the Portola Inn, the Blacksmith Shop & Livery Stable, a doctors office, the Old City jail, Libby School and the Blade newspaper building.

California Surf Museum

The museum displays surfboards, photographs, surf clothing and surfing equipment. Exhibits are changed annually and generally highlight a surfing pioneer or legend. The museum sells surf-related merchandise.

Location:	223 N. Coast Highway, Oceanside
Hours:	Thurs-Mon 10am-4pm. Closed holidays
Admission:	Free
Phone:	760-721-6876
Website:	www.surfmuseum.org

HOW TO GET THERE
Exit I-5 at Mission Street and proceed west. Turn right at N. Coast Highway.

Camp Pendleton Paintball Park

This paintball park is located on 75 acres in a box canyon on Camp Pendleton Marine Corps Base. Players begin the day with a brief orientation and then begin play on either a Beginner or Advance Team. Players rotate between eight fields and usually play two games per field. There is a wide variety of terrain with bunkers, buildings, trees, trenches and sandbag fortifications. On average, twelve to sixteen games are played per day. Each game lasts fifteen to twenty minutes and typically involves Capture The Flag, Center The Flag, Elimination or Attack & Defend. The games are not recommended for children younger than twelve years old. The park allows players to use their own equipment and paintballs or rent. Call ahead for rental availability.

Location:	Camp Pendleton, Oceanside
Hours:	Sat & Sun 9am-4:30pm
Admission:	Walk-On Rates: $12/Person Entrance; $44/Person Entrance, Equipment Rental, 500 Paintballs & Unlimited CO2 Supply
Phone:	800-899-9957
Website:	www.cppaintball.com

HOW TO GET THERE
Exit I-5 at Ocean Harbor Drive/Camp Pendleton and proceed east to the Camp Pendleton main gate. Explain you are visiting the paintabll park and present your valid driver's license, registration and insurance. Proceed straight for 7.5 miles. The staging area is on the right. Look for signs.

Mission San Luis Rey

This 1798 mission is the 18th of the 21 California missions and is considered the "King of Missions". The remarkable architecture reflects Spanish, Mexican, and Moorish styles built of adobe and faced with brick. Visitors may enjoy the picnic areas, sunken gardens, museum and gift shop. Guided and self-guided tours of the grounds and church are welcome. An English mass is held Saturday at 5:30pm followed by a Spanish mass at 7pm.

The museum relates the tumultuous history of this mission. With the American conquest of California and secularization in the 1830s, the mission grounds were used for bullfights and a U.S. military post, but President Lincoln returned the property to the Catholic Church in 1865 and in 1893 it was rededicated as a Franciscan seminary.

Location:	4050 Mission Avenue, Oceanside
Hours:	Daily 10am-4pm
	Closed Thanksgiving, Dec 25 & Jan 1
Admission:	General-$5; Students-$3;
	Family-$15; Under 7-Free
Phone:	760-757-3651
Website:	www.sanluisrey.org

HOW TO GET THERE

Exit I-5 at Highway 76 and proceed east or exit I-15 at Highway 76 and proceed west. Exit Highway 76 at Rancho del Oro and proceed north to the Mission.

Oceanside Museum of Art

Housed in a 1930s classic Irving Gill designed building, this downtown museum presents five provocative exhibits each year showcasing the finest art of regional and international artists. Shows run the gamut, from classic landscape paintings to neon sculpture, from art quilts to architectural glass. In addition to contemporary art, OMA offers art instruction at the OMA School of Art and chamber music in the museum galleries as part of the Pier View Way Concert Series.

Location:	704 Pier View Way, Oceanside
Hours:	Tues-Sat 10am-4pm & Sun 1pm-4pm
Admission:	General-$5; Seniors(65+)-$3;
	Students & Military (with ID)-$3
Phone:	760-721-2787
Website:	www.oma-online.org

HOW TO GET THERE

Exit I-5 at Mission Street/Downtown and proceed west. Turn right at Ditmar Street. The museum is on the right.

Buena Vista Lagoon & Audubon Society

This coastal wetlands habitat is run by the Buena Vista Audubon Society. The lagoon, which at one time had a natural outlet to the ocean, is the only fresh water lagoon in California and caters to both fresh and salt water fowl. Dozens of bird species and plant life can be viewed via two trails near the Nature Center. Guest may call in advance to request a free guided tour. The educational Nature Center has real animal displays, featuring a white pelican, barn owl, red-shouldered hawk, bobcat and raccoon. A hands-on activity table lets visitors examine bones, feathers and nests.

Location:	2202 S. Coast Highway, Oceanside
Hours:	Tues-Sat 10am-4pm & Sun 1pm-4pm
Admission:	Free
Phone:	760-439-2473
Website:	www.bvaudubon.org

HOW TO GET THERE

Exit I-5 at Highway 78 and proceed west. Turn left at S. Coast Highway and proceed south. The Nature Center is on the left.

Carlsbad & Oceanside

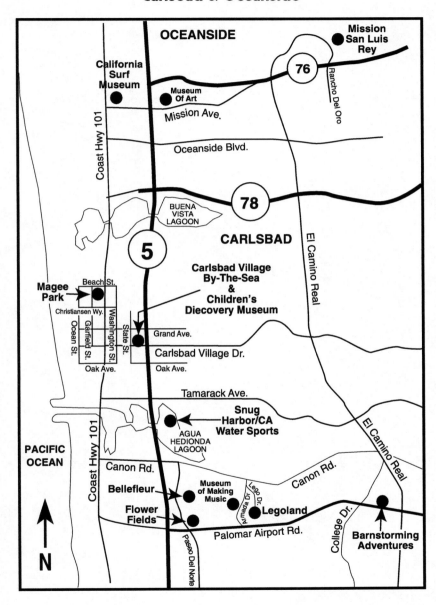

San Diego County

NORTH COUNTY

- Escondido
- Fallbrook
- Poway
- Rancho Bernardo
- Rancho Santa Fe
- Scripps Ranch & Miramar
- Valley Center
- Vista

SAN DIEGO COUNTY - NORTH COUNTY

Escondido

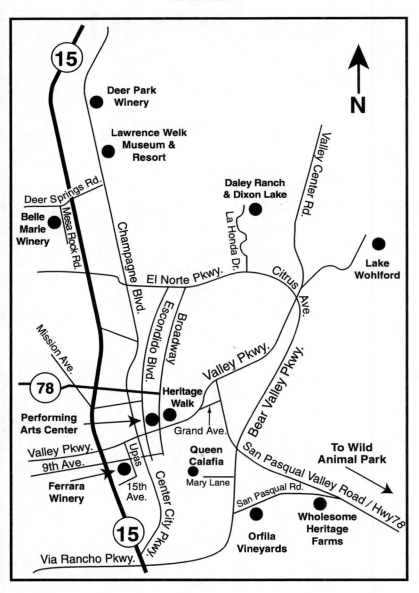

ESCONDIDO

This city was once a small farming town that lived up to its name, meaning "hidden place." But the warm inland climate and scenic rolling hills attracted many. Today the area boasts several golf courses and wineries, dozens of recreational hiking trails and parks, three sizeable lakes, a large shopping mall and a quaint historic downtown. The city's largest attraction is the San Diego Wild Animal Park, located in San Pasqual Valley, a 10,000 acre agricultural preserve and natural habitat.

Tree-lined Grand Avenue in downtown Escondido has its own unique character with eclectic antique stores and art galleries, down-to-earth restaurants and coffee shops and other varied storefronts. The Mingei International Museum is a welcome addition to Grand Avenue. The museum is a sister location to the popular Balboa Park Mingei. A small extension of the Children's Museum is already located on Grand Avenue. Every Tuesday afternoon a section of the thoroughfare is blocked from 3pm-6pm for the weekly Farmer's Market. April through September, classic cars line the street bumper to bumper as people showcase vintage vehicles for the Cruisin' Grand event every Friday night 5pm-9pm. Annual street festivals are held the third Sundays of May and October.

Another remarkable city treasure is the late artist Niki de Saint Phalle's *Queen Calafia's Magical Circle* sculpture garden in Kit Carson Park. A mirrored mazelike entrance lures visitors into the sizeable mosaic playground. The installment is special in that it was de Saint Phalle's final project before her death in May 2002. The park is also home to Escondido Sports Center, which features arena soccer, roller hockey and skate park facilities. The park backs up to the large Westfield North County Fair mall.

California Center For The Arts & Heritage Walk at Grape Day Park

The contemporary performing arts complex is Escondido's cultural core. A 1,500-seat concert hall and 400-seat theatre accommodate an impressive roster of national performers year-round. As one of North County's premier venues, a broad range of shows are offered, including comedy, dance, contemporary music concerts, plays and musicals. There is a museum that hosts intriguing painting, sculpture and photography exhibits. On weekend show nights, the museum holds extended hours until curtain and ticket holders are admitted for free. Admission is always free the first Wednesday of every month. Tours of the 12-acre complex are available.

Beside the Center for the Arts is Grape Day Park, creating a backyard of sorts for the complex. The park has paved walkways, picnic tables and horseshoe pits. Fountains and garden art, as well as the nostalgic Heritage Walk create ambiance. Heritage Walk was formed to honor the 1976 Bicentennial. Historic buildings were saved from demolition, moved to Grape Day Park and preserved to create the outdoor complex. Buildings include Escondido's first library, the 1888 Santa Fe Depot and a railroad car, the working Bandy Blacksmith shop used for demonstrations, a Victorian house, a 1900s barn and a windmill. A time capsule was buried on October 8, 1976 and will not be opened until the same date in 2076. The walk is self-guided and there is a gift shop. Grape Day Festival is held the first Saturday after Labor Day, a tradition held since 1908.

Location:	Art Complex: 340 N. Escondido Boulevard, Escondido Heritage Walk: 321 N. Broadway, Escondido
Hours:	Box Office: Mon-Fri 10am-5pm, Sat 12pm-5pm Museum: Tues-Sat 10am-5pm, Sun 12pm-5pm Heritage Walk: Thurs-Sat 1pm-4pm
Admission:	Show prices vary Museum: General-$5; Seniors & Military-$4; Students & Youth(13-18)-$3; Under 13-Free Free 1st Wednesday of every month Heritage Walk: Free
Phone:	800-988-4253 Box Office 760-839-4120 Art Museum 760-743-8207 Heritage Walk
Website:	www.artcenter.org

HOW TO GET THERE

Exit I-15 at Valley Parkway and proceed east one mile. Turn left at Escondido Boulevard. The Art Complex is three blocks down on the right side. Heritage Walk and Grape Day Park are behind the Complex along Broadway.

Dixon Lake & Daley Ranch

Tucked into the foothills of northeast Escondido is an outdoor playground for fishermen, hikers, bikers and equestrians alike with the neighboring Dixon Lake and Daley Ranch.

Dixon Lake covers 76 acres and is surrounded by 527 acres of verdant grounds used for picnicking, walking and camping. The lake, which measures 80 feet deep, is stocked with bass, catfish and trout. Every year, Dixon hosts a trout derby for prizes. A concession building rents boats and three fishing floats enable shore fishing. Since the lake is a drinking water reservoir, no swimming is allowed.

Visitors enjoy nature walks through the primitive area and appreciate barbecues and tables for picnics. No pets, wood fires or alcohol are permitted in day use areas. There are 45 campsites with tables, stoves and food lockers. Ten of those sites are set up for RVs with water, electric and sewer hookups.

Dixon Lake

Location:	1700 N. La Honda Drive, Escondido
Hours:	Daily 6am-Dusk. Closed Dec 25
	Reservations Mon-Fri 7am-4pm
Admission:	Weekdays-Free
	Weekends & Holidays- $2/Vehicle;
	$3/Vehicle Over 19'
	Call for fishing & camping fees
Phone:	760-839-4680 Information
	760-741-3328 Reservations
Website:	www.ci.escondido.ca.us

Above Dixon Lake lies Daley Ranch, a 3,058-acre habitat preserve with dozens of trails for recreational day use by hikers, mountain bikers and equestrians. Before the young English immigrant Robert Daley arrived in this valley in 1869 and built a small log cabin, which remains on the ranch to this day, the area was frequented by native Californians of the Kumeyaay and other local tribes. In 1997, Escondido acquired the land to protect it as a habitat preserve.

Among the 20+ miles of trails, popular routes are the 2.4-mile Boulder Loop with nice city views and the 2.5-mile Ranch House Loop, which passes two ponds and Daley's original log cabin site. Free trail maps are available onsite. Common trailside sights are rare oak trees, sage scrub, and a number of birds and reptiles such as lizards and snakes. Be aware of poison oak, rattlesnakes and the occasional mountain lion.

Daley Ranch

Location:	3024 N. La Honda Drive, Escondido
Hours:	Daily Dawn-Dusk
Admission:	Free
Phone:	760-839-6266 Information
	760-839-4345 Ranger Station
Website:	www.ci.escondido.ca.us

HOW TO GET THERE

Exit I-15 at El Norte Parkway and proceed east. Turn left at La Honda Drive. Parking for Daley Ranch is on the left and the entrance to Dixon Lake is on the right.

Dixon Lake

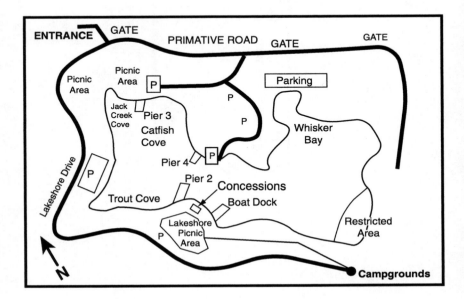

Lake Wohlford

Lakeside trails for hikers and nature walkers are matched by stocked waters for fishermen. bass, trout and catfish are common catches. There are fishing and boat launch fees. Boat rentals are available and there is a small café. Canoes and kayaks are welcome. Swimming and pets are not allowed.

Location:	25453 Lake Wohlford Road, Escondido
Hours:	Late Dec-early Sept: Daily 6am-Dusk
	Open weekends rest of year
	Closed Dec 25
Admission:	Free. Boat and fishing fees
Phone:	760-839-4346

HOW TO GET THERE

Exit I-15 at Valley Parkway and proceed east through Escondido. Turn right at Lake Wohlford Road. Follow the road up hill to the lake, which is on the right.

Lawrence Welk Museum & Resort Village

While this scenic 600-acre golf resort primarily indulges vacationers with several luxurious amenities, visitors enjoy the museum and theater shows along with shopping and dining.

The museum, which displays memorabilia from Lawrence Welk's long career, is free and opens at 10am daily. In the same building, an intimate 340-seat theatre is active 52 weeks of the year with four Broadway-style musicals and an annual Christmas show. Curtain time for a matinee is 1:45pm and for an evening performance is 8pm.
Seating begins 15 minutes prior to curtain. A buffet meal is served two and a half hours before each performance. Both package and show-only tickets are available.

Location:	8860 Lawrence Welk Drive, Escondido
Hours:	Weekdays 8am-5pm, Weekends 10:30am-5pm
	Most restaurants open until 9pm
	Matinee Shows: Tues-Thurs, Sat-Sun
	Evening Shows: Tues, Thurs, Sat
Admission:	Resort & Museum-Free
	Show prices vary. Expect $30-$45/Ticket
	Youth pricing for ages 3-12
Phone:	760-749-3000 Resort Information
	760-749-3448 or 888-802-7469 Shows
Website:	www.welkresort.com

HOW TO GET THERE

Exit I-15 at Deer Springs Road and proceed east. Turn left at Champagne Boulevard. Turn right at Lawrence Welk Drive to enter the resort.

San Diego Wild Animal Park

This lush 2,200-acre wildlife sanctuary lives up to its accreditation as a

botanical garden. The naturally landscaped grounds allow visitors to observe more than 3,500 rare and exotic creatures representing 260 species in surroundings close to their native habitats. The *Kilimanjaro Safari Walk* is a must and the bird show and elephant show are timeless favorites.

Nairobi Village has shops, restaurants and favorite exhibits including the *Petting Kraal* and *Lorikeet Landing* where visitors feed animals and birds straight from their hands. *Hidden Jungle* is a favorite rainforest exhibit. *Condor Ridge* is a popular recent attraction featuring these incredible endangered birds.

The *Wgasa Bush Line* is a 50-minute guided monorail safari allowing close views of free roaming animals of Asia and Africa. For an additional charge, visitors can get up close and personal with the animals on a Photo Caravan Tour that takes guests inside the large animal enclosures. Call 800-934-2267 for required caravan reservations.

Location:	15500 San Pasqual Valley Road/Highway 78, Escondido
Hours:	Daily 9am-4pm. Summer: Open until 8pm
Admission:	General-$26.50; Seniors(60+)-$23.85; Youth(3-11)-$19.50; Under 3-Free Memberships & Two-Park Passes available, which include San Diego Zoo admission Parking-$6 (Free for Members)
Phone:	760-747-8702 Press "0" for operator 760-480-0100 Recorded Information
Website:	www.wildanimalpark.org

HOW TO GET THERE

Exit I-15 at Via Rancho Parkway and proceed east. Turn right at San Pasqual Road. Follow signs to Wild Animal Park. Turn right at Highway 78 and proceed east. The park is on the left.

San Dieguito River Park
& Lake Hodges

The vision of this preservation project is to create a continuous 55-mile Coast-To-Crest Trail from the desert east of Volcan Mountain, the San Dieguito River's source, to the mouth of the river in Del Mar. There are further proposals for an open space park system that will link the Anza Borrego State Park to the Pacific Ocean. Currently, parts of this trail are open around the San Pasqual Valley, Highland Valley and Lake Hodges areas of Escondido. There are no facilities at trailheads.

San Dieguito River Park Updates & Information

Location:	18372 Sycamore Creek Road, Escondido
Phone:	858-674-2270
Website:	www.sdrp.org

San Dieguito River Park Trails

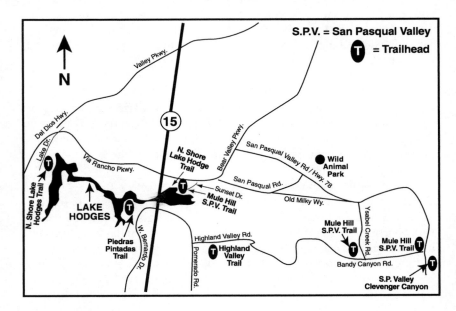

The following trails can be covered individually or combined for longer routes.

San Pasqual Valley Clevenger Canyon Trail

This trail has both a north trailhead and a south trailhead ascending either side of the Santa Ysabel Creek canyon. The north trail is longer and more difficult with several switchbacks, large elevation changes and side trails for spectacular views at about twenty miles round trip. This trail eventually forks into an east branch and west branch. The south trail is much shorter and relatively easy in comparison. This trail climbs gently to a fork as well, also with an east and west branch. Both trails provide stunning views and are for hiking only. Leashed dogs are allowed. No bikes or horses are allowed on this trail.

HOW TO GET THERE

Exit I-15 at Via Rancho Parkway and proceed east. Turn right at San Pasqual Valley Road. Follow signs to the Wild Animal Park. Turn right at Highway 78 and proceed 5 miles east of the Wild Animal Park to reach the south trail parking lot on the right and the north trail parking lot on the left.

Mule Hill Historic Trail & San Pasqual Valley Trail

These two trails converge to create twenty-two miles roundtrip with parking lots at each end and near the middle for shorter options. Expect a wide variety of terrain and scenery along the eleven miles, from flat straight aways to hillside climbs and shady oak tree groves to sunny sprawling farmland. A historic point of interest is the 131-year-old Sikes Adobe Farmhouse being restored near Mule Hill. The relatively easy Mule Hill Trail shares its starting point with the North Shore Lake Hodges Trail, east of San Pasqual Valley. The longer and more challenging San Pasqual Valley Trail begins at the east end of the agricultural valley at Bandy Canyon Road. However, the

Ysabel Creek Road parking lot in the heart of the valley is between the two trailheads and provides an 8-mile roundtrip option winding east into the valley and a 14-mile roundtrip option winding west through the valley towards Mule Hill.

HOW TO GET THERE

To reach *Mule Hill Trailhead*, exit I-15 at Via Rancho Parkway and proceed east. Turn right onto Sunset Drive. The parking lot is at the end of Sunset Drive to the right.

To reach *Ysabel Creek Trailhead,*exit I-15 at Via Rancho Parkway and proceed east. Turn right at San Pasqual Valley Road. Turn right at Milky Way Road. Where Milky Way merges with Highway 78, make an immediate right onto the poorly marked dirt Ysabel Creek Road. The parking lot is at the far end of the dirt road on the left.

To reach *Bandy Canyon Trailhead*, exit I-15 at Via Rancho Parkway and proceed east. Turn right at San Pasqual Valley Road. Follow signs to the Wild Animal Park. Turn right at Highway 78 and proceed east past the Wild Animal Park and San Pasqual Battlefield Visitor's Center. Turn right at Bandy Canyon Road. The parking lot is to the immediate right at the corner of Highway 78 and Bandy Canyon Road.

Highland Valley Trail

This is an easy 4-mile roundtrip option for hikers, joggers and equestrians. Dogs are allowed on leashes. Bikes are not allowed. The first section of the trail is the Ruth Merrill Children's Interpretive Walk, a 1.5-mile roundtrip option for youngsters. Beautiful oak trees and a few small streams provide

some shade along this mostly exposed and sunny trail.

HOW TO GET THERE
The trailhead is near the corner of Highland Valley Road and Pomerado Road, near Rancho Bernardo. Exit I-15 at W. Bernardo Drive/Pomerado Road. Proceed east and turn left at Highland Valley Road. Make an immediate right into the dirt parking lot.

Piedras Pintadas Interpretive Trail
This is an easy 4-mile roundtrip trail along the south Lake Hodges shore for hikers and mountain bikers. Dogs are allowed on leashes. Equestrians are not allowed. Trailside displays relate the native Kumeyaay lifestyle. Several side trails offers many more miles of hiking and trail running.

HOW TO GET THERE
The trailhead is located on W. Bernardo Drive. Exit I-15 at W. Bernardo Drive/Pomerado Road and proceed west. Turn right into the parking lot.

North Shore Lake Hodges Trail
This trail is fifteen miles roundtrip and allows hikers, mountain bikers and equestrians. The easy to moderate trail winds west through Escondido along the lake's northshore towards Del Dios and continues further south along the lake. The scenic trail is shaded in parts by oak and eucalyptus trees. Near the lake you pass the Boat Dock & Launch and Del Dios community with a park, general store and restaurants. The trail ends with a view of the Lake Hodges Dam.

March through October, Lake Hodges is open for recreation. The Aquatic Center provides windsurfing lessons and outdoor rental equipment such as mountain bikes, windsurfers, kayaks and canoes. There is also a fishing and snacks concession. Call 760-735-8088 or visit www.lakehodges.net for details.

HOW TO GET THERE
The trailhead is located at the end of Sunset Drive off of Via Rancho Parkway. Exit I-15 at Via Rancho Parkway and proceed east. Turn right at Sunset Drive. The parking lot is at the end of Sunset Drive on the right.

To start from a Lake Hodges trailhead for a shorter route, start at Del Dios Community Park. Exit I-15 at Via Rancho Parkway and proceed west. Turn left onto Lake Drive. The park is on the left.

Wineries

Escondido's desirable climate has made it prime real estate for a handful of wineries. Four of those wineries offer tastings and beautiful grounds for picnicking.

Belle Marie Winery

This winery is located on Wine Haven Campus, which features a demonstration vineyard with 29 different grape varieties from around the world and an educational center. The grounds include grape arbors and gazebos, picnic areas, a gift shop and tasting rooms, where you can sample five wines for $5.

Location:	26312 Mesa Rock Road, Escondido
Hours:	Daily 11am-5pm. Summer: Open until 6pm
	Closed Tuesdays & Holidays
Admission:	Free. Tastings: $5/Person
Phone:	760-796-7557
Website:	www.bellemarie.com

HOW TO GET THERE

Exit I-15 at Deer Springs Road and proceed west. Turn left at Mesa Rock Road. The winery is on the right.

Deer Park Winery & Auto Museum

This 15-acre respite is enjoyed by wine connoisseurs and car buffs alike. Shady oaks, orchards, vineyards and grape arbors create a nice backdrop for picnics. There are several shady tables and a gazebo. The impressive market has a gourmet deli and gift shop with many collector items. Vintage cars and nostalgia, lend character to the store and Coca Cola memorabilia decorates the side of the gift shop.

The wine is produced by locally-grown grapes and grapes from the main Napa Valley Deer Park Winery. Visitors may taste any two wines for free or taste six wines in a keepsake glass for $5. Dry reds are their specialty.

The auto museum holds more than 100 immaculately restored antique cars, motorcycles and bicycles in three different buildings, comprising the world's largest museum of vintage convertibles and Americana. Old radios, TVs, cameras, Barbie dolls, signs and advertisements represent yesteryears.

Location:	29013 Champagne Boulevard, Escondido
Hours:	Thurs-Mon 10am-5pm. Museum until 4pm
	Closed Thanksgiving, Dec 25 & Jan 1
Admission:	Free. Tastings: $5/Person
	Museum: General-$6; Seniors(55+)-$5;
	Under 13-Free
Phone:	760-749-1666 Press "03" for operator
Website:	www.deerparkwinery.com

HOW TO GET THERE
Exit I-15 at Deer Springs Road and proceed east. Turn left at Champagne Boulevard. The winery is on the right.

Ferrara Winery
This winery has been a State Historical Point of Interest since 1971 as the Ferrara's are the oldest active, grape-growing, winemaking family in the county. Since 1932, the family has been producing wine. The winery lies in the heart of Escondido and has a tasting room that offers free wine samples as well as grape juice, wine marinade and wine vinegar. A deli is open 11am-2pm for lunch options on the winery's patio.

Location:	1120 W. 15th Avenue, Escondido
Hours:	Daily 10am-5pm. Closed Holidays
Admission:	Free
Phone:	760-745-7632

HOW TO GET THERE
Exit I-15 at 9th Avenue and proceed east. Turn right at Upas. The winery is on the right at the corner of Upas and 15th Avenue.

Orfila Winery

This winery boasts a beautiful view of San Pasqual Valley. Visitors may tour the hillside grounds on their own and picnic beneath grape arbors at their leisure or experience the wine-making process firsthand via a guided tour at 2pm daily. Annually, the winery hosts a grape stomp during late summer. Whites, reds and dessert wines are available for tasting. The first tasting is free and five more tastings may be purchased in a keepsake glass for $4. There is also a roadside tasting room off Highway 78 in Julian. The tasting works the same way and costs $1 less. The gift shop carries wine related merchandise, including unique hand-painted bottles and personalized labels.

Location:	13455 San Pasqual Road, Escondido
Hours:	Daily 10am-6pm. Open until 5pm Jan-Feb
	Closed Jan 1, July 4, Thanksgiving & Dec 25
Admission:	Free. Tastings: $4/Person
Phone:	760-738-6500 or 800-868-9463
	760-765-0102 Julian Tastings
Website:	www.orfila.com

HOW TO GET THERE

Exit I-15 at Via Rancho Parkway and proceed east. Turn right at San Pasqual Road. The vineyard is one mile up on the right

.Wholesome Heritage Farm

More than meets the eye at this unique farm filled with exotic animals. Perhaps the most interesting bit of trivia is that this farm is home to pop legend Michael Jackson's beautiful old ostrich. Visitors are guaranteed to be captivated by any number of things, including several Bactrian and Dromedary camels, thick-horned African Watusi cattle, a llama and a miniature donkey. The ostrich and emu do more for the farm than attract visitors. Seasonally, they lay one egg every three days. Both natural and elaborate hand-painted ostrich and emu eggs are for sale, as well as feathers and ostrich purses. An impressive bird collection includes rare spectacular pheasants, white doves and a talking macaw. Goats, turkeys, peacocks, ducks and geese round out this ever-changing farm, which provides educational tours and hosts ostrich talks. A selection of fresh produce, meat and homemade jerky is available.

Location:	Highway 78 at San Pasqual Road, Escondido
Hours:	Wed-Fri 12pm-Dark, Sat-Sun 9am-Dark
	Call ahead to confirm hours
Admission:	Free
Phone:	760-746-3276

HOW TO GET THERE

Exit I-15 at Via Rancho Parkway and proceed east. Turn right at San Pasqual Road. Continue to the Highway 78 stop light. The farm is on the right just before the light.

FALLBROOK

Fallbrook's charm lies in the community's ability to maintain a pace that allows one to be down right friendly. Many of Main Street's storefronts date back to the 1890s and are filled with authentic antiques and period memorabilia. Some house more modern art galleries. Social events often take place at Village Square on the historic corner of Main Street and Alvarado Street, which was once Harrison's Drug Store whose sign still stands. Historic houses and an 1880 church are also of interest in the area.

The Gem & Mineral Museum at 260 Rocky Crest Road is open Thursday through Sunday from 1pm to 4pm. The downtown museum is at 123 W. Alvarado Street and is open Tuesdays and Thursdays from 10am to 2pm. The museum features educational exhibits and mining displays, as well as offers gold panning. Other highlights include a whale fossil, a florescent mineral and a gift store. Call the museum at 760-723-1728 or the downtown branch at 760-728-1130 for further directions and details.

Endless citrus and avocado groves, outdoor murals, bronze sculptures and several windmills and notable bridges, including the dramatic Lilac Bridge arching over Interstate 15, all make for endless roadside scenery. Live Oak Park is a favorite destination with locals for its giant ancient oak trees, nature trails, streams and gardens at 2746 Reche Road.

While events such as art and flower shows, vintage and classic auto rallies and golf tournaments occur monthly, Fallbrook's largest event is the Avocado Festival in April. The spring festival draws thousands of people who attend for the abundance of delicious food and the opportunity to shop for fresh produce, plants, trees and gifts among hundreds of booths. Several avocado-focused events and contests round out the event, most notably the annual 10-, 20- and 50-mile Guacamole Grande bike ride.

Fallbrook

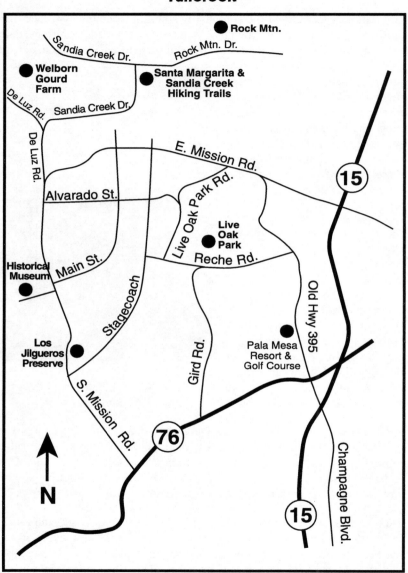

Santa Margarita River & Sandia Creek Trails

One of the few remaining wild rivers in Southern California, the Santa Margarita River provides hikers and equestrians a unique waterside trail experience. Various hiking and riding trails run along both sides of the river providing loops of a few miles or as long as ten miles. There are no bridges, but several places are low enough for crossings. At the east end of the trail indian grinding holes called morteros can be found in the rocks. Nearby Rock Mountain, north of the river, features coastal sage and riparian habitats.

The two trailheads are on either side of Sandia Creek Road. The Santa Margarita Trail is east of the road and the Sandia Creek Trail is west of the road. Dogs are allowed, but must be on a leash at all times.

Location:	Sandia Creek Road, Fallbrook
Hours:	Daily Dawn-Dusk
Admission:	Free

HOW TO GET THERE

Exit I-15 at Mission Road and proceed west to town. Turn right at Pico Avenue which turns into De Luz Road. Turn right on Sandia Creek Road. The parking lot is on the right.

Los Jilgueros Preserve

This 46-acre preserve offers a place to walk, jog or simply relax. An 1889 map of Fallbrook identified the property's stream as "Arroyo de los Jilgueros," hence its name which means "house finch" in Spanish. The finch is still common to the property, along with 50 other bird species. Other highlights include a 1.5-mile loop trail, two ponds and a Firescape Garden featuring over 100 different fire retardant and drought tolerant plants.

Location:	South Mission Road, Fallbrook
Hours:	Daily Dawn to Dusk
Admission:	Free

HOW TO GET THERE
Exit I-15 at Highway 76 and proceed west. Exit Highway 76 at Mission Road and proceed north. The preserve is on the right.

Welburn Gourd Farm

The country's largest supplier of quality hard-shell gourds resides on a 60-acre certified organic farm in Fallbrook. For more than 20 years, Welburn has been producing over 300,000 gourds annually for artists, crafters and musicians. Visitors are welcome to tour the beautiful farm and purchase gourds at good prices. The selection process is an adventure in itself. The farm has several suggestions for use and creative projects and holds monthly classes. Harvest season peaks in March and the annual Welburn Summer Gourd Fest happens in June.

Location:	40635 De Luz Road, Fallbrook
Hours:	Mon-Sat 10am-4pm. Closed Holidays
Admission:	Free
Phone:	760-728-4271
Website:	www.welburngourdfarm.com

HOW TO GET THERE
Exit I-15 at Mission Road and proceed west to Fallbrook through Main Street. Turn right at Pico Avenue. Pico turns into De Luz Road after one block. Continue on De Luz Road for 11 miles until the pavement ends. The farm entrance is on the right.

POWAY

Poway's location nestled up against the foothills makes it an ideal place for outdoor recreation and the city's commitment to natural preservation is rewarded with the popularity of its busy parks, lakes and vast trail system. Trails to the peaks of Mt. Woodson and Iron Mountain entice with views of the area.

A weekly Farmer's Market is held Saturdays 8am-11am at Old Poway Park. In September, the Annual Poway Rodeo takes place. Call 760-736-0594 or visit www.powayrodeo.com for details.

Blue Sky Ecological Reserve

This 700-acre wilderness park is frequented by nearly 40,000 hikers each year. The trail system provides many options, including hikes to Lake Poway, Lake Ramona or Mount Woodson. Streambeds are hugged by lush riparian woodland and chaparral and wildlife such as fox, coyote and deer are common to the area. It is the only staffed state reserve in San Diego County with a full-time naturalist on duty and nearly 40 docents who offer programs to the public, including guided hikes. Free slow-paced wildlife and plant walks geared for families take place on weekends at 9am. Bikes are not allowed.

Location:	Green Valley Road, Poway
Hours:	Daily Dawn-Dusk
Admission:	Free
Phone:	858-679-5469
Website:	www.ci.poway.ca.us

HOW TO GET THERE

Exit I-15 at Rancho Bernardo Road and proceed east. After crossing Pomerado Road, Rancho Bernardo Road becomes Espola Road. Immediately after Espola Road bends south, turn left into the parking lot.

Poway

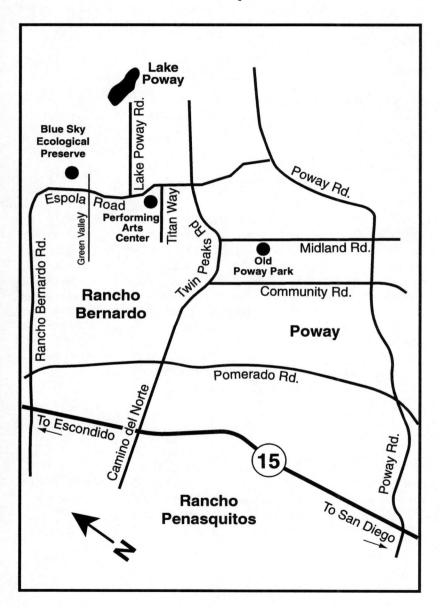

Center for the Performing Arts Foundation

Broadway shows, comedy, concerts and a variety of artistic offerings are presented at this cultural center.

Location:	15498 Espola Road, Poway
Hours:	Daily 9am-5:30pm. Opens at 10am Sat-Sun
Admission:	Ticket prices vary
Phone:	760-748-0505
Website:	www.powayarts.org

HOW TO GET THERE

Exit I-15 at Rancho Bernardo Road which becomes Espola Road. Turn right at Titan Way. The center is on the right.

Lake Poway

The lake itself is tailored to sailing, boating and fishing. Swimming is prohibited, but the surrounding park is ideal for picnics, hiking and camping. A lake concession rents boats and sells mandatory licenses, bait and tackle for those interested in catching trout, bass, catfish and bluegill. Seasonally, the park hosts a summer concert series and night fishing events.

Location:	14644 Lake Poway Road, Poway
Hours:	Daily 7am-Sunset
	No lake activity Mon-Tues
	Call for June-Oct seasonal hours
Admission:	Weekdays-Free
	Weekends(April-Oct): Non-Residents-$4
Phone:	858-679-5466 or 858-679-5470 Information
	858-679-4342 Reservations
Website:	www.ci.poway.ca.us

HOW TO GET THERE

Exit I-15 at Rancho Bernardo Road and proceed east. After crossing Pomerado Road, Rancho Bernardo Road becomes Espola Road. Turn left at Lake Poway Road.

Old Poway Park & Heritage Museum

A tribute to Poway's past, this 4.75-acre historical park offers a variety of sights and activities year-round. In 1948, John S. Porter retired to Poway with the dream of revitalizing the old west in a historic village. His early acquisitions, the Porter House, the Hamburger Factory and the Heritage Museum, were refurbished and remain in Old Poway Park. The city added two historic buildings, Poway's first public assembly building and the Nelson House. The Heritage Museum is open Saturdays and Sundays 9am-4pm and the Nelson House is open Saturdays 9am-4pm and Sundays 11am-2pm.

Porter had also bought a 1907 Baldwin No. 3 Steam Engine. The city built a barn to house this along with a San Francisco Cable Car, a 1938 Fairmont Speeder and a 1894 L.A. Yellow Trolley. Train rides are available every Saturday 10am-4pm and Sunday 11am-2pm. Rides cost 50¢-$2, but are not offered the second Sunday of the month. Every Saturday morning a Farmer's Market takes place 8am-noon. The Boardwalk Craft Market happens the first Saturday each month 8am-2pm. It runs every Saturday from Labor Day to Christmas for the holiday season. Contemporary artists work in old-fashioned craft areas and sell one-of-a-kind handcrafted gifts. The Overshiners Blacksmith operates the last two Saturdays of the month 11am-4pm.

Location:	14134 Midland Road, Poway
Hours:	Park: Daily Dawn-Dusk
	Museum & Activities: Weekends Only
Admission:	Free
Phone:	858-679-4313
Website:	www.ci.poway.ca.us

HOW TO GET THERE

Exit I-15 at Poway Road and proceed east. Turn left at Midland Road. The park is on the left.

North County

RANCHO BERNARDO

While technically part of the City of San Diego, Rancho Bernardo runs independent of the city. In the 1960s, a corporation known as Rancho Bernardo, Inc. was formed and eventually bought by developers who created the community as it exists today. The original concept of a planned residential community with light industry, shopping areas, parks and golf courses remains intact today.

The first recorded individual owner of the area was a former sea captain who became a Mexican citizen and received land grants in 1842 and 1845 to establish a cattle ranch. At the time, California was a Mexican territory. The area remained farming land for sheep and cattle for several years, even as the land changed ownership numerous times. It was during the late 1800s that the popular Bernardo Winery was established. Fortunately, the historic vineyard survived area development and still operates as San Diego's oldest winery.

The area largely remains a residential community with few major attractions beyond Bernardo Winery and the elegant Rancho Bernardo Inn, a 265-acre golf resort and spa. A weekly Farmer's Market is held Friday mornings 9am-noon at the winery and RB ALIVE! Annual Street Fair welcomes thousands the first Sunday in June for food, entertainment and shopping among several arts and crafts booths.

Rancho Bernardo

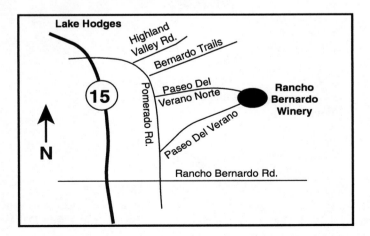

Bernardo Winery

Dating back to 1889, the winery's warm and relaxed setting is apropos. The land it rests on was originally a Spanish Grant and purchased by the Rizzo

family in 1928. Today it is the oldest operating winery in San Diego with some vines planted over 100 years ago. Visitors are welcome to tour the lush grounds independently. Grape vines, olive trees, old rustic farm implements, machinery and winery equipment from the turn of the century contribute to the romantic ambiance of this winery.

The tasting room offers four samples at no charge. A wide variety of red, white and dessert wines are sold and can be personalized with custom labels. Estate made olive oil, wine sauces, jellies and jams are also available. There are several village shops that comprise a plaza of specialty boutiques. The annual grape stomp and dinner is a favorite autumn event as well as the Art, Wine & Culinary Festival the first Sunday in October.

Location:	13330 Paseo Del Verano Norte, Rancho Bernardo
Hours:	Daily 9am-5pm
Admission:	Free
Phone:	858-487-1866
Website:	www.bernardowinery.com

HOW TO GET THERE

Exit I-15 at W. Bernardo/Pomerado Road and proceed east towards Pomerado Road. Proceed south on Pomerado Road. Turn left at Paseo Del Verano Norte. Proceed 1.5 miles to the winery.

RANCHO SANTA FE

Rancho Santa Fe is a Southern California anomaly with 6,200 acres populated by less than 4,500 people in fewer than 1,500 households. This exclusive area forbids sidewalks and street lights in residential areas, where the average lot size is greater than two acres, creating a privileged rural environment. A drive through the area will reveal ornate landscaping around large private gates that conceal Spanish, Mediterranean or Ranch style homes surrounded by pristine open spaces of citrus groves and native foliage.

In the early 1920s, Rancho Santa Fe was developed in the Spanish Colonial Revival style it is known for today. Female architect Lilian Rice had a great understanding of Southern California's history and traditions and thoughtfully transformed a eucalyptus forest into a community reminiscent of a Spanish village. She and the city's project manager intentionally designed Rancho Santa Fe's signature winding roads to guarantee drivers would pass slowly enough to absorb each awe-inspiring view.

Several of the buildings lining Paseo Delicias, Rancho Santa Fe's main thoroughfare, are Rice's designs, including the famous Inn at Rancho Santa Fe. The Inn was a popular meeting place for movie stars such as Errol Flyn, Bette Davis and Jimmy Stewart. The area still remains a Hollywood favorite. A walk down Paseo Delicias and through the side streets delights visitors with unique boutiques, wonderful restaurants and cafes and endless sophisticated ambiance. Thyme on the Ranch is a quaint cafe and bakery

that serves excellent breakfasts, lunches and fresh baked goods at 16905 Avenida De Acacias. The deserts have been rated some of the best in the county. Take home a cake, pie or handful of cookies or tarts.

The Rancho Santa Fe Historical Society, located in the historic La Flecha House on the corner of La Flecha and Via de Santa Fe, reveals the area's interesting past. It was an Indian rancheria until 1831 when 8,824 acres were bestowed to one family in a formal land grant. A scandalous history followed the possession of that desirable land grant and by 1906 only 200 acres remained tied to the original endowment.

HOW TO GET THERE

Exit I-5 at Lomas Santa Fe Road and proceed east for several miles. The road winds inland and drops you onto Paseo Delicias, leading you to the quaint downtown.

Exit I-15 at Via Rancho Parkway and proceed west. Turn left onto Del Dios Highway and proceed west. The highway turns into Paseo Delicias. Continue west to the quaint downtown.

Rancho Santa Fe

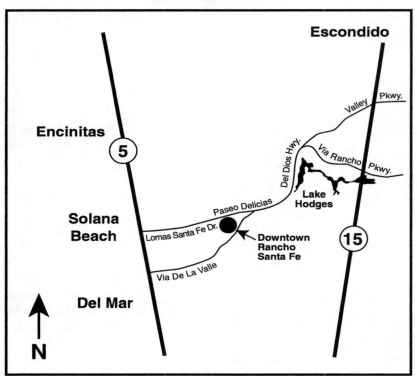

SCRIPPS RANCH & MIRAMAR

Newspaperman E.W. Scripps visited this area in 1890 and with his half-sister, Ellen Browning Scripps, purchased 400 acres of the area known today as Scripps Ranch. Appreciation for the landscape and arid climate led him to build a home he named Miramar.

Scripps Ranch is almost entirely a residential neighborhood with community clubs, centers and a local theatre. This tight-knit community was devastated by the fires of 2003, which destroyed hundreds of homes in this area. A Farmer's Market is held Saturday mornings at Ellen Browning Scripps Elementary School. Lake Miramar is a popular scenic recreational outlet. Across the road from Lake Miramar is Scripps Ranch Library in beautiful mission revival architecture, Evans Pond and the historic 200-foot Meanley Stone Wall.

In 1914, the military acquired the area known as Miramar, which was a cattle and citrus ranch, for Army infantry training and named it Camp Kearny. After WWI, Miramar became an auxiliary field for the Navy and a major air base for the Marine Corps, which rapidly expanded with WWII. After the war, the Marines moved to El Toro and Miramar became a Master Jet Station. Miramar's claim to fame began in 1973 when E-2C Hawkeye Squadrons joined the Miramar fighters. "Fightertown" was created to provide tactical training for the Tomcat Fighters and Hawkeye Wizards, inspiring the movie *Top Gun* which was filmed in the area. Highly technical aviation maintenance schools provided aircraft repair and maintenance training. In 1997, Naval Air Station Miramar became the Marine Corp's largest aviation facility relocating fighter and helicopter squadrons from El Toro to create Marine Corps Air Station. Each year, the Miramar Air Show features the U.S. Navy's Flight Demonstration Team called the Blue Angels. Vintage airplanes, more than 100 military and civilian aircraft, simulation rides, as well as food and novelties are other show highlights.

Scripps Ranch, Mira Mesa & Miramar

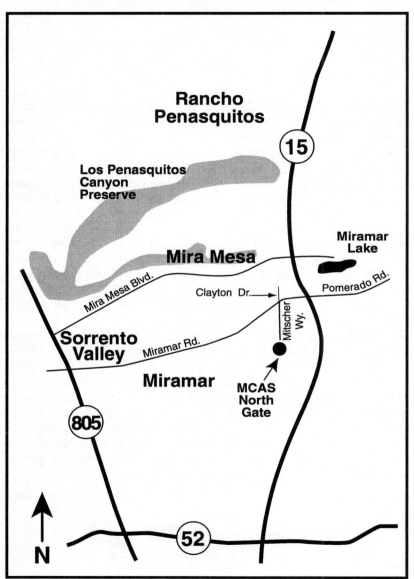

Lake Miramar

The attractive natural landscape combined with 48 picnic tables, 18 barbecues and a concession stand make the lake a popular fishing, boating and relaxation spot. The lake covers 162 acres when full with depths reaching 114 feet. Boat fishing, shore fishing and float tubes are used to catch bass, bluegill, channel catfish, sunfish, and trout, which is stocked November to May. An annual bike ride is held every Fourth of July.

The wide paved path along the lake perimeter makes it popular with bikers, joggers, walkers, rollerbladers, and families with strollers. Unfortunately, the 5 mile path no longer loops around the entire lake as crossing the dam is now prohibited. However, visitors can reach the 3.5 mile point and return for 7 total miles.

Location:	Scripps Lake Drive, Scripps Ranch
Hours:	Daily Sunrise-Sunset
	Boating & Fishing are seasonal
Admission:	Free
Phone:	619-465-3474 Recorded Info
	619-390-0222 Concession/Boat Rentals
Website:	www.sandiego.gov/water/recreation

HOW TO GET THERE

Exit I-15 at Mira Mesa Boulevard and proceed east. Turn right at Scripps Ranch Boulevard. Turn left at Scripps Lake Drive. The lake is on the left beyond a gate entrance.

MCAS Miramar & Flying Leatherneck Aviation Museum

This historical museum is the only official Marine Corps aviation museum in the western U.S. It houses the most complete exhibit of women in the Marine Corps, representing their history from 1918 to today with original uniforms and memorabilia. Several artifacts and over 20 aircraft are on display, including the F4U (Corsair) made famous by WWII Marine Aviators. However, the museum owns as many as 40 historically significant aircraft. Funds needed for restoring the aircraft are raised through the museum gift shop and donations.

Location:	MCAS North Gate off Miramar Road, Miramar
Hours:	Mon-Sat 9am-3pm
Admission:	Free
Phone:	858-693-1723
Website:	www.flyingleathernecks.org

HOW TO GET THERE

Exit I-15 at Miramar Road and proceed west. Turn left at Clayton Drive. Enter the base through the North Gate. When you arrive, tell the guard you want to visit the museum and have a photo ID ready. The guard will direct you from the gate.

VALLEY CENTER

Valley Center is a picturesque agricultural town located in a high valley near San Diego's backcountry. A visit to the area offers several options for spending time on farms and ranches or hitting a few casinos as you wind along oak tree-lined roads.

Bates Nut Farm

Wide open green belts with picnic areas in a beautiful farm setting decorated with unusual country antiques give this ranch a friendly atmosphere. It is a perfect place to bring young children, who can feed ducks and geese or pet sheep and goats, while others sort through a wide variety of nuts, dried fruits and candy from all over the world or shop for gifts at the Farmer's Daughter boutique. The farm roasts and packages their own products and even presses fresh peanut butter on-premise. During autumn, Bates plants a pumpkin patch it is famous for and then  offers Christmas trees for the holidays. Car shows, craft fairs and fine art shows are held throughout the year.

Location:	15954 Woods Valley Road, Valley Center
Hours:	Daily 9am-5pm
Admission:	Free
Phone:	760-749-3333
Website:	www.batesnutfarm.biz

HOW TO GET THERE

Exit I-15 at Valley Parkway and proceed east through Escondido. Continue on this road for approximately 6 miles uphill as it becomes Valley Center Road. Turn right at Woods Valley Road as you enter Valley Center. The farm is on the left 3.5 miles up the road.

Valley Center

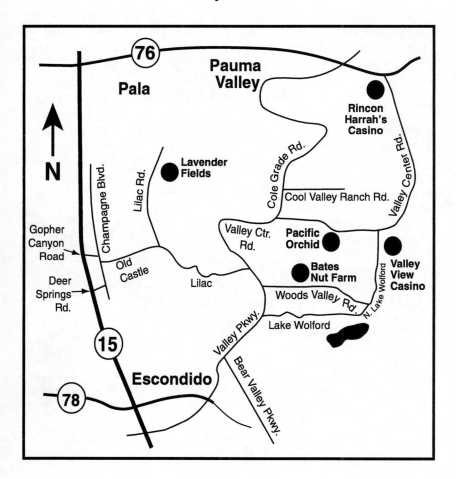

The Lavender Fields

This fragrant 9-acre organic lavender farm offers seasonal "you pick" dates, teaches classes and has a charming General Store with homemade lavender essential oil, creams, lotions, soaps, candles and more. Call ahead or check the website for public dates and events or to request a private group tour.

Location:	12460 Keys Creek Road, Valley Center
Hours:	Hours vary. Peak Season: May/June
Admission:	Free
Phone:	760-742-8790 or 877-449-8945
Website:	www.thelavenderfields.com

HOW TO GET THERE

Exit I-15 at Gopher Canyon/Old Castle Road and proceed east. Turn right at Champagne Boulevard. Turn left at Old Castle Road and proceed 5 miles. Turn left at Lilac Road and proceed 3 miles. Turn right at Old Lilac. This turns into (a dirt) Keys Creek Road. The farm is about 1.5 miles down on the left side.

Pacific Orchid Express

On Fridays and Saturdays the public is welcome to visit this orchid grower and importer's greenhouses. Through a reliable supply network with Asian and Thai orchid growers, the nursery can offer several varieties of high- quality plants and cut flowers including popular hybrids, select species and Mericlone orchids.

Location:	29837 Valley Center Road, Valley Center
Hours:	Fri 8am-4pm & Sat 9am-3pm
Admission:	Free
Phone:	760-749-8411
Website:	www.pacificorchid.com

HOW TO GET THERE
Exit I-15 at Valley Parkway and proceed east though Escondido. Climb the grade and proceed on Valley Center Road. The greenhouses are on the right about a mile past Cole Grade Road.

Casinos

Valley Center has two casinos, Harrah's Rincon Casino & Resort and Valley View Casino. Nearby Pala and Pauma Valley have casinos as well.

Harrah's Rincon Casino & Resort

This casino marked the first Las Vegas-style gambling venue in North County

when it opened late-summer 2002. A 200-room hotel complements the casino, complete with a sundeck, oversized pool, poolside bar, four restaurants, a coffee shop and an entertainment bar lounge. The 45,000 square-foot casino has 1,500 reel and video slots, as well as video poker machines and table games. The casino features Total Rewards, Harrah's national player rewards program, and points earned are good at any of their 26 casinos.

Location:	777 Harrah's Way, Valley Center
Hours:	Daily 24 Hours
Admission:	Free
Phone:	877-777-2457
Website:	www.harrahs.com

HOW TO GET THERE

Exit I-15 at Valley Parkway and proceed east through Escondido. Continue east up the grade as Valley Parkway turns into Valley Center Road. Continue along Valley Center Road. Turn left at Harrah's Way.

Exit Highway 76 at Valley Center Road and proceed south on Valley Center Road. Turn right at Harrah's Way.

Valley View Casino

This casino has over 750 popular reel and video slot machines and friendly dealers at blackjack and poker tables. Bets range from $5 to $500. A free membership program earns cash-back rewards. Membership cards are attained at the VIP Club Center. Fresh food is prepared in person by chefs for the all-you-can-eat buffet.

Location:	16300 Nyemii Pass Road, Valley Center
Hours:	Daily 24 Hours
Admission:	Free
Phone:	866-726-7277
Website:	www.valleyviewcasino.com

HOW TO GET THERE

Exit I-15 at Valley Parkway and proceed east through Escondido. Continue east up the grade as Valley Parkway turns into Valley Center Road. Continue along Valley Center Road. Turn right at North Lake Wohlford Road. Turn right at Nyemii Pass Road.

VISTA

Many of the attractions in Vista have a historic bend to them and take one back to the romance of early California at the turn-of-the-century. The adobe haciendas and ranchos of the area are a true national treasure and the impressive Antique Gas & Steam Engine Museum is a must-see during the museum's semiannual exhibitions in June and October.

While the area's history has been well-preserved via several attractions including the Vista Historical Museum, most of the city's countryside is now residential. Several city parks offer numerous green spaces. Brengle Terrace Park is home to Moonlight Amphitheater, which hosts outdoor plays and shows. The renovated art-deco Avo Playhouse in nearby Vista Village provides a more intimate indoor theatre option with only 382 seats. For current shows, call Moonlight Amphitheater and Avo Playhouse at 760-724-2110. On Saturdays, more than fifty vendors sell produce from 7:45am-11am at the county's oldest Farmers' Market at Eucalyptus Street and Escondido Avenue.

Vista

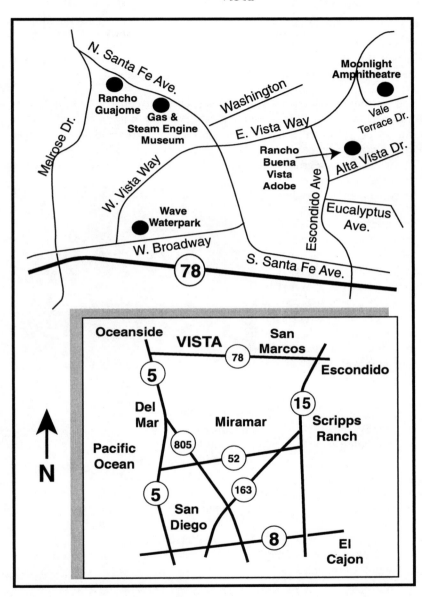

Antique Gas & Steam Engine Museum

This 40 acre museum in the rolling hills of Guajome Regional Park is unique in that the exhibits are not just displays, but well-maintained working mechanical items associated with 1849-1949 farm communities.

The museum collection highlights agriculture, construction and early industrial trades with blacksmith and wheelwright shops, a country kitchen and parlor, steam and gas industrial power units, grist and saw mills, and horse-drawn to modern row crop farm equipment. Dry-land crops, such as wheat and oats, are grown on the property so visitors can see crops harvested from the field and prepared for cooking in the farmhouse.

The last two weekends in June and October are the best times to see the equipment in action and watch the crafts and trades of farmers, weavers, soap and broom makers and wood carvers. Overnight camping, crafts, food and entertainment are part of the biannual revel.

Location:	2040 N. Santa Fe Avenue, Vista
Hours:	Daily 9am-4pm
Admission:	General-$3; Seniors(60+)-$2;
	Youth(6-12)-$2; Under 6-Free
	Fairs: General-$7; Youth(6-12)-$4
Phone:	760-941-1791
Website:	www.agsem.com

HOW TO GET THERE

Exit Highway 78 at Melrose Drive and proceed north 3 miles. Turn right at N. Santa Fe Avenue.

Rancho Buena Vista Adobe

This single-story Monterey style adobe hacienda is the best-preserved of the land-grant ranchos. Its original Pio Pico land grant of 1,184 acres was issued in 1845. Guided 45-minute tours relate the interesting history and legends of this rancho Wed-Fri 10am-2:15pm and on Saturdays at 10am. There is also an art gallery and La Tiendita gift shop.

Location:	651 East Vista Way, Vista
Hours:	Wed-Sat 10am-3pm
Admission:	General-$4; Youth(Under 13)-50¢;
	Seniors (60+), Residents & Students-$3
Phone:	760-639-6164
	760-639-6139 Recorded Information
Website:	www.ci.vista.ca.us/adobe

HOW TO GET THERE

Exit Highway 78 at Escondido Avenue and proceed north. Turn right at East Vista Way. Rancho Buena Vista is on the right in Wildwood Park.

Guajome Regional Park & Rancho Guajome Adobe

This gigantic 22-room hacienda was built on a 2,219-acre Pio Pico land grant in 1853 and is one of California's best examples of Anglo-Hispanic architecture. Guided tours relate the lively and extravagant history of this national landmark, which grew to include a school, chapel, store, and the famous inner courtyard. All proceeds from an onsite gift shop benefit the adobe.

The adobe is part of Guajome County Park, a riparian area with marshes, spring-fed lakes, picnicking, hiking, horseback riding, fishing, and camping. San Diego County Parks allow camping reservations to be made 2 days to 3 months before the desired date. Check-in is at 2pm and check-out is at 1pm. Up to 8 people may stay in one campsite and maximum stay is 14 nights.

Location: 2210 N. Santa Fe Avenue, Vista
Hours: Park: Daily Sunrise-Sunset
                 Adobe Tours: Sat-Sun 11am, 12:30pm & 2pm
                 Reservation Line: Daily 8am-5pm
Admission: Park: $2/Vehicle
                 Adobe: General-$3; Youth(5-12)-$1
                 Overnight: $16/Night + $3 Reservation
Phone: 760 724-4082 Adobe
                 858-694-3049 Park Information
                 877-565-3600 / 858-565-3600 Reservations
Website: www.co.san-diego.ca.us/parks

HOW TO GET THERE

Exit Highway 78 at Melrose Drive and proceed north 3 miles. Turn right
at N. Santa Fe Avenue.

The Wave

This 3-acre water park is owned and operated by the city. It features a wave machine for body boards called *Flow Rider*, four 35-foot waterslides, a free-flowing river, a competition size pool and a children's water playground. No food can be brought into the park, but there are concession stands. Call to confirm seasonal dates and hours.

Location:	161 Recreation Drive, Vista
Hours:	Open Memorial Day-Labor Day
	Daily 10:30am-5:30pm
Admission:	General-$12; Seniors(60+)-$9;
	Youth prices based on height:
	Over 42"-$12; Under 42"-$9;
	Under 2-Free
Phone:	760-940-9283
Website:	www.ci.vista.ca.us

HOW TO GET THERE

Exit Highway 78 at Vista Village Drive and proceed north 3 blocks. Turn right at Recreation Drive.

San Diego County

SOUTH BAY

- Bonita
- Chula Vista
- Imperial Beach

San Diego's South Bay

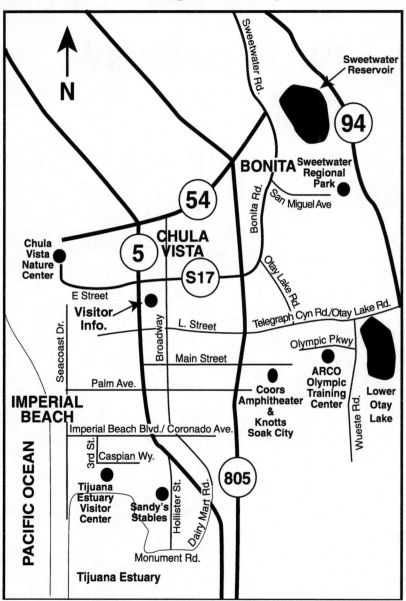

BONITA

This community, which means "pretty" in Spanish, was originally part of the Bonita Ranch of 1884. The community is a welcome environment for horses and equestrians.

Sweetwater Summit Regional Park

This county park caters to both day users and overnight campers. Fifteen miles of trails through a variety of habitats welcome hikers, mountain bikers and equestrians alike. At the park's Summit Site panoramic views reveal the Pacific Ocean and San Diego Bay to the west, the Tijuana hills to the south and Sweetwater Reservoir to the east. The Sweetwater Reservoir Riding & Hiking Trail allows pedestrians and pets, bikers and equestrians to hug the south side of the reservoir for nearly five miles. There are no restrooms or drinking fountains along the trails.

There are park restrooms and hot showers for all campers and each of the 53 sites is equipped with water and electricity. Tent camping is as common as trailer and RV camping at this park. Some campsites have horse corrals. San Diego County Parks allow reservations to be made two days to three months before the desired date. Check-in is at 2pm and check-out is at 1pm. Up to eight people may stay in one campsite and maximum stay is 14 nights.

Location:	3218 Summit Meadow Road, Bonita
Hours:	Daily Sunrise-Sunset
	Reservation Line: Daily 8am-5pm
Admission:	Day-Use: $2/Vehicle
	Overnight: $16/Night + $3 Reservation
	Horses: $2/Night
Phone:	858-694-3049 Information
	877-565-3600 / 858-565-3600 Reservations
Website:	www.sdparks.org

HOW TO GET THERE

Take I-8 to CA-125 South. Exit CA-125 at Spring Street/Highway 94 and turn left. Turn right at Broadway. Turn left at Sweetwater Road and proceed along this road. Turn left at Bonita Road. Turn left at San Miguel Road. Turn left at Summit Meadow Road.

CHULA VISTA

Chula Vista Harbor has relatively uncrowded waters and spectacular views as one might expect of a place meaning "beautiful view".

Three parks offer great recreational opportunities. Bayside Park & Pier features a fishing pier, picnic tables, bike paths and walkways surrounded by marinas, restaurants and shopping. Bayfront Park boasts a public boat launching ramp and beautiful landscaping. Slightly inland, Marina View Park at 200 Marina Parkway caters to children with play equipment, picnic tables and an open play area with views of the bay.

Every Thursday, a Farmer's Market takes place downtown from 3pm-6pm at Third Avenue and Center. During the summer, the market stays open until 7pm. May through September, Third Avenue is graced with over 125 classic cars and motorcycles for the Blast From the Past Car Show on Wednesday nights 5pm-8:30pm. In August, the annual Lemon Festival brings live entertainment, hundreds of craft and food vendors, a beer garden, a car show, a kids fun zone and "everything lemon." In December, the Annual Starlight Yule Parade runs along Third Avenue with floats and marching bands in conjunction with a craft fair. For details on all events, call 619-422-1982 or visit www.downtownchulavista.com.

Chula Vista Heritage Museum

This museum relates the history of Chula Vista and the South Bay area using many artifacts and interesting old photographs. A Walk of History Tour featuring historic sites in downtown Chula Vista and a Historic Home Tour featuring special residences of the area can be downloaded from the museum's website.

Location:	360 Third Avenue, Chula Vista
Hours:	Mon-Thurs & Sat 1pm-4pm
Admission:	Free
Phone:	619-427-8092
Website:	www.chulavista.lib.ca.us/museum/

HOW TO GET THERE

Exit I-5 at Fourth Avenue/Highland Avenue. Turn right at Fourth Avenue. Turn left at C Street. Continue on Third Avenue.

Chula Vista Nature Center

Walking trails, aquariums and aviaries equally lure visitors to this impressive place. Inside the modern 11,000-square foot Nature Center a 4,500-gallon petting pool is populated by bat rays, stingrays, horned sharks, sea hares and other sea life specimens. Detailed exhibits explain the ecology of salt marshes, the diversity and migratory patterns of the area's birds and highlight some rare plants and animals.

Although used for spotting area wildlife, the two outstanding observation platforms offer views of San Diego's beautiful bay, the Coronado Bridge and downtown San Diego. Nearly 200 species of migratory birds arrive and depart annually from the center's marsh, many of which are endangered

species. Many rare birds, including the light-footed clapper rail, Belding's savannah sparrow and the California least tern, can be seen nesting in the marsh or skimming the water in search of fish.

The onsite classrooms, photo darkroom and auditorium facilitate in the center's education efforts. Nature souvenirs and books are sold at the gift shop.

Location:	1000 Gunpowder Point Drive, Chula Vista
Hours:	Tues-Sun 10am-5pm
	Last shuttle to Nature Center at 4pm
	Daily during summer. Closed holidays
Admission:	General-$5; Seniors(55+)-$3;
	Youth(12-17)-$3; Youth(5-11)-$2;
	Under 5-Free
Phone:	619-409-5900
Website:	www.chulavistanaturecenter.org

HOW TO GET THERE

Exit I-5 at E Street and proceed west to the parking lot. Free shuttle rides take visitors from the parking lot to the center.

Coors Amphitheater

First-rate national acts are common to this venue, which is managed by House of Blues Concerts. The outdoor theater, designed specifically for music concerts, seats 20,000. Half are reserved, while the other half are general admission lawn seats. Gates open one to two hours before showtime. Non-alcoholic tailgating is allowed before shows. Visitors can bring blankets, but chairs, food, drink, umbrellas, cameras and video recorders are not permitted inside. Last minute tickets may be purchased at the amphitheater Box Office on show days 10am-9pm. Call or visit the website for upcoming shows.

Location:	2050 Entertainment Circle, Chula Vista
Hours:	Varies by show
Admission:	Varies by show
Phone:	619-671-3600 Information
	619-220-8497 Ticketmaster
Website:	www.hob.com/venues/concerts/coors/

HOW TO GET THERE
Exit I-805 at Main Street/Auto Park and proceed east on Main Street for 2.5 miles. Turn right at Entertainment Circle.

Lower Otay Reservoir

This lake is home to the US Olympic Training Center's rowing sports. It also serves as a great fishing spot and picnic location for visitors. The lake features over a dozen picnic tables and barbecues. Visitors are also allowed to bring their own self-contained barbecues for use in designated areas. Private and rental boats are allowed on the lake. Boat, float tube and shore fishing are permitted. Leashed dogs are allowed, but must stay 50 feet from the water at all times.

Location:	Wueste Road, Chula Vista
Hours:	Open February-September
	Wed, Sat & Sun Sunrise-Sunset
Admission:	Free
Phone:	619-465-3474
Website:	www.sannet.gov/water/recreation/lotay

HOW TO GET THERE
Exit I-805 at Telegraph Canyon Road and proceed east for about 8 miles. Turn right at Wueste Road.

South Bay

Knott's Soak City U.S.A.

This 32-acre water park offers 22 rides in a themed 1950s San Diego setting of long boards and surf woodies. *La Jolla Falls* features high-speed drop slides while *Palisades Plunge* and *Solana Storm Watch Tower* features tube slides. *Imperial Run* has six different body slides and *Tykes Trough* offers slides for young children. Families enjoy the lazy river ride at *Sparkletts Sunset River* and the raft ride at *Coronado Express*. A wave pool is the highlight at *Balboa Bay*. *Gremmie Lagoon* and *Dick's Beach House* cater to young children. Food may not be brought into the park. Locker rentals, food, drink and souvenirs are available. Special rates are offered for groups of fifteen or more with advance reservations.

Location:	2052 Entertainment Circle, Chula Vista
Hours:	Daily 10am-6pm Memorial Day-Labor Day
	Weekends 10am-6pm Late April & September
Admission:	General-$23.95, After 3pm-$13.95;
	Youth(3-11)-$16.95, After 3pm-$9.95;
	Under 3-Free; Season Passes available
	Parking-$6/Vehicle; $8/RV
Phone:	619-661-7373
Website:	www.knotts.com

HOW TO GET THERE

Exit I-805 at Main Street/Auto Park and proceed east on Main Street for two miles. Turn right at Entertainment Circle.

US Olympic ARCO Training Center

This $65 million state-of-the-art athletic training facility is active year-round and is the largest of its kind in the world. Roughly 4,000 athletes visit the training center each year. Track and field, canoe/kayak, cycling, field hockey, soccer, softball, tennis, archery and rowing are all supported by the 150-acre facility. A gymnasium and aquatic center are being considered for future additions.

The facility can house 150 athletes at any one time and caters to their needs with a Sports Science & Medicine Center and an 18,000 square foot kitchen and dining area with 300 seats. The Visitor Center offers free guided tours hourly Mon-Sat 9am-4pm and on Sunday 11am-4pm. Reservations are not necessary.

Location:	2800 Olympic Parkway, Chula Vista
Hours:	Daily 9am-4pm
Admission:	Free
Phone:	619-656-1500 Information
	619-482-6222 Visitor Center
Website:	www.olympic-usa.org/about_us/

HOW TO GET THERE

Exit I-805 at Telegraph Canyon and proceed east for about 8 miles. Turn right at Wueste Road and proceed to the Visitor's Center on the left.

South Bay

IMPERIAL BEACH

Imperial Beach, which happens to be the most southwesterly city in the continental U.S., is a quaint seaside town best enjoyed at the ocean. Within an hour, one can walk the three-and-a-half miles of city beach front among surfers, boogie borders and fishermen. Public fishing is free off the 1,500-foot pier. Across the way, Portwood Pier Plaza Park features colorful public art called "Surfehenge". Looking south just across border, Tijuana's famous "Bullring by the Sea" called Plaza De Monumental is visible. The beach runs along Seacoast Drive.

In mid-May, Imperial Beach hosts an annual Chili & Jazz Festival. However, the city is best known for the international U.S. Open Sandcastle Competition held each year in late July. During the competition, Seacoast Drive shuts down to invite music, entertainment, food, children's rides, art and the Sandcastle Parade. Fireworks are launched from the end of the Imperial Beach pier at dark. Visit www.usopensandcastle.com or call 619-424-5380 for more information.

HOW TO GET THERE
Exit I-5 at Palm Avenue and proceed west to the ocean.

Border Field State Park &
Tijuana River National Estuarine Reserve

Both these wildlife habitats represent the natural U.S. Mexico Border environment at its western edge and provide a place for picnicking, exploring and enjoying ocean views. They both have Visitor Centers as well.

The intertidal Tijuana Estuary, which spans 2,500 acres, provides miles of walking trails through a wildlife habitat. There is beach access and one can view where the river mouth meets the Pacific Ocean. On weekends, free guided walks are offered. Some tours detail the reliance that more than 370 species of migratory and native birds place on the rare salt marsh as a feeding and nesting ground. Six of these birds are known to be endangered species. Depending on weather patterns, the typically shallow stream flow can change dramatically and the ever-changing topography can include sand dunes, marshes, uplands, the river bed, mud flats and tidal sloughs.

Border Field State Park, which merges with the southwest corner of the Tijuana River National Estuarine Research Reserve, is oftentimes closed. Call ahead. Situated on a bluff, one can view the ocean and the estuary as well as the Plaza De Monumental Mexican bull ring located on the south side of the border. Highlights include hiking, biking and horseback nature trails, a wildlife viewing area used primarily for birding and ocean access allowing for surf fishing and swimming.

South Bay

Location:	301 Caspian Way, Imperial Beach
Hours:	Daily 10am-5pm
	Trails close at Sunset
Admission:	Free
Phone:	619-575-3613
Website:	www.parks.ca.gov

HOW TO GET THERE

Exit I-5 at Coronado Avenue in Imperial Beach (not the Coronado Bridge exit) and proceed west about 3 miles. The road becomes Imperial Beach Boulevard. Turn left at Third Avenue. Follow the road around the corner. The Visitor Center is on the right.

Sandy's Rental Stable

With fifteen years of experience, Sandy's knows how to guide visitors through this best-kept secret corner of San Diego. Across from the national estuary and wildlife reserve, this outfitter offers an experience that allows riders to view rare birds, plants and wildlife, while enjoying the natural landscape on horseback. Over sixty horses are available to accommodate all ages and all riding levels. Riders must be seven years or older. Reservations are not necessary as the stables operate on a first-come, first-serve basis, unless you have a group of ten or more. Groups of up to forty people are welcome.

The most common rides are the one hour Nature Trail ($30) and three hour Beach & Trail Combo ($60) rides. When weather forbids the beach rides, a two hour Scenic Preserve Trail ($45) is offered and Moonlight Rides are also available by request. For groups of at least ten people, you can reserve a one hour Hay Wagon Ride for $20 per person or add a Chuckwagon Meal to any ride for an extra $25 per person.

Location:	2060 Hollister Street, Imperial Beach
Hours:	Daily 9am-4pm
Admission:	Prices vary $30-60/Person
Phone:	619-424-3124
Website:	www.sandysrentalstable.com

HOW TO GET THERE

Exit I-5 at Coronado Avenue in Imperial Beach (past the Coronado Bridge) and proceed straight through the traffic light. The street becomes Hollister. The stables are a mile up the road on the right.

San Diego County

EAST COUNTY

- Alpine
- Boulevard
- Campo
- Guatay
- Jacumba
- El Cajon
- Flinn Springs
- Jamul
- La Mesa
- Lakeside
- Lemon Grove
- Spring Valley

Alpine, Boulevard, Campo, Guatay & Jacumba

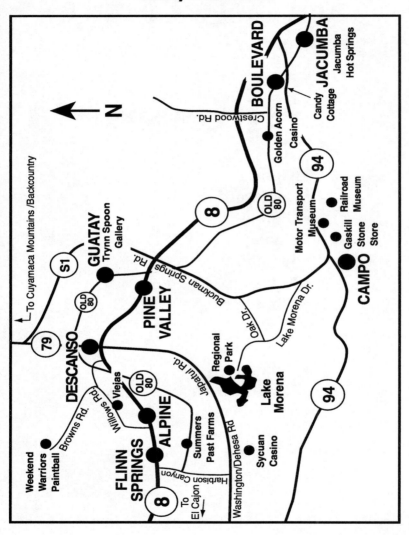

ALPINE

Although the casino is the obvious draw, Alpine has lesser known treasures to please visitors, especially the outdoor types. Nestled at the foothills of the Viejas Mountains near Cleveland National Forest, Alpine provides easy access to the Cuyamaca and Laguna Mountains for camping and trail activities (see Backcountry chapter). The town itself is a National Wildlife Habitat and the Annual Sage & Songbirds Festival held in May celebrates this designation. Other annual events that draw crowds are the Alpine Viejas Western Days & Parade in September and the Alpine Village Christmas Light Parade held the last Saturday of November. During summer months a free Summer Concert Series takes place on select Sunday evenings. Call 619-445-1818 for concert details.

Another little known attraction in Alpine is Roy Athey's Descansco, Alpine & Pacific Railway where the enthusiastic conductor takes visitors on a free Sunday afternoon ride between 1pm-3pm in his own real train June through September at 1266 Alpine Heights Road. Call 619-445-4781 for further details.

The quaint and rustic Alpine Creek Shopping Center is the small town's area of activity with restaurants, a little shopping and some services. Beside the popular Bread Basket bakery and restaurant are green belts perfect for picnicking.

Sadly, Alpine was greatly affected by the fires that swept through the county in late 2003. Be prepared that much of the beautiful countryside is burned out in and around the Alpine area.

HOW TO GET THERE
Exit I-8 at Tavern Road and proceed south straight to the town's only stop light.

Viejas Casino & Outlet Center

For more than a decade now, the Viejas Village has entertained visitors with gambling, shopping, dining, concerts and shows. The Native American village setting adds ambiance and charm to the casino and outlet activities.

Gamblers take their chances at Poker, Blackjack, Bingo, Double Hand Baccarat, Pai Gow, Caribbean Stud and Let It Ride. Those that prefer slots over tables can play anything from pennies to $100 hands at video and pull-handle machines, including progressives like Superball and Megabucks. Satellite wagering is also popular at Viejas. A VIP Rewards Card, which is free, allows visitors to earn points every time they gamble, as well as free valet parking and discounts at outlet stores. Five restaurants offer a wide selection of dining choices, from a steakhouse dinner to a deli-style sandwich. A full-service bar is on-premise.

The Viejas Outlet Center is an open-air shopping and entertainment hub with award winning architecture. Over 50 top-name outlet stores and several eateries lie within a nicely landscaped plaza of fountains, gardens and parks. Free family-friendly entertainment is common at Center Show Court and special performances are offered during the outdoor Viejas Concerts In The Park series. Nightly water show spectaculars with lasers and special effects include The Legend of Nightfire, Splash Tracks and The Legend of the Ice Princess.

Location:	Casino: 5000 Willows Road, Alpine
	Outlet: 5005 Willows Road, Alpine
Hours:	Casino Daily 24 Hours
	Outlets Daily 10am-9pm
	Open until 7pm Sundays
Admission:	Free
Phone:	619-445-5400 Casino
	619-659-2070 Outlets
Website:	www.viejas.com / www.shopviejas.com

HOW TO GET THERE
Exit I-8 at Willows Road and proceed north. Continue east along Willows Road to Viejas.

Weekend Warriors Paintball Park

Driving through Alpine one would likely miss this once-in-a-lifetime adventure, but a thrilling game of paintball awaits at San Diego's largest outdoor paintball park.

Adults and children alike enjoy this game that combines Tag with Hide-Go-Seek using pellet markers filled with non-toxic vegetable oil paints. Players move through trees and hide behind rocks as they dodge and shoot paintballs at the opposing team. The adrenaline-filled experience can accommodate large groups and teams, as well as individual walk-ons or a few friends that will be placed or combined with other groups to create a team.

Several different pricing packages exist to accommodate all needs. There are packages for those that have never tried the game and need everything from guns, goggles, face-shields and paint-balls. A basic entry fee will cover those that just want to play and already have their own equipment and paintballs. An all-day air supply of CO_2 and N_2O is included in the entrance price. Prepaid rates are the most economical and parents can oftentimes play free with their children. Most players shoot 50 paintballs per game and participate in about half of the dozen games held each day. Paintball packages start at 200 paintballs for $12 and run as high as 2,000 paintballs for $100.

Players can register online to reserve a space and pay at the time of registration to get better rates. All players need to show ID and sign a release form. Weekend Warriors rents private fields to large groups and has a Battle Bus Store with discount equipment sales.

Location:	25 Browns Road, Alpine
Hours:	Sat-Sun 8am-5pm. Last game at 4pm
	Call for holiday openings
	Weekday group reservations available
Admission:	Walk-On Rates: $15 Entrance & Air;
	$25 Entrance, Air & Equipment
	Prepaid rates are less expensive
Phone:	619-445-1217
Website:	www.paintballfield.com

HOW TO GET THERE

Exit I-8 at Willows Road and proceed north past the Casino & Outlet Center. Turn left at Browns Road. Stay to the right and you will see the fields.

BOULEVARD

When traveling along Interstate 8 or Old Highway 80 near Boulevard, one should always drop into town for a little sugar. The one-street town is as charming as its residents. Across from the mainstay candy shop is the equally luring Boulevard Gift Shop, filled with antiques and small country collectibles.

Wisteria Candy Cottage

This historical building has been a candy shop and kitchen since 1921. Stepping inside the small house, one can hardly believe that it was once the

community's single-room high school. The old-fashioned candies are still handmade with fresh ingredients by the family that has owned the cottage for more than eighty years. The confections are created from scratch using original recipes for toffees and brittles, truffles and fudges, nut rolls, clusters and their famous turtles. Endless combinations of milk, semisweet and white chocolate complement cashews, almonds, pecans and more. There are several other candies for those that prefer sweets other than chocolate. Visitors that become hooked on the confections can order their candies online.

Location:	39961 Old Highway 80, Boulevard
Hours:	Daily 9am-5pm. Open until 5:30pm Fri-Sat
Admission:	Free. Candy prices are by the pound
Phone:	619-766-4453 or 800-458-8246
Website:	www.candycottage.com

HOW TO GET THERE

Exit I-8 at Jewel Valley Road and proceed south to Old Highway 80. Proceed east along Old Highway 80. The Candy Cottage is on the right.

CAMPO

Campo is a haven for vintage train and railroad aficionados. The San Diego Railroad Museum and its popular 16-mile train expedition, as well as the historic Gaskill Brothers Stone Store and Motor Transport Museum make for active weekends in this town. Campo also has a county park with a lake and nice camping facilities, as well as a casino.

Gaskill Brothers Stone Store Museum

The Gaskill Brothers Stone Store was built in 1885 and is now a museum with exhibits on the history of the Mountain Empire Region. Displays feature old time gadgets, photos, furniture and area legends. There are also extensive displays on the region's military history, a book store and research archive that is available by appointment.

The Gaskill Brothers, Luman and Silas, owned the store and were notorious for their brutish attitudes. When a gang of outlaws led by Cruz Lopez tried to rob the store, one of early California's bloodiest battles broke out. Three of the bandits were killed and the others hung. Luman and a friend were injured, but recovered.

Location:	31130 Highway 94, Campo
Hours:	Sat & Sun 11am-5pm. Open select holidays
Admission:	General-$2; Under 13-Free
Phone:	619-478-5707
Website:	www.sdrm.org/border/

HOW TO GET THERE

Exit I-8 at Buckman Springs Road (S1) and proceed south for about 10 miles to its end. Turn right at Campo Road/Highway 94.

Golden Acorn Casino

Slots may be the draw at this casino with 750 video slot machines, including some of the more popular games like *$1,000,000 Pyramid*, *American Bandstand* and *Jeopardy* among many other Vegas favorites like *Wheel of Fortune*. Thirteen tables offer a range of limits from $2 Blackjack to $10 Double Deck as well as Pai Gow, 3-Card Poker and Let it Ride. The Player's Gold Club rewards program allows gamblers to accrue points while playing. Points are redeemable for promotions, cash back, food and merchandise. Monthly drawings award cash, trips and vehicles. Other highlights include free valet parking, a 24-hour restaurant, full-service bar, pizza shop and the popular Travel Center.

Location:	I-8 at Crestwood Drive, Campo
Hours:	Daily 24 Hours
Admission:	Free
Phone:	866-794-6244
Website:	www.goldenacorncasino.com

HOW TO GET THERE

Exit I-8 at Crestwood Drive and and proceed south. The casino is on the east side of the street just south of I-8.

Lake Morena Regional Park

This county park offers year-round picnicking, camping, hiking, boating and fishing among 3,250 acres of chaparral, oak trees and grasslands surrounding Morena Reservoir. Wildlife sightings are common and occasionally a bald eagle is spotted. There are plenty of trails, including a portion of the famous Pacific Crest Trail.

Two nice campgrounds on either side of the lake provide easy access to the water, which allows boats, kayaks, canoes and sailboards. Swimming is not allowed and boats can not exceed 10mph. One campground is equipped to accommodate RVs and trailers with partial hook-ups, while the other caters to tent-campers who prefer private and scenic primitive sites with fire rings. There are eight cabins available at $25 per night. Restrooms, warm showers, a boat launch ($4 use fee), boat rentals ($6-$30) and a country store satisfy any need. State and daily fishing licenses are required.

San Diego County Parks allow reservations to be made two days to three months before the desired date. Check-in is at 2pm and check-out is at 1pm. Up to eight people may stay in one campsite and maximum stay is 14 nights.

Location:	2550 Lake Morena Drive, Campo
Hours:	Day-Use: Daily Sunrise-Sunset
	Reservation Line: Daily 8am-5pm
Admission:	Day-Use: $2/Vehicle
	Overnight: $12-$16/Night + $3 Reservation
Phone:	858-694-3049 Information
	877-565-3600 / 858-565-3600 Reservations
Website:	www.sdparks.org

HOW TO GET THERE

Exit I-8 at Buckman Springs Road (S1) and proceed south 4 miles. Turn right at Oak Drive and proceed west 3 miles to Lake Morena Drive and the park entrance.

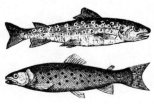

Motor Transport Museum & Truck Yard

This volunteer museum aims to create and nurture an appreciation for vintage trucks and motor transport. The truck yard is a place for restoration and visitors are welcome to view the fleet as long as the gates are open. Volunteers are usually present on Wednesdays, Fridays and Saturdays. Antique trucks, old photos, literature and memorabilia are in the museum. The museum resides in the historic 1929 Campo Feldspar Mill, which processed porcelain for sparkplugs and fixtures.

Location:	31949 Highway 94, Campo
Hours:	Saturdays 9am-5pm
Admission:	Free
Phone:	619-478-2492
Website:	www.sdrm.org/border/

HOW TO GET THERE

Exit I-8 at Buckman Springs Road (S1) and proceed south for about 10 miles to its end. Turn right at Campo Road/Highway 94.

San Diego Railroad Museum

For more than 15 years, this museum has been operating 90-minute weekend train excursions between Campo and Miller Creek on Saturdays and Sundays. The ride is a 16-mile backcountry historic tour of the Pacific Southwest railroad industry aboard restored locomotives and refurbished cars from the museum's collection. The San Diego and Arizona Railway was active in east county in the early 1900s. Upon return to Campo Depot, visitors are taken to the museum's restoration area for a guided tour of locomotives, freight equipment, passenger cars and cabooses.

Railroad artifacts, displays and memorabilia are museum highlights. The gift shop, which is housed in the original Campo Depot, sells snacks, books and souvenirs.

Occasionally, an all-day trip south to Tecate, Mexico runs. In addition, two special occasion trains are sometimes offered. Twilight Dinner Trains, departing at 6:30pm, feature five-course elegant meals served on china over white linens. Private observation cars are usually pulled at a leisurely pace by a vintage diesel-electric locomotive. Reserve ahead as only thirty passengers can be accommodated. One-and-a-half hour Brunch Trains run on some Sundays, departing at 11am. For reservations, call 619-938-1943.

Location:	31123 Highway 94, Campo
Hours:	Sat & Sun 10am-5pm
	Train Departs 11am & 2:30pm
Admission:	Campo-Miller Creek Excursion:
	General-$15; Seniors(60+)-$12;
	Youth(6-12)-$5; Under 6-Free
	Twilight Dinner Train: $75/Person
	Brunch Train: General-$35; Youth(2-12)-$20
Phone:	619-478-9937 Weekends (Campo)
	619-465-7776 Weekdays
Website:	www.sdrm.org

HOW TO GET THERE

Exit I-8 at Buckman Springs Road (S1) and proceed south for about 10 miles to its end. Turn right at Campo Road/Highway 94. Turn left at Forest Gate Road and proceed to Museum Drive.

East County

GUATAY

Tryyn Wooden Spoon Gallery

This unassuming gallery is a find and one of the county's best kept secrets. Reminiscent of Vermont's Simon Pierce glass or New Mexico's Nambe silver, Tryyn Gallery uses  wood to create signature items that include beautiful spoons, kitchen utensils, bowls, toys, collectibles, bookmarks, jewelry and custom orders. Each piece is directed by its natural shape and grain, so every single hand-carved treasure is one-of-a-kind. Each piece is signed and dated by internationally-acclaimed artist William Chappelow.

Over twenty years ago, a huge oak tree fell on Chappelow's property after a bad storm. An intriguing twisted limb inspired him to create a large spoon, resulting in a new passion and what is the Tryyn Gallery today. His love for the art is evident in each creation. Chappelow has spent up to two months perfecting one spoon. Hundreds of woods from across the world, including the rare Ebony, Purpleheart, and Tulipwood, are used for certain pieces, such as Wedding & Anniversary Spoons. Tryyn spoons are featured in the Smithsonian, New York's American Craft Museum, San Diego's Mingei International Museum and many private collections, including those of British and U.S. heads-of-state. The gallery has been featured on television and the pieces are sold in fine galleries and gift shops across the country.

Location:	27540 Old Highway 80, Guatay
Hours:	Tues-Sun 1pm-4pm. Open at 10am weekends
Admission:	Free. Items range in price from $10-$2,500
Phone:	619-473-9030
Website:	www.tryyn.sandiego411.net

HOW TO GET THERE

Exit I-8 at Japatul Valley Road (Descanso exit) and proceed north. Turn onto Old Highway 80. Continue past Highway 79 towards Guatay. Tryyn Gallery is on the left.

JACUMBA

Jacumba loosely means "hut by water" and was originally settled due to the healing effects of the hot waters from the natural springs. This funky town of less than 1,000 residents drew several visitors and Hollywood stars such as Clark Gable and Marlene Dietrich during the 1920s. At that time more than 5,000 residents lived in the town known for the fine Vaughn Hotel, which remained until the early 90s, and the natural hot springs, which still remain today. Visitors should note the large painted mural on a wall near the edge of town recalling the day Jacumba actually experienced a rare California hurricane.

Jacumba Hot Springs

This outdoor mineral hot springs pool is volcanically heated and varies between 70 and 90 degrees depending on the season. Several chaise lounge chairs invite one to linger for the day and enjoy the springs. An indoor Jacuzzi, sauna, restaurant and bar are also open to visitors. Swimsuits are required and there are changing rooms.

A connected motel offers rooms starting at $55-65 per night. Visitors planning to stay the night should make reservations one week in advance.

Location:	44500 Old Highway 80, Jacumba
Hours:	Daily 8am-11pm
Admission:	Day-Use: $10/Person. Free to motel guests
Phone:	619-766-4333

HOW TO GET THERE

Exit I-8 at Carrizo Gorge Road (Jacumba exit) and proceed south along Corrizo Gorge Road. Turn right at Old Highway 80 and proceed for two miles. The springs are on the right.

El Cajon, Flinn Springs, Jamul, La Mesa, Lakeside, Lemon Grove & Spring Valley

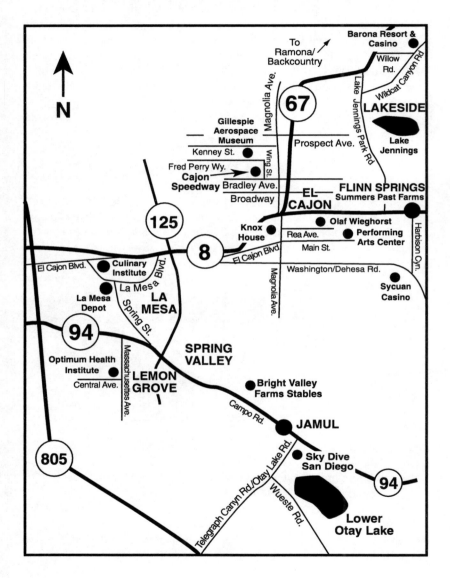

EL CAJON

Downtown El Cajon's Main Street is lined with eclectic shops, galleries and restaurants. Every Wednesday a Farmer's Market is held 4pm-7pm at the historic intersection of Main Street and Magnolia Avenue. In 1880, this intersection was a crossroads for two wagon trails and so a seven room hotel was built there.  The hotel still remains as the 1876 Knox House Museum. Public tours are offered on Thursdays, Saturdays and Sundays at 280 N. Magnolia Avenue. Call the El Cajon Historical Society at 619-444-3800 to confirm a tour or for further details. The society maintains a website at www.elcajonhistory.org.

Another cultural treasure in El Cajon is the Heritage of the Americas Museum open Tuesday-Friday 10am-4pm and Saturday 12pm-4pm. This educational center features both the prehistoric and the historic art, culture and natural history of these two continents at 12110 Cuyamaca College Drive West. Call 619-670-5194 or visit www.cuyamaca.net/museum for more details.

The El Cajon Art Association hosts gallery showings Wednesday-Saturday 11am-4pm at 1246 East Main Street. Call 619-588-8875 for gallery details. May through September, Concerts on the Green are held at 5:30pm on Fridays at Main Street's Prescott Promenade. Call 619-401-8858 for concert details. The annual Mother Goose Parade is a big draw each Thanksgiving morning. Call 619-444-8712 for parade details.

HOW TO GET THERE

Exit Interstate 8 at Magnolia Avenue/Civic Center and proceed south to Main Street and downtown El Cajon.

Cajon Speedway

Six thousand fans can pack the stands to witness a diverse group of cars race along this paved 3/8-mile oval track with banks angled between five and eighteen degrees at the turns. Cajon Speedway is one of roughly 100 short tracks that participate in the national NASCAR Weekly Racing Series presented by Dodge. While nationally recognized championship series do race at this track, regular shows create local racing champions whose records are tracked and kept using a point system. Various divisions race to the same format during regular shows: a 4-lap Trophy Dash, two 8-lap Heat Races and a Main Event ranging from 20-40 laps. The track was at its height in the mid-70s when nearly a hundred Super Stocks crowded the pits. Since the late 80s, Sportsman Stocks have replaced the Super Stocks. Grand American Modifieds, Street Stocks, Pony Stocks and Bomber Stocks all race the Cajon Speedway that rests on forty acres next to Gillespie Airport.

Location:	Wing Street at Fred Perry Way, El Cajon
Hours:	Races Fri & Sat. Hours vary
	Gates open around 4pm-5pm
Admission:	General-$10; Youth(6-12)-$3; Under 6-Free
	Special event pricing varies
Phone:	619-448-8900
Website:	www.cajonspeedway.com

HOW TO GET THERE

Take I-8 to Highway 67. Exit Highway 67 at Bradley and turn left. Turn right at Wing Street and proceed to the track entrance.

East County

East County Performing Arts Center

This intimate theater with only 1,140 seats has attracted top name performers such as Tony Bennett, Herbie Hancock and the Preservation Hall Jazz Band.

Location:	210 East Main Street, El Cajon
Hours:	Box Office: Mon-Sat 11am-4pm
	Concert times vary. Most shows at 7:30pm
Admission:	Prices vary
Phone:	619-440-2277
Website:	www.ecpac.com

HOW TO GET THERE

Exit I-8 at Magnolia/Civic Center and proceed south on Magnolia. Turn left at Julian and proceed straight to the center. The theater is on the right.

Gillespie Field Aerospace Museum

This museum started as a small one-hanger site for aircraft restoration. Today the annex is a major part of the restoration and replica reproduction program for the San Diego Aerospace Museum. Several historically significant aircraft and aviation artifacts are on display at this facility. Highlights include the F-14A Tomcat, F-8J Crusader, F-86F Sabre and the F-16N Viper just to name a few. The C.A.F.-Air Group One is a large part of this volunteer restoration project. They also fly the WWII aircraft at Gillespie's annual air show in May.

Location:	335 Kenney Street, El Cajon
Hours:	Mon, Wed & Fri 8am-3pm
Admission:	Free. Donations accepted
Phone:	619-234-8291
Website:	www.aerospacemuseum.org/gillespie
	www.cafairgroup1.org

HOW TO GET THERE
Exit I-8 at Highway 67 and proceed north. Exit Highway 67 at Prospect Avenue and proceed west. Turn left at Magnolia. Turn right at Kenney Street.

Olaf Wieghorst Museum & Western Heritage Center

Western art lovers look no further. Olaf Wieghorst is known as the "Dean of Western Art" and his art and his story are the highlight of this museum. The Western Heritage Center is dedicated to preserving his legacy and the art and heritage of the American West. Horses are a major theme in Wieghorst's work, which encompasses oil, watercolor, bronze sculptures, copper etchings and ink sketches. Exhibits by other talented Western artists are sometimes on display. The gallery sells lithographs of Wieghorst's work as well as western gifts.

Next to the museum, Wieghorst's rustic home studio has been relocated and is undergoing renovation.

Location:	131 Rea Avenue, El Cajon
Hours:	Tues-Fri 10am-3pm
Admission:	Free
Phone:	619-590-3431
Website:	www.wieghorstmuseum.org

HOW TO GET THERE
Exit I-8 at Magnolia Avenue/Civic Center and proceed south. Turn left at Rea Avenue. The museum is on the right.

Sycuan Casino

Two thousand slot machines, popular table games, off-track betting and a 1,200-seat Bingo Palace and are just the beginning at Sycuan. Unique to this casino are the upscale, smoke-free Poker Room and a High Limit Room reserved for serious players. Table games include Blackjack, Pai Gow, Caribbean Stud, Let It Ride and Baccarat. Club Sycuan rewards program offers discounts and cash back rewards. There are four restaurants and a state-of-the-art 457-seat Showcase Theater provides weekly entertainment.

Singing Hills Country Club at Sycuan offers overnight accommodations, award-winning restaurants, two top-rated 18-hole golf courses, several tennis courts and a pool. Call 800-457-5568 or 619-442-3425 for prices and reservations.

Location:	5469 Casino Way, El Cajon
Hours:	Daily 24 Hours
Admission:	Free
Phone:	619-445-6002 or 1-800-2sycuan
Website:	www.sycuancasino.com

HOW TO GET THERE

Exit I-8 at El Cajon Boulevard and proceed east. Turn right at Washington Avenue. Continue on this road as it becomes Dehesa Road and proceed for several miles past Singing Hills Resort. Turn right to stay on Dehesa Road at the Harbison Canyon intersection and follow the signs to Sycuan.

FLINN SPRINGS

Summers Past Farm Herbal Garden

This beautifully landscaped property is memorable. The lush and aromatic grounds feature grape arbors and pathways leading to flower fields, herb gardens and a French-style lavender field.

The farm harvests their plants for several different handmade, pure herbal

offerings sold in a soap shop. Gifts and soap-making supplies are also sold. A garden coffee shop and several animals add to the experience.

Many of their products are offered at a satellite location at Old Town State Historic Park (see Downtown & Central chapter). On specific dates, different classes and "how-to" workshops are offered on-premise. Call or visit their website for recent offerings and special events.

Location:	15602 Old Highway 80, Flinn Springs
Hours:	Wed-Sat 9am-5pm. Open at 10am on Sundays
	Call for holiday hours
Admission:	Free
Phone:	619-390-1523 Farm
	619-390-3525 Soap Shoppe
Website:	www.summerspastfarms.com
	www.soapmaking.com

HOW TO GET THERE
Exit I-8 at Harbison Canyon/Dunbar Lane and proceed north under the   freeway. Turn left immediately at Old Highway 80. The barn is one mile up on the right.

JAMUL

Sky Dive San Diego

Sky Dive San Diego offers thrill-seekers two kinds of jumps, a tandem jump where you are connected to an instructor or an accelerated freefall where you're in control with the help of two instructors. Both require ground school prior to the dive and jump from 13,000 feet. The thrill lasts up to one minute and speeds get up to 120mph. About 22 people jump together. Those that are seeking certification can jump with this company. Divers must be 18 years old. Reservations are required. The company offers a $25 discount by booking online.

Location:	13531 Otay Lakes Road, Jamul
Hours:	Daily 10am-6pm. Open at 8am weekends
Admission:	$199-$299/Jump
Phone:	619-216-8416
Website:	www.skydivesandiego.com

HOW TO GET THERE

Exit I-805 at Telegraph Canyon Road/L Street. Bear right on Telegraph Canyon Road and continue as it becomes Otay Lakes Road. Sky Dive San Diego is on the right.

LA MESA

La Mesa is a residential community with a charming downtown area, close

proximity to Lake Murray, the historic La Mesa Depot Museum and the San Diego Culinary Institute.

At the heart of La Mesa Village in downtown is the Spring Street and La Mesa Boulevard intersection, home of the La Mesa Depot Museum. The Depot is the city's oldest building in its original form and the only authentic station from the San Diego Cuyamaca Railway. Free tours are offered on weekend afternoons. The quaint cobblestone, tree-lined sidewalks are filled with antique stores and cafes. A Classic Car Show takes place Thursdays 6pm-9pm and a Farmer's Market takes place Fridays 3pm-7pm. In October, La Mesa Village hosts an annual Oktoberfest. Call 619-440-6161 for details.

HOW TO GET THERE
Exit I-8 at Spring Street and proceed towards downtown La Mesa.

San Diego Culinary Institute

Although SDCI exists to train aspiring professional chefs, the public can tap into their expertise through the Hands-On Home Chef series where cooking enthusiast can spend a day or evening learning culinary techniques to take home with them. The school offers everything from knife skills to couples cooking classes to traditional classes tailored to individuals. There are also special classes for teens and kids. Classes usually run two to four hours and involve hands-on cooking with the chef. Call the school or visit the website for current course offerings. SDCI is the only professional culinary school in the area to offer courses to the public.

Location:	8024 La Mesa Boulevard, La Mesa
Hours:	Call for dates & times
Admission:	$45-$125/Person
Phone:	619-644-2100
Website:	www.sdci-inc.com

HOW TO GET THERE

Exit I-8 at Spring Street and proceed towards downtown. Turn right at La Mesa Boulevard. The school is in a shopping center on the right.

LAKESIDE

A resort-style casino, the great outdoors and the popular Annual Western Days Parade & Lakeside Rodeo in April bring people to this scenic community.

Lakeside is paradise for those that love to fish, hike, camp and enjoy a day at the park. With four lakes and eight parks, there are endless recreational opportunities. El Capitan Reservoir & Open Space Preserve offers hiking, rock climbing, fishing, boating and even water-skiing when the reservoir is full. Louis A. Stelzer Park has a Nature Studies Interpretive Center and rustic campsites, while Lake Jennings offers well-equipped campsites open year-round. Oak Oasis also provides camping opportunities. Fishermen appreciate San Vicente Reservoir, which holds the California State Blue Catfish record at 101 pounds. Birders will enjoy Silverwood Wildlife Sanctuary owned by the Audubon Society. For more information on these places call 619-561-1031 or visit www.lakesideca.com.

Lake Jennings

Located in the hills above Lakeside, this is a great place for an overnight camp, some hiking, boat fishing (especially for catfish) or a daytime escape. Roughly one hundred acres of open space surrounds the lake. Fishing is allowed sunrise to sunset Friday through Sunday and until midnight during the summer. There is a boat launch ramp ($5 use fee), row boat and motor boat rentals ($8-25) and a fish-cleaning facility. Kayaks, canoes, paddle boats and float tubes are not allowed on this lake. Boats can not exceed 10mph and state and daily fishing licenses are required. Several year-round campsites cater to RVs, campers and tents. There are restrooms and hot showers. Some sites have partial or full hook-ups.

San Diego County Parks allow reservations to be made two days to three months before the desired date. Check-in is at 2pm and check-out is at 1pm. Up to eight people may stay in one campsite and maximum stay is 14 nights.

Location:	10108 Bass Road, Lakeside
Hours:	Day-Use: Daily Sunrise-Sunset
	Reservation Line: Daily 8am-5pm
Admission:	Day-Use: $1/Person; Under 16-Free
	Overnight: $14-18/Night + $3 Reservation
Phone:	619-443-2510 Information
	877-565-3600 / 858-565-3600 Reservations
Website:	www.sdparks.org

HOW TO GET THERE

Exit I-8 at Lake Jennings Park Road and proceed north. Turn right at Harritt Road. Veer right where Harritt Road divides and proceed to the south entrance on Bass Drive.

Barona Valley Ranch Resort & Casino

This resort is reminiscent of the old west with earthy stone and wood buildings set against shade trees and an old water wheel . The gambling hall has over fifty table games with an emphasis on high-stakes Blackjack, but also features various Poker games, Pai Gow, Let It Ride, Caribbean Stud, Mini-Baccarat and Casino War. Bingo and off-track betting are also available. There are 2,000 slot machines, including progressives with large jackpots. Several quality restaurants are in the casino.

The resort was crafted by the same visionaries that created The Mirage, Paris Hotel & Casino and Caesars Palace in Las Vegas. Barona Creek Golf Club has been receiving high praise for its course ever since opening in 2001. Casual elegance defines the 397-room hotel which offers a fitness center, business center, pool, spa and 24-hour room service. There is even a wedding chapel.

Location:	1932 Wildcat Canyon Road, Lakeside
Hours:	Daily 24 Hours
Admission:	Free
Phone:	619-443-2300 or 888-722-7662 Information
	877-287-2624 Hotel Reservations
	619-387-7018 Golf Reservations
Website:	www.barona.com

HOW TO GET THERE

Exit Highway 67 at Willow Road and proceed east. Turn left at Wildcat Canyon Road and proceed six miles to the resort.

LEMON GROVE

For a little culture in Lemon Grove head to City Center Park where the Historical Society preserves and maintains two sister museums, the 1897 Victorian Parsonage Museum and the 1928 Tudor Revival H. Lee House. The Parsonage Museum resides in the former Atherton Chapel and features permanent displays related to agricultural, social, civic and architectural history of the area in addition to revolving exhibits on art, literature and science. The museum is located at 3185 Olive Street and open to visitors Fridays 1pm-3pm and Saturdays 10am-4pm, except in August and on holidays. Call 619-462-6494 or 619-460-4353 for more details.

Optimum Health Institute

This alternative lifestyle center, which has received national press along with its sister facility in Austin, Texas, teaches its students how to detoxify and then rejuvenate the mind and body through a three week program. The institute focuses on nutritional, physical, mental, emotional and spiritual balance and harmony for a longer life.

The concept is actually quite basic and adheres to what Hippocrates taught centuries ago: wholesome natural foods can restore health. Based on the fact that the human body is self-regenerating and self-cleansing, students cleanse their bodies with 100% living foods on a limited vegetarian diet and lots of pure wheatgrass juice. Through diet and colonics, the body goes through changes over the course of three weeks. Massage and chiropractic services are offered, but not part of the program. The program always starts on Sundays and the minimum stay is one week. OHI offers a Sunday evening open house with a tour of the grounds, a lecture and a dinner starting at 4pm for people interested in the program. Reservations are recommended and a dinner donation is appreciated.

Location:	6970 Central Avenue, Lemon Grove
Hours:	Daily 7am-8pm
Admission:	Prices vary. Starting at $400/Week
Phone:	619-464-3346
Website:	www.optimumhealth.org

HOW TO GET THERE

Take I-8 to I-805 and proceed to Highway 94. Exit Highway 94 at Massachusetts and proceed south to Central Avenue.

SPRING VALLEY

Spring Valley is primarily a residential community. The Spring Valley Historical Society is incredibly knowledgeable on the area and operates the Bancroft Ranch House as a free museum dedicated to preserving and relating the area history. The museum is generally open Friday through Sunday 1pm-4pm at 9050 Memory Lane. Call 619-469-1480 for details.

Bright Valley Farms Horse Stables

The horses that fill the stables at this working farm are bred, raised and trained by the owners. Accordingly, the guides are incredibly knowledgeable about their horses and have an animal suited to any level rider, including beginner. There are more than 800 acres of scenic riding trails with access to thousands more near Bright Valley Farms. Guides take groups on English and Western trail rides through canyons, streams, meadows and hills. Half-hour pony rides are offered to children at $15. Reservations are not required as weekend rides leave every hour.

Location:	12310 Campo Road/Highway 94, Spring Valley
Hours:	Tues-Sun 8:30am-4pm
	Open until 5pm during daylight savings
	Closed Thanksgiving & Dec 25
Admission:	$25/Hour
Phone:	619-670-1861
Website:	www.brightvalleyfarms.com

HOW TO GET THERE

From I-8, merge onto CA-125 South. Take the Spring Street/Highway 94 East exit and turn left at Spring Street. Merge onto CA-94 East.

San Diego County

BACKCOUNTRY

- Cuyamaca
- Julian
- Laguna Mountain
- Pala
- Palomar Mountain
- Pauma Valley
- Ramona
- Santa Ysabel
- Warner Springs

San Diego's Backcountry

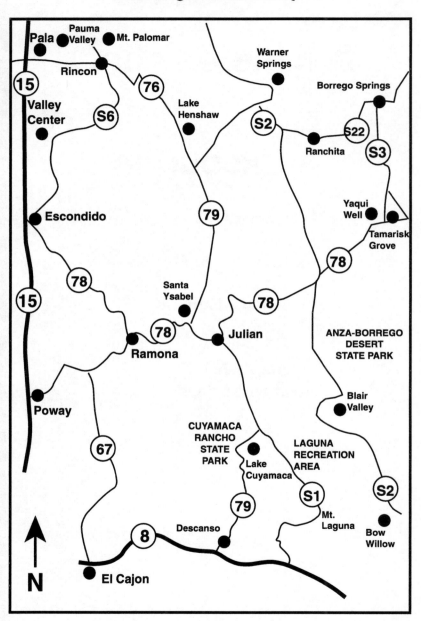

CUYAMACA

South of Julian, off the Sunshine Highway (SR 79), some wonderful camping areas, outdoor recreation opportunities and scenic driving adventures were highlights of the Cuyamaca Mountains. At an elevation upwards of 4,000 feet, Cuyamaca has four distinct seasons. This pristine area was a landmark location for hiking and camping before the 2003 fires swept through the area, devastating Cuyamaca Rancho State Park. While the forest will replenish itself, it will takes years and years to mtach its pre-fire beauty. The Cuyamaca region was graced by acre upon acre of tall pine trees and healthy ancient oaks. It was among the best places in the county to see spring wildflowers, autumn-colored leaves and winter snow. The loss is shocking and visitors should take this into considerations before making a trip in or around the Cuyamaca Mountains.

Nearly 750,000 acres burned in the Southern California fires that persisted for over a week in late October and early November of 2003. Over 4,800 homes and buildings were destroyed. There were 22 deaths and over 180 firefighter and civilian injuries. At the peak of the fires, more than 15, 625 firefighters from across the country worked to save lives, homes and land.

Cuyamaca Rancho State Park

About half of Cuyamaca Rancho State Park's 25,000-acre wildlife habitat is classified as a wilderness area, restricting vehicles from these areas and adding to the pristine outdoor experience. Sadly, the state park was one of the county's biggest losses during the 2003 fires. Over a hundred miles of hiking and horseback trails and fifty miles of mountain biking trails swept by streams and high peaks across varied terrain including alpine meadows, dense forests and narrow valleys that are now burned out. Call before visiting to get current information on the park's progress and for details on what areas of the park are open or still closed for reconstruction.

The Visitor Center and Museum, which provided trail maps and details on recreational opportunities in the park, burned down as did the campgrounds. Hiking through the park will not be as rewarding for several years to come due to the devastation. The two-mile, 900-foot climb along Stonewall Peak Trail rewards with incredible views. Cuyamaca Peak at 6,512 feet, reveals offshore islands and parts of Mexico on a clear day. Easier nature trails abound.

Before the fires, Paso Picacho and Green Valley campgrounds provided picnic tables, fire rings, potable water and nearby restrooms with coin-operated hot showers. Camping fees covered one vehicle and up to eight people. Additional vehicles were $4 per night. There were also a handful of primitive cabins, which typically slept four people, although eight people were allowed. There was also room for a tent on these sites. There were three horse camps in the park, Stonewall Mine, Los Caballos and Los Vaqueros, which allowed for two horses per paid entrance. Check-in was at 2pm. Check out was at noon. At press time, plans for rebuilding were not yet decided. Call for current camping details and recommendations.

Location:	Park Headquarters:
	12551 Highway 79, Cuyamaca
Hours:	Daily Sunrise-Sunset
Admission:	Day-Use: $5/Vehicle
	Camping: $12-15/Night
	Cabins: $27-31/Night
	Horse Camps: $19/Night
Phone:	760-765-0755 Park Headquarters
	800-444-7275 Reservations
Website:	www.cuyamaca.statepark.org

HOW TO GET THERE

From I-8, exit at Highway 79 and proceed north. From Highway 78, proceed east past Julian and turn south at Highway 79. The park is on the east side of Highway 79 between Descanso and Julian.

Backcountry

6 - 4

Lake Cuyamaca

Surrounded by beautiful oak trees and pine forests, this modest size alpine lake is a great place for some easy trail walks along the lake's shore or a decent day of fishing. Trout is stocked all year long and fly fishing is quite common at this lake. State and day fishing permits are required and available at the lake. Catches usually include catfish, bass, crappie, and bluegill. Day permits run $5 per adult and $2.50 per child. An on-site store doubles as a tackle shop with everything one needs to fish. Boat rentals cost $12-28 per day. All boats must stay at or under 10mph. During the summer, paddleboats and canoes are rented at $7 per hour for those who are not interested in fishing, but would like to be out on the water. Fishing classes and guided nature walks are sometimes offered for free.

There is a full-service restaurant with outside dining overlooking the lake. Two cabins, which can accommodate up to eight people each, are rented at $135-$165 per night for four persons. There is a $10 charge for each additional person. Cabins have a full kitchen, fireplaces and a covered outside patio with a gas grill and dining area. The kitchen does not have utensils. RV sites with hook-ups and tent camping sites are available on a first-come, first-serve basis at $14-$20 per night. Water and flush toilets are nearby.

The area surrounding Lake Cuyamaca was devastated by the 2003 fires. Be aware that most of the beautiful pines are charred and will take years, if not decades to recover.

Location:	15027 Highway 79, Cuyamaca
Hours:	Daily 6am-Sunset
Admission:	Day-Use: $6/Vehicle
Phone:	760-765-0515 Cuyamaca Lake
	760-765-0700 Store & Retaurant
Website:	www.lakecuyamaca.org

HOW TO GET THERE
From I-8, exit at Highway 79 and proceed north. From Highway 78, proceed east past Julian and turn south at Highway 79. The lake is on the east side of Highway 79, near the State Park.

JULIAN

Simply put, Julian is a historic gold-mining town known for its apple pie. But few things are that simple and Julian is no exception with all there is to do in this backcountry junction. The four seasons are exaggerated in this quaint town, with spring wildflowers, autumn breezes, changing leaves and

even snow. Families, nature lovers and romantics embrace everything Julian has to offer, from historic gold mines and primitive camping to modern wineries and charming bed and breakfasts.

Picture perfect Main Street with its wooden sidewalks is even more charming when a visitor decides to indulge in a horse-drawn carriage ride from Country Carriages located at the corner of Washington and Main Street. Call the outfitter at 760-765-1471 for further details or to make reservations. Half hour or hour rides are offered at $25-$35 per couple or small family. The century-old Town Hall, the 1886 drug store with its 75-year-old soda fountain and numerous antique and collectible-filled shop windows make for endless eye candy. Historic walking tours of the town are commonly offered.

If one is inspired by the scenic countryside to go horseback riding, Julian Stables can accommodate trail rides with mountain and ocean views by appointment. For inquiries, call 760-765-1598 or visit www.julianactive.com.

The fall apple harvest beginning in September is arguably the best seasonal attraction, but Julian celebrates its heritage year-round. The Annual Julian Mayfest & Wildflower Show is in May and the Annual Mountain Blues Festival is in June. Call 760-765-0887 or visit www.julianbluesfestival.com for details. The Annual Julian Grape Stomp Festa at the Menghini Winery is each September and the Annual Fall Julian Apple Festival is each October. Call 760-765-1857 for further festival information.

There are endless bed and breakfasts, hotels, motels, lodges and cabins in the Julian area. Julian Hotel is listed on the National Register of Historic Places in Washington D.C. and the State of California's Points of Historic Interest. Call Julian Hotel at 760-765-0201.

It is important to know that several areas near downtown Julian were burned during the 2003 fires. Firefighters were successful in saving historic downtown, but the surrounding backcountry was greatly affected by the tragedy. Nevertheless, a visit to downtown is as charming as ever.

HOW TO GET THERE

Exit I-5 or I-15 at Highway 78 and proceed east through the towns of Escondido and Ramona to Julian. Exit I-8 at Highway 67 and proceed north to the town of Ramona. Continue east along Highway 78 to Julian.

Eagle Mining Company

Eagle and High Peak mines are two of the original gold mines in the area. At the north end of C Street, visitors may enter part of the intricate tunnel paths in a hard rock mine via a one-hour guided tour. The entertaining tour in-cludes narration about the area's gold mining history. Local lore and trivia are tour highlights.

Location:	At the end of C Street, Julian
Hours:	Daily 10am-3pm
Admission:	General-$8; Youth(5-15)-$4; Under 5-$1
Phone:	760-765-0036

HOW TO GET THERE

Take Highway 78 eastbound to Julian. Turn right at Main Street. Turn left at C Street and proceed to the street's end.

Julian Pioneer Museum

A collection of turn-of-the-century items including clothing, photos, furnishings, household items and mining equipment have helped coin this museum "Julian's Little Attic." An impressive assortment of lace, Victorian-era pianos, an original Julian City buggy and an origianl sleigh are highlights.

Location:	2811 Washington Street, Julian
Hours:	Tues-Sun 10am-4pm
	December-March: Sat & Sun only
Admission:	General-$2; Youth(8-18)-$1; Under 8-Free
Phone:	760-765-0227

HOW TO GET THERE

Take Highway 78 eastbound to Julian. As you approach town, Highway 78 doubles as Washington Street. The museum is on the left before reaching Main Street.

Julian Tea & Cottage Arts

High tea in the high country is possible at this 100-year-old cottage that offers a full-service afternoon tea with finger sandwiches, scones and dessert. A simple tea service with your choice of scones or dessert is also available. A lunch of soups, salads and sandwiches is another option. The cottage gift store features china, tea accoutrements, tea and items from local artisans. Reservations are recommended.

Location:	2124 Third Street, Julian
Hours:	Tea Daily 12pm, 1:30pm & 3pm
Admission:	$12.50/Person
Phone:	760-765-0832
Website:	www.juliantea.com

HOW TO GET THERE
Take Highway 78 eastbound to Julian. Highway 78 doubles as Washington Street. Proceed straight along Washington Street. Turn right at Third Avenue. The cottage is on the left.

Pine Hills Lodge Dinner Theater

On Friday and Saturday nights, the Pine Hills Players perform a comedy, drama or musical in this historic theater. What is now the theater was

originally built as professional boxer Jack Dempsey's training gym for his 1926 fight against Gene Tunney, who won the fight. Each year, five productions are staged for the dinner theater which serves barbecued baby-back ribs and baked chicken with the trimmings. Reservations are recommended.

The lodge also has a pub open Friday through Sunday, which often comes alive with open mic nights, poetry slamms and karaoke. Lodge rooms, cabins and suites are available for overnight stays starting at $72 per night. There are eight wooded acres surrounding the lodge, which opened in 1912.

Location:	2960 La Posada Way, Pine Hills
Hours:	Fri-Sat Dinner 6:30pm, Show 8:00pm
Admission:	Dinner & Show-$30/Person
	Friday Show Only-$15/Person
Phone:	760-765-1100
Website:	www.pinehillslodge.com

HOW TO GET THERE

Take Highway 78 eastbound towards Julian. Before reaching the town of Julian, turn right at Pine Hills Road. Drive through the Pine Hills area and turn right at Blue Jay. Turn left at La Posada Way and proceed to the lodge.

William Heise County Park

Giant oak trees and auburn manzanita trees make this park one of the most scenic camping places in the county. There are over 900 acres of hiking and equestrian trails. Campers have their choice of tent, cabin or RV sites. All sites have fire rings and tables. The cabins have six rustic bunks, but campers need to supply their own linens. Running water, toilets and showers are available.

San Diego County Parks allow reservations to be made two days to three months before the desired date. Check-in is at 2pm and check-out is at 1pm. Up to eight people may stay in one campsite and maximum stay is 14 nights.

Location:	4945 Heise Park Road, Julian
Hours:	Daily Sunrise-Sunset
Admission:	Day-Use: $2/Vehicle
	Camping: $12-16/Night; Cabins-$35/Night
Phone:	760-765-0650 or 858-694-3049 Information
	858-565-3600 Reservations
Website:	www.sdparks.org

HOW TO GET THERE
Take Highway 78 towards Julian. Before reaching the town of Julian, turn right at Pine Hills Road and continue straight. Turn left at Frisius Drive and proceed to the park.

Wineries

Four welcoming tasting rooms in and around downtown Julian make this a perfect afternoon activity. All four tasting rooms can be visited in one afternoon. En route to Julian, heading east along Highway 78, start with Orfila Winery. Continue east to the town of Julian. At Main Street, drop into Witch Creek Winery. Proceed north along Main Street as it becomes Farmers Road and end your afternoon adventure at J. Jenkins Winery and Menghini Winery.

Orfila Winery

Orfila's vineyard is in Escondido's San Pasqual Valley. This backcountry location is a satellite location to the main winery at the vineyard. One tasting is free. Five more tastings may be purchased in a keepsake glass for $3.

Location:	4470 Highway 78, Julian
Hours:	Daily 10am-6pm
Admission:	Free. Tastings: $3/Person
Phone:	760-765-0102 Julian Tastings
	760-738-6500 Escondido Winery
Website:	www.orfila.com

HOW TO GET THERE

Take Highway 78 eastbound towards Julian. The tasting room is on the north side of Highway 78 en route to Julian.

Witchcreek Winery

This tasting room is a satellite location to the main Witch Creek Winery in Carlsbad. It is located upstairs in downtown Julian's Stonewall Building. Visitors can sample a variety of wines for $3 and keep the souvenir glass.

Location:	2000 Main Street, Julian
Hours:	Daily 11am-5pm
Admission:	Free. Tastings: $3/Person
Phone:	760-765-2023 Julian Tastings
	760-720-7499 Carlsbad Winery
Website:	www.witchcreekwinery.com

HOW TO GET THERE

Take Highway 78 eastbound to Julian. Turn left at Main Street.

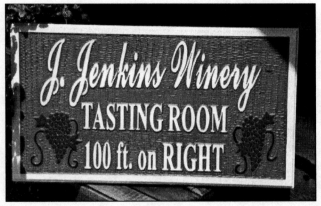

J. Jenkins Winery

In a beautiful backcountry location, this winery has a roadside tasting room next to several rows of grape vines that are harvested for their label. They specializes in Pinot Noir, Pinot Grigio and apple wines.

Location:	1255 Julian Orchards Drive, Julian
Hours:	Sat-Sun 11am-5pm
Admission:	Free
Phone:	760-765-3267

HOW TO GET THERE

Take Highway 78 eastbound to Julian. Turn left at Main Street. Follow Main Street north as it becomes Farmers Road and proceed three miles. Veer right at Julian Orchards Drive. The winery is on the right.

Menghini Winery

Menghini has ten acres of grape vineyards and apple orchards that invite visitors to picnic. The tasting room welcomes visitors to sample the wines free of charge.

Location:	1150 Julian Orchards Drive, Julian
Hours:	Daily 10am-5pm
	Open until 4pm November-May
Admission:	Free
Phone:	760-765-2072

HOW TO GET THERE

Take Highway 78 eastbound to Julian. Turn left at Main Street. Follow Main Street north as it becomes Farmers Road and proceed 3 miles. Veer right at Julian Orchards Drive. Follow signs.

LAGUNA MOUNTAIN

On a clear day, the Laguna Mountains will reveal views of the Anza Borrego Desert, the Salton Sea, San Diego, the Pacific Ocean and Mexico. Winter months in the Lagunas are popular for bestowing San Diegans with some treasured snow. During cold spells, snow sledding and cross-country skiing are impromptu sports at the Burnt Rancheria Campground and Laguna Campground in the Laguna Mountain Recreation Area. In warmer months hang gliding from Kwaaymii Point is a favorite pastime. Remote camping is only allowed outside the Laguna Mountain Recreation Area. A National Adventure Pass is available at the Visitor's Center and is necessary if you were to park anywhere within the Unites States Forest Services boundaries.

Laguna Mountain Recreation Area

In 1926, 8,000 acres of Cleveland National Forest were designated as Laguna Mountain Recreation Area. The Laguna Mountain Volunteer Association is largely the reason this area remains so pristine and popular with campers, hikers, equestrians, mountain bikers and nature lovers. At 6,000 feet, the four seasons are in full force year-round. The area is marked with pine trees, oak trees, native brush, fields, meadows and seasonal streams. Stargazing in the Lagunas is rewarding. The Mount Laguna Observatory, which is operated by San Diego State University, has four telescopes and a Visitors Center.

There are endless hiking options for all skill levels. Area trail maps can be purchased at the Laguna Mountain Lodge General Store along Highway S1.

Hikers and nature walkers treasure Desert View Nature Trail for the spectacular panoramic views that are revealed while summiting. The summit of Wooded Hills Nature Trail also provides nice vistas. Desert View has a picnic area with tables, stoves, water and flush toilets. Pioneer Mail is another picnic area with the same amenities, except water. The historic Pacific Crest Trail, Noble Canyon Trail and Indian Creek Trail are roughly 10 miles each one-way for those seeking an all day adventure.

There are four campgrounds to choose between. Laguna and Burnt Rancheria are the largest. Boulder Oaks, which is tailored to families and equestrians, and Cibbets Flat are more remote. All have water, pit toilets, tables, stoves or fire rings and the Laguna campground has pay showers. Reservations are recommended. There is a fourteen day maximum stay within any thirty day period. Each site is allowed up to eight people and two cars. Leashed dogs are allowed. Check-out is at 2pm. Call for campsite pricing.

Location: General Store & Visitor's Center:
10678 Highway S1, Mount Laguna
Hours: Daily Sunrise-Sunset
Admission: Day-Use: $5/Vehicle(Adventure Pass)
Phone: 619-445-6235 Descanso Ranger District
619-473-8547 Laguna Visitor Info Center
877-444-6777 Camping Reservations
Website: www.lmva.org

HOW TO GET THERE

Exit I-8 at Sunrise Highway (S1) and proceed north. The top of the mountain is about 9 miles from I-8.

Exit Highway 78 just outside of Julian at Highway 79. Proceed south along Highway 79 for about 6 miles. Turn onto Sunrise Hwy (S1). Follow Sunrise Highway for about 15 miles to reach the store, lodge and Visitor Information Center.

Cuyamaca, Julian & Laguna Mountain

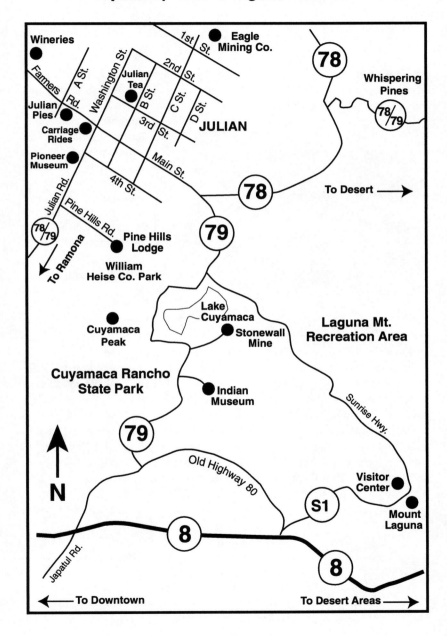

PALA

Gems of Pala

An unusual adventure awaits at Gems of Pala and the world-famous Stewart Mine that feeds it. The Stewart Mine produces a gem quality natural pink tourmaline that is five times as rare as gem diamond and at least ten times as

valuable as pure gold. Tourmaline has the most color variety of any gem and is highly reflective when cut, making for beautiful gemstones. Bi-color gems are the most valuable. The mine also produces less valuable kunzite, morganite and lepidolite.

Federal restrictions prohibit visitors from entering the mine's underground tunnels, but the Gems of Pala Mineral Shop figured an innovative way for the public to take their chance at mining for precious stones. In a "grab bag" fashion, visitors can purchase a bucket of underground mine gravels. Mine run from the "Bridal Chamber" costs $50. It costs $25 from what is called the "pocket zone" and $10 from general spillage. Once visitors purchase their bucket, they grab a screen and head to a table where a 5-minute video shows them how to sift through the gravel to find precious stones. The favored tourmaline colors are hot pink, cranberry and raspberry. To find a pink tourmaline, which has been coveted by kings, pharaohs and world rulers for centuries, is incredibly lucky. Mineral specimens, gemstones, jewelry, carvings, and gifts are sold at a country store.

Location:	Magee Road, Pala
Hours:	Thurs-Sun 10am-4pm March-December
	Call for winter hours
Admission:	$10, $25 & $50/Bucket. Reserve ahead
Phone:	760-742-1356
Website:	www.mmmgems.com

HOW TO GET THERE
Exit I-5 or I-15 at Highway 76 and proceed east 7 miles past I-15. Turn left at Magee Road just past the Calmat Conrock Division Plant.

Pala Casino

Frank Lloyd Wright-inspired architecture set against a mountain backdrop is a refreshing contrast to the lights and sounds of the casino's 2,000 slot machines and fifty Vegas-style table games. There are six restaurants, one with patio seating, and two distinctly different lounges with live entertainment. The Palomar Lounge has floor-to-ceiling windows with views of Palomar Mountain while the Promenade Lounge is a dark cozy candlelit venue featuring jazz and acoustic entertainment. A 2000-seat Events Center hosts larger events. For those wanting to stay the night, a 507-room luxury hotel is connected to the casino complete with a full-service day spa.

Location:	11154 Highway 76, Pala
Hours:	Daily 24 Hours
Admission:	Free
Phone:	877-946-7252
Website:	www.palacasino.com

HOW TO GET THERE
Exit I-5 or I-15 at Highway 76 and proceed east 5 miles past I-15.

Mission San Antonio De Pala

The most unique thing about this 1816 mission is that it is the last remaining California Mission to be operating as it

was when first established. It is an active church to this day. Just as Santa Ysabel Mission was an annex to San Diego de Alcala, Pala Mission was established as an annex to nearby Mission San Luis Rey.

The bell tower, which is modeled after one similar in Ciudad Juarez, Mexico, is unusual in that it is detached from the building, which is atypical of missions. If one looks carefully they will see the cactus plant that Padre Peyri planted when the mission was completed as a symbol of Christ conquering the desert in California and in the human soul.

Wooden crosses still mark a few of hundreds of Indian graves in "Old Luiseno Cemetery." Many of the fallen and misplaced crosses have been placed in a commemorative pile.

Location:	Pala Mission Road, Pala
Hours:	Daily 10am-4pm
	Services: Sat 5pm, Sun 8:30am & 12pm
	Spanish Service: 10:30am
Admission:	Museum: General-$2
Phone:	760-742-3317

HOW TO GET THERE

Exit I-5 or I-15 at Highway 76 and proceed east to the Pala Indian Reservation. Turn left at Pala Mission Road and proceed to the mission.

PALOMAR MOUNTAIN

This alpine community high in the Cleveland National Forest offers a wide variety of outdoor activities and one very famous attraction, the 200-inch Hale Telescope. While most people head to Julian for the fall apple harvest, Palomar Mountain is a lesser known area for apple picking and spectacular color change. It also receives quite a bit of snow in winter months.

The summit lies at the intersection of Highway S6 and Highway S7. Here visitors will find the helpful and friendly Palomar General Store. It has a wealth of information on the area and a fun souvenir shop with crystals, gems, amber, fossils and Indian jewelry. The store can be reached at 760-742-3496. Next door, Mother's Kitchen offers a wide selection of fresh vegetarian meals. A quaint U.S. Post Office can provide the stamp for a postcard from this beautiful hiking and camping destination.

By following Highway S7, visitors can reach Palomar Mountain State Park in one direction and Palomar Mountain Lodge in the other direction. The lodge is a nice bed and breakfast alternative to camping.

The alternate Highway S6, leads to the Palomar Observatory, Observatory Campground and Fry Creek Campground, both operated by the United States Forest Service.

HOW TO GET THERE

Exit I-5 or I-15 at Highway 76 and proceed east past Pala and Pauma Valley to Highway S6. Veer left up the mountain along Highway S6.

Palomar Observatory

Palomar Mountain is a star gazers dream. It's no wonder there are five domes at the Palomar Observatory. The largest of these domes is open to the public and holds the Hale Telescope, which visitors may view from a glass-enclosed observation deck. The ground floor of the observatory shows pictures and findings from this large instrument. The California Institute of Technology runs the observatory as a research lab. A gift shop sells relevant gifts and books.

Location:	End of Highway S6, Palomar Mountain
Hours:	Daily 9am-4pm. Closed Dec 24 & 25
Admission:	Free
Phone:	760-742-2119
Website:	www.astro.caltech.edu/observatories/palomar/

HOW TO GET THERE

Exit I-5 or I-15 at Highway 76 and proceed east past Pala and Pauma Valley to Highway S6. Veer left up the mountain along Highway S6. Once at the summit, veer left towards the General Store. Before reaching the General Store, turn right to continue along Highway S6. Proceed along Highway S6 about 5 miles to the road end at the parking lot. A walking path leads to the observatory.

Palomar Mountain
Camping, Riding & Hiking Trails

There are plenty of designated camping areas and trails on the mountain managed by the USFS Palomar Ranger District. The Palomar Ranger District is located on Highway S6 just before Palomar Observatory on the left side of the highway. During summer months, rangers hold programs such as "Explore the Stars" for campers.

When hiking, stay on designated trails. Cutting through the switchbacks causes erosion and soil damage. Note that a permit, which can be obtained from any Forest Service Office or Station, is required to enter Aqua Tibia Wilderness and horses are not permitted in this area overnight. Also obtain a permit before doing any remote camping, which is allowed. To park along any of the roads within the USFS boundaries, a National Adventure Pass must be visible. The passes are available for purchase at the General Store.

Note that there are several private campgrounds in the area as well.

Location:	Highway S7, Palomar Mountian
Hours:	Mon-Fri 8am-4:30pm
Admission:	Day-Use: $5/Vehicle (Adventure Pass)
Phone:	760-788-0250 Palomar Ranger District
	877-444-6777 Camping Reservations
Website:	www.fs.fed.us/r5/cleveland

Barker Valley Trails
(Location: Barker Valley, Southeast of Palomar Observatory)

Off Barker Valley Spur Road, Deer Flats provides access to two hiking and equestrian trails that descend into Barker Valley from 5,700 feet in elevation to 4,000 feet. The two trails, both of which measure two and a half miles, intersect half way into the valley. One trail begins at Deer Flats Trailhead and quickly descends into the valley. The other trail is a more gentle descent and can be caught at Palomar Divide Truck Trail east of the Deer Flats Trailhead. Portions of the trails can be challenging. Mixed chaparral blankets the mountainside that leads to an oak woodland environment in the valley. Palomar Observatory and Mendenhall Valley are visible from the trails. Seasonally, streams flow into the valley, eventually leading to the San Luis Rey River and Lake Henshaw. When the streams are heavy, waterfalls can occur in the canyons below.

Pacific Crest Trail & Remote Camping
(Location: Between Scissors Crossing & Riverside County Line)

Parts of the famous Pacific Crest Trail (PCT) can be accessed in a few places on Palomar Mountain. In its entirety, over 53 miles of the PCT can be continuously covered on foot or horseback through the Palomar Mountain region, which is still just a smidge of this path that leads from Mexico to Canada. Indian Flats Trail, Highway 79, Highway S2 and Highway S22 all provide access to the PCT. Excellent views of the Warner Springs area, Hot Springs Mountain, Anza Borrego Desert, Coyote Canyon and the Santa Rosa and San Bernardino mountain ranges can all be enjoyed at various points along the trail. Chaparral is the prevailing vegetation, but in higher elevations timber surrounds travelers along this peaceful trail of solitude. The elevation varies between 2,250 feet and 5,600 feet across the Palomar portion of the trail. Water is scarce and warmer months can be very hot on this exposed trail.

Remote camping is allowed by obtaining a permit from any Forest Service office or station. There are no restroom facilities or treated water in these areas. Natural water from the mountain should be boiled or treated before consumption. No fires or barbecues are allowed in remote camping environments due to the high fire dangers. Liquid fuel stoves may be used within a 10-foot cleared area.

Observatory Campground &
Observatory National Recreation Trail
(Location: Highway S6)

This 2 mile hiking-only trail takes trekkers from 4,800 feet at the campground to 5,550 feet at the Palomar Observatory. Passing through mixed conifer and some scattered chaparral along this National Scenic Trail, there are great views of the Mendenhall and French Valleys. Trail maps are often available at the campground trailhead.

Fry Creek Campground &
Fry Creek Trail
(Location: Highway S6)

This easy loop hiking trail is only a mile and a half with a gain of 200 feet. Wildlife sightings are common along this heavily forested area of mixed conifer and chaparral. There is also a Penny Pines Plantation along the trail.

Palomar Mountain State Park

Nearly 2,000 acres are designated as Palomar Mountain State Park. Within this park are picnic areas for day use, family campsites, group campsites,  hiking and biking trails and Doane Pond for year-round trout fishing. Spectacular views of the Pacific Ocean and a fragrant pine forest perched above the dry lowlands make this a favored destination on the mountain.

Year-round camping is offered at the family camgrounds. Each site can accommodate up to eight people. Check-in is at 2pm and check-out is at noon. Reservations are recommended and required on weekends during the summer. Mountain bikes nor dogs are allowed on the twelve miles of scenic trails that pass by streams, meadows, vistas and forests. A valid state fishing license is required at Doane Pond for those over 15-years-old.

Location:	19952 State Park Road, Palomar Mountain
Hours:	Day-Use: 8am-Sunset
Admission:	Day-Use: $4/Vehicle; Seniors-$3/Vehicle
	Family Campsites-$12-$15/Night
	Group Campsites-$20-$65/Night
Phone:	760-742-3462 Information
	800-444-7275 Reservations
Website:	www.palomar.statepark.org

HOW TO GET THERE

Exit I-5 or I-15 at Highway 76 and proceed east through Pala and Pauma Valley. Proceed up the mountain along Highway S6 and turn left at the summit to connect to Highway S7 at the junction near the store. Proceed west along Highway S7 which doubles at State Park Road.

PAUMA VALLEY

Pauma Valley has been inhabited by the La Jolla Band of Luiseno Indians for many generations. The beautiful San Luis Rey River and ancient oak trees line this scenic valley.

La Jolla Indian Reservation Campground

This year-round camping spot offers hundreds of primitive tent sites, many with fire rings and tables. These sites are given out on a first-come, first-serve basis and allow for four persons per site. Showers and restrooms are nearby most camping sites. RV sites should be reserved and include water and electric hook-ups. Recreation includes hiking and biking through the hills. When Lake Henshaw opens the dam, there is inner tubing and fishing in the San Luis Rey River. Inner tubes can be rented for $6. Pets  are not allowed at this campground.

Location:	Highway 76, Pauma Valley
Hours:	Daily 6am-6pm
Admission:	Tents-$18/Night; RV-$25/Night
Phone:	760-742-1297
Website:	www.lajollaindians.com

HOW TO GET THERE

Exit I-5 or I-15 at Highway 76 and proceed east. The campground is on the south side of Highway 76.

Sengme Oaks Water Park

This 10-acre water park is modest compared to most, but still offers a lot of fun at a great price. Two giant *Serpentine Slides* twist and turn into a large main pool. Two side-by-side *Speed Slides* make for a great racing opportunity. A *Rampage Slide* is used with a sled board. There is a large Kiddie Pool with three small slides for young children.

River Tubing down the real San Luis Rey River is a more authentic water adventure and can be a thrill when the rapids flow. Horseshoe pits, volleyball, barbecue grills, a snack bar and gift shop are other highlights.

Location:	Sengme Oaks Road at Highway 76, Pauma Valley
Hours:	Open Memorial Day-Labor Day Fri-Sun 11am-7pm. Open until 6pm Sundays
Admission:	$12/Person Over 47"; $8/Person Under 48"
Phone:	760-742-1921
Website:	www.lajollaindians.com

HOW TO GET THERE
Exit I-5 or I-15 at Highway 76 and proceed east. Continue 28 miles past I-15. Turn right at Sengme Oaks Road.

Casino Pauma

Casino Pauma has over 750 slot machines that accept everything from pennies to five dollar bills. There are also video poker and video keno machines. Balckjack tables can be played with hands ranging from $2 to $500. Other table games include 3-Card and Pai Gow Poker.

This casino is one of the few to offer card versions of Craps and Roulette. These games are typically played Wednesday night through Sunday. They perfectly simulate the statistical outcome of thrown dice. Pauma Bay Café is open twenty-four hours and Red Parrot Lounge is a full service bar.

Location:	777 Pauma Reservation Road, Pauma Valley
Hours:	Daily 24 Hours
Admission:	Free
Phone:	760-742-2177
Website:	www.casinopauma.com

HOW TO GET THERE

Exit I-5 or I-15 at Highway 76 and proceed east. Turn left at Pauma Reservation Road and proceed to the casino.

Pala, Palomar Mountain & Pauma Valley

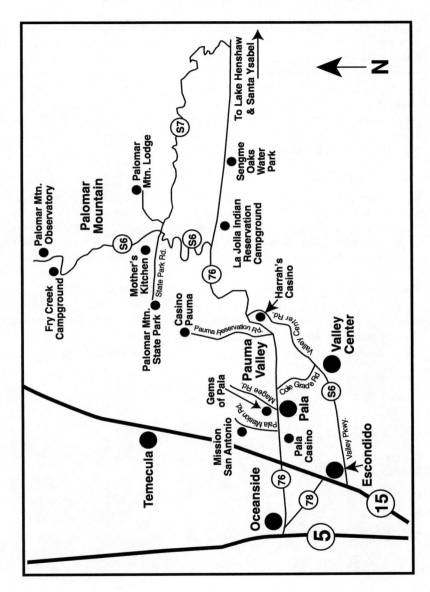

RAMONA

Between San Diego's inland cities and the east county desert and mountains is the charming country town of Ramona. The surrounding backcountry provide endless outdoor recreation and Main Street preserves small town charm with home-style restaurants and antique shopping. Once called the "Turkey Capital of the World," the town was one of the nation's largest producers of turkeys. It is fairly common to see a stray wild turkey or two running through the fields. Ramona is also well known for Hope Street's Mailboxes that line a dirt road on the outskirts of town. Passersby often stop for this matchless photo opportunity.

Two golf courses and one winery add to the ever-growing list of things to do in this backcountry community. Lake Sutherland Reservoir provides water recreation for boaters, fishermen and picnickers. Hikers gravitate towards Mount Woodson and Iron Mountain for their taxing switchbacks and impressive views. Mt. Gower Open Space Preserve is less demanding and offers eight miles of trails among hundreds of acres of untouched land.

The town comes alive each May for an annual Rodeo and early June for an annual Air Fair. For information on the Ramona Rodeo at Fred Grand Arena, call 760-789-1484 or visit www.ramonachamber.com. For information on the Ramona Air Fair at Ramona Airport, call 760-788-6174 or visit www.ramonaairfair.org. Smaller events are held throughout the year.

Dos Picos County Park

This 79-acre park is graced with beautiful old oak trees and sits among mountians as its name, which mean "two peaks", indicates. A beautiful duck-filled pond and large boulders add to the park scenery.

There are horseshoe pits, play areas, a nature trail, a soccer field and several picnic areas for day use. The park caters to both tent and RV campers. There are partial hookups and hot showers available.

San Diego County Parks allow reservations to be made two days to three months before the desired date. Check-in is at 2pm and check-out is at 1pm. Up to eight people may stay in one campsite and maximum stay is fourteen nights.

Location:	17953 Dos Picos Park Road, Ramona
Hours:	Daily 9:30am-Sunset
Admission:	Day-Use: $2/Vehicle; Camping: $12-16/Night
Phone:	760-789-2220
	877-565-3600 Reservations
Website:	www.sdparks.org

HOW TO GET THERE

Exit Highway 78 or Highway 67 at Ramona and proceed east. Turn right at Mussey Grade Road. Veer right at Dos Picos Park Road.

Guy B. Woodward Museum

Ramona's history unfolds here with the preservation of historic buildings, shops, wagons and antique exhibits.

Location:	645 Main Street, Ramona
Hours:	Fri-Sun 1pm-4pm. Closed holidays
Admission:	General-$3; Youth Under 12-$0.50
Phone:	760-789-7644

HOW TO GET THERE

Take Highway 78 or Highway 67 to Ramona and continue along Main Street.

Lake Sutherland

This lake has over five miles of shoreline, measures 145 feet deep and spans over 555 surface acres when full. Fishing is allowed from boats, float tubes and the shore. A state fishing license is required. Catches include bass, catfish, crappie and other species. A cash-only onsite concession sells bait and tackle, motor rentals, state fishing licenses and food. Rowboats are available for rent at $8-$12 per day. Motorboats are also available for rent at various prices. Private boats must pay a $5 launch fee. Windsurfing, waterskiing, tubing and kneeboarding are allowed, but there is a water use fee.

Barbecues and picnic tables make this a great place for picnicking. Visitors may also bring their own barbecues for use in designated areas. Leashed dogs are allowed, but must stay fifty feet from the water at all times.

Location:	22850 Sutherland Dam Road, Ramona
Hours:	Fri-Sun Sunrise-Sunset
	Open mid-March-October
Admission:	Free
	Fishing & Water Use:
	General-$5; Youth(8-15)-$2.50
Phone:	619-465-3474 or 619-698-3474
Website:	www.sandiego.gov/water/recreation

HOW TO GET THERE

Exit Highway 78 at Sutherland Dam Road and proceed north to the reservoir.

Schwaesdall Winery

This local winery got its start from some vines that were planted in the 1950s. The vintner has since planted nearly five acres of various red and white grape varieties used for his wine, which is served and sold at local establishments in addition to the winery. The winery has a wide range of varietals, including Zinfandel, Petite Sirah, Port, Merlot, Chardonnay and Cabernet Sauvignon. Tastings are $4 per person and includes a souvenir glass. The tasting includes six to eight wine samplings.

The charming and down-to-earth winery also has trademark boulders on its property, most notably the 80-ton rock that looks like a huge cat and inspired the winery's label "Gato Grande".

Location:	17677 Rancho de Oro Drive at Highway 67, Ramona
Hours:	Sat-Sun 10am-6pm
Admission:	Free. Tastings: $4/Person
Phone:	760-789-7547
	760-789-7542 Tasting Room
Website:	www.schwaesdallwinery.com

HOW TO GET THERE

Exit Highway 78 or Highway 67 at Ramona and proceed east. Turn right at Rancho de Oro Drive.

SANTA YSABEL

Where Highway 78 and Highway 79 intersect, the crossroad town of Santa Ysabel welcomes road weary travelers. At one time, this area was called "Elcuanan" by the Digueno, Cupeno and Cahuilla tribes who supported one of the largest Indian villages in Southern California at this crossroads.

Dudley's Bakery with mouth watering cinnamon rolls and seventeen varieties of fresh baked breads is a must stop for anyone passing by. Inside the bakery, a boutique called Crossroads Treasures sells Indian jewelry, rocks, minerals, pottery and gifts. The bakery is open Wednesday through Sunday 8am-5pm. Call 760-765-0488 or visit www.dudleysbakery.com for further details. Behind the bakery, Don's Market is an impressive grocery and general store. The adjacent restaurant carries a good menu of homestyle meals and boxed lunches for those who are spontaneously inspired by the scenery to picnic in the backcountry. Nearby attractions include Lake Henshaw and Santa Ysabel Mission.

Lake Henshaw

Between Santa Ysabel and Palomar Mountain, this lake is a locals favorite and a welcome day outing or overnight escape. Lake Henshaw Cafe offers dining with a lake view and is popular for its all-day breakfasts and occasional live music on weekend nights.

The lake is available for fresh water fishing and boating at $5 per person. Children under thirteen do not need the lake use permit. Fishing yields bass, crappie, bluegill, bullhead and catfish. An on-site store sells tackle and licenses. Boat rentals are available at $8-30 per day and private boats up to ten feet can use the launch for $5. Rafts and canoes are not allowed. Campsites with modern restrooms and showers accommodate tents and RVs. Water is available throughout the camping areas and pets are welcome. Cabins are available for those that desire a bed and some housekeeping. Pets are $1per night.

Location:	26439 Highway 76, Santa Ysabel
Hours:	Daily 6am-7pm
	Office: Mon-Thurs 7am-6pm
	Fri-Sat 6am-9pm, Sun 6am-6pm
Admission:	Day-Use: $5/Person; Under 13-Free;
	Camping: $14-19/Night; Cabins: $45-60/Night
Phone:	760-782-3501 Store
	760-782-3487 Camping Reservations
Website:	www.lakehenshawca.com

HOW TO GET THERE

Exit I-5 or I-15 at Highway 76 and proceed east past Pala to the lake.

Santa Ysabel Mission

Santa Ysabel Mission looks more modern than others in the area for good reason. It is. Unfortunately, the original 1818 site of adobe buildings eroded away over the years and a new structure was built in 1924 to serve as a spiritual center for the local Indian reservations and Santa Ysabel community. A small museum, Indian burial ground and murals relate the historical significance of this mission, which was built as a sub-mission of San Diego de Alcala for those in the backcountry. After 10 years of erosion, the Indians bought two bells for the mission with six burrow loads of barley. The bells were hung in a frame in 1846 as the only remains of the original chapel. The early-to mid-1700 bells were among the oldest in California. In 1926 the bells disappeared and still have not been found.

Location: Highway 79, Santa Ysabel
Hours: Daily 8am-Dusk
Admission: Free
Phone: 760-765-0810

HOW TO GET THERE
Exit I-15 at Highway 78 and proceed east past Ramona to Santa Ysabel. Turn left onto Highway 79 at the Highway 78/Highway 79 intersection. The mission is on the right.

Exit I-8 at Highway 67 and proceed north to Ramona. Proceed east along Highway 78. Continue east through Ramona to Santa Ysabel. Turn left onto Highway 79 at the Highway 78/Highway 79 intersection. The mission is on the right.

WARNER SPRINGS

Warner Springs is a community at the foothills of Palomar Mountain, best known for the Warner Springs Ranch resort.

Shadow Mountain Vineyards

Shadow Mountain Vineyards is a limited production winery founded in 1944 by Agusto & Helen Mase. The current owners acquired the vineyard in 1990 and continue the estate grape growing and winemaking business operation. This vineyard has a unique micro-climate at 3,500 feet in the mountains. High summer temperatures are cooled by coastal breezes and cold mountain temperatures at night create a prime grape growing location.

The vineyard has a tasting room with a large selection of their wines for sampling. A few tastings are offered at no charge and a full tasting can include as many as a dozen different wines for $3, which includes a souvenir glass.

Location:	34680 Highway 79, Warner Springs
Hours:	Wed-Sun 10am-5pm. Open most holidays
Admission:	Free. Tastings: $3/Person
Phone:	760-782-0778
Website:	www.shadowmountainvineyard.com

HOW TO GET THERE

Exit I-15 at Highway 78 and proceed east past Ramona to Santa Ysabel. In Santa Ysabel, turn left at Highway 79 and continue to Warner Springs. The winery is a 1/2-mile up a dirt road off Highway 79.

Exit I-8 at Highway 67 and proceed north to Ramona. Proceed east along Highway 78. Continue east through Ramona to Santa Ysabel. In Santa Ysabel, turn left onto Highway 79 and continue to Warner Springs. The winery is 1/2-mile up a dirt road off Highway 79.

Sky Sailing

Sky Sailing offers peaceful yet invigorating flights in sleek sailplanes, also called gliders, from Warner Springs Airport. The planes are manned by FAA certified pilots and provide a smooth and quiet ride with few blind spots and incredible birds-eye views of the surrounding scenery, providing several "Kodak moments."

Sailplanes are incredibly safe as they do not rely on fuel and are   engineered for slow short landings in natural field landscapes. For take-off, the planes are towed by a rope that is attached to a powered aircraft and released once the glider has lift. These one or two passenger adventures can last anywhere from twenty to forty minutes depending on weather, although the planes are capable of keeping flight for several hours. Passengers can do as much or as little of the flying as they like. For $125, thrill seekers can take an adrenaline-filled 25 minute Aerobatic Flight with loops, rolls and a parachute vest which is required-by-law. Reservations are required during the week and are appreciated, but not required, for weekend flights.

Location:	31930 Highway 79, Warner Springs
Hours:	Daily 9am-Sunset
	By appointment after 5pm
Admission:	$45-85/Person
Phone:	760-782-0404
Website:	www.skysailing.com

HOW TO GET THERE

Exit I-15 at Highway 78 and proceed east past Ramona to Santa Ysabel. In Santa Ysabel, turn left at Highway 79 and continue to Warner Springs Airport, which is about 2 miles past Warner Springs Ranch.

Exit I-8 at Highway 67 and proceed north to Ramona. Proceed east along Highway 78. Continue east through Ramona to Santa Ysabel. In Santa Ysabel, turn left at Highway 79 and continue to Warner Springs Airport, which is about 2 miles past Warner Springs Ranch.

Ramona, Santa Ysabel & Warner Springs

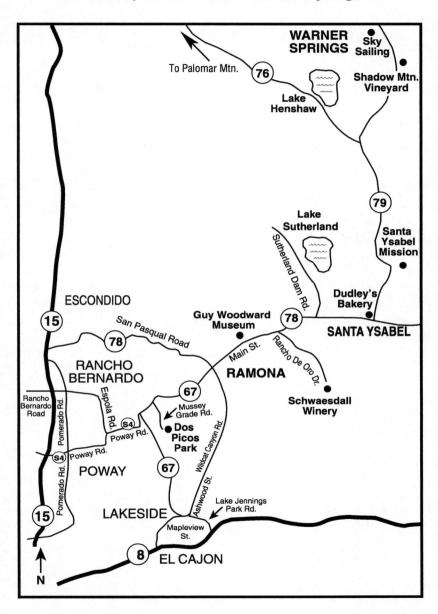

In & Around San Diego County

DESERT AREAS

- **Anza-Borrego Desert**
- **Death Valley**
- **Imperial Valley Desert**
- **Indio**
- **Joshua Tree**
- **Mojave Desert**
- **Palm Springs**

Anza-Borrego Desert
San Diego County

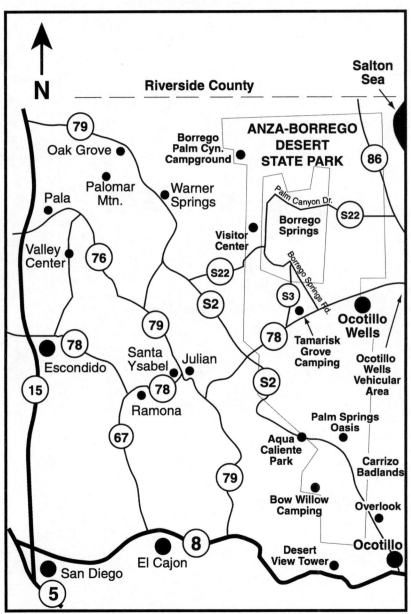

ANZA-BORREGO DESERT

Anza Borrego is San Diego's backyard desert. En route to the nearby recreational destination, an intriguing attraction for passersby is the offbeat California Historical Landmark Desert View Tower and Boulder Park Caves at Interstate 8's In-Ko-Pah exit. The 70-foot tower is a four-story, stone museum and gift shop with a miscellaneous collection honoring the area's pioneer days. The highlight of this attraction is the observation deck over-looking the Anza Borrego Desert. The view alone makes this stop worth-while. Boulder Park features naturally wind-blown caves and walkways among an intriguing garden of large quartzite boulders carved into all sorts of three-dimensional creatures such as lizards, snakes and faces. The mu-seum is open daily 9am-5pm. General admission is $2 and children are $1. Call 760-766-4612 for further details.

The Anza Borrego landscape is intriguing with mountains as a distant backdrop for boulder gardens, stark badlands and occasional palm oases. The best time to visit is late February and early March when colorful wildflowers take over this 600,000-acre desert. It is said that one year out of every five or ten, an ideal combination of moisture and temperature create the perfect climate for the desert's annual flower bloom. In these years, the entire desert appears to be brightly painted by bright fuschia verbena, yellow desert sunflower and red chuparosa. Other years, the flowers bloom in patches and visitors must seek out the most colorful areas. The winter's moisture and temperature are what decide the spring's bounty of flowers. Picking flowers or digging up plants is not allowed, and in many cases illegal. Anza Borrego is a favorite subject for photographers during flower season.

Year-round the curious visitor or photographer can seek out the cherished petroglyphs and pictographs etched on the surface of the richly colored desert rocks by native Indians ages ago. The rock drawings, which are widely considered art, are scattered throughout various locations in the Anza Borrego. They relate the religion, mythology and customs of the native tribes. There is always the chance that a hiker will happen upon these ancient treasures while exploring the desert canyons. Study the rock walls carefully.

Note that summer months are harsh, usually maintaining triple digit status. Always bring plenty of water, a hat and sunscreen. Be mindful the desert is not an ideal climate for pets.

Agua Caliente County Park

This 900-acre park sits at 1,300 feet. Native trees, small streams and water trenches from seismic activity spot the area. Palm trees, mesquite, chaparral and creosote add color and life to the desert landscape. Over 250 migratory and permanent bird species can be seen, including quails, roadrunners and hummingbirds. Coyotes and reptiles inhabit the park, but are not threatening to visitors. Hiking trails are throughout the area.

A therapy pool fed by underground hot mineral springs is what makes this county park unique. The glass-enclosed indoor pool maintains a temperature of 102 degrees. A smaller, shallow outdoor pool is beside the main pool. Many people seek out the spring for therapeutic benefits. There are even some permanent residency campsites for people who gain medicinal value from the pool and carry a physician's certificate claiming so. Showers and a changing room are provided for pool use.

There is a very developed campground with 140 sites. The campground has plenty of restrooms, even laundry facilities, children's play areas and RV hookups. Before the park entrance, Agua Caliente General Store has propane, food and miscellaneous supplies. Pets are not allowed.

San Diego County Parks allow reservations to be made two days to three months before the desired date. Check-in is at 2pm and check-out is at 1pm. Up to eight people may stay in one campsite and maximum stay is 14 nights.

Location:	39555 Highway S2, Agua Caliente
Hours:	Daily Sunrise-Sunset. Closed June-August
	Reservation Line: Daily 8am-5pm
Admission:	Day-Use: $5/Vehicle
	Overnight: $14-18/Night + $3 Reservation
Phone:	858-565-3600
Website:	www.sdparks.org

HOW TO GET THERE

From points south, exit I-8 at Highway S2 and back track west on Highway S2 25 miles to the park.

From points north, take Highway 78 through Ramona and Julian. Proceed along Highway 78 down Banner Grade to Scissors Crossing. Turn onto Highway S2 and proceed south for 23 miles. There are signs to the park.

Anza Borrego Desert State Park

Undeveloped nature trails wind through desert canyons and the adventurous hiker will be the most rewarded in Anza Borrego Desert State Park. It's best to delve into the narrow canyons in the morning or evening when the sunlight plays with the twisting rock of the canyon walls.

Off Highway S2, Bow Willow Canyon and Carrizo Canyon in the southern Carrizo Badlands vicinity are good areas for canyon exploration. From Carrizo Canyon, hikers can access Rockhouse Canyon. Also along Highway S2, just past the Carrizo Badlands Overlook, Canyon Sin Nombre has a hiking trail.

The Calcite Mine parking area off of Highway S22 is a good area to explore. Hike down into the canyon via a road that is left of the sign that tells the history of the Calcite Mine. The canyon floor provides access to several off shoot canyons where there is great hiking among sandstone walls. For one of the few areas with greenery, head to Cougar Canyon near the Borrego Springs Visitor Center. The historic Anza Trail runs along a stream in this canyon. You can catch the Canyon Trailhead near the Desert Gardens Picnic Area.

Part of the historic San Diego Emigrant Trail runs through the Anza Borrego. Famous legends such as Kit Carson, The Mormon Battalion and General  Kearny traversed this trail. Passengers on John Butterfield's Overland Mail rode stage coaches on this path between 1858 and 1861. Visitors can easily view parts of the trail from the roadside or even hike it. To view the trail, visit the Badland Overlook to see its southern section. Nearly ten miles north of this overlook, one can hike to Palm Spring Oasis, a respite for many weary travelers along the trail. Palms and an historic mile marker designate the spot. On foot the trail can be over three miles to the historic marker, but with a four wheel drive it can be just over a mile and a half. From Blair Valley one can view the northern section of this historic trail. There are several vantage points that reveal the long winding trail throughout the desert. Keep an open eye. The Nature Center at 652 Palm Canyon Drive in Borrego Springs provides free brochures detailing a self-guided auto tour of the trail.

Borrego Palm Canyon and Tamarisk Grove camping areas provide sites with fire grills, tables, piped water, flush toilets and showers for tent campers and RVs. A popular 1.5-mile nature trail from the Borrego Palm Canyon campground leads to a palm grove and waterfall. Open camping is permitted and several primitive campgrounds speckle the desert. Bow Willow has primitive sites. Dogs are allowed in campgrounds, but not on trails. Be mindful that the desert temperatures are often unkind to animals. Family campsites may be reserved up to six weeks in advance. Individual sites are on a first come, first serve basis.

Location:	Palm Canyon Road at Highway S22, Anza Borrego
Hours:	Daily 9am-5pm Information Line
Admission:	Free. Camping: $15-$16/Night
Phone:	760-767-5311 Information
	760-767-4205 Visitor Center
	760-767-4684 Wildflower Hotline
	800-444-7275 Camping Reservations
Website:	www.desertusa.com/anza_borrego

HOW TO GET THERE

From points south, exit I-8 at Highway 67 in El Cajon and proceed north to Ramona. Follow Highway 78 east to Santa Ysabel. Turn left at Highway 79 and proceed north along Highway 79. Turn right at Highway S2 and proceed to Highway S22. Turn left at Highway S22 and proceed to the park.

From points north, exit I-5 or I-15 at Highway 76 and proceed east to the dead end at Highway 79. Turn left at Highway 79 and proceed north. Turn right on Highway S2. Follow Highway S2 to Highway S22. Turn left at Highway S22 and proceed to the park.

Borrego Springs

This community of about 3,000 year-round permanent residents is located in the middle of Anza Borrego State Park. The population doubles in the winter months. There are several public golf courses, tennis courts and swimming pools, as well as off-road vehicle adventures in this desert resort town. The most popular resort is the luxurious Casa Del Zoro. Call the resort at 800-824-1884 or visit www.lacasadelzorro.com for details.

A weekly Farmer's Market is held Saturdays 7am-12pm at Christmas Circle. In April, the Borrego Springs Grapefruit Festival brings in music, food, arts and crafts. Borrego Days Festival is held the last weekend in October and the De Anza Trail Relay Ride occurs in November. The Saturday before April 1st, the annual Peg Leg Liar's Contest is held where participants sit around a fire and tell a story, or rather a lie. The liar's contests requires one to tell a story and somehow incorporate Peg Leg Smith, the 1830s legend who apparently struck gold but misplaced his mine, stole mules, frequented saloons and ended up with a stocky wooden leg that caused him to wander the desert in circles. So it is said.

As the hub of this desert, Borrego Springs is home to the Anza-Borrego Desert State Park Visitor Center. The center, which is west of Highway S22 on Palm Canyon Drive, provides information on recreational opportunities and events in the area October through May 9am-5pm and on weekends June through September 10am-3pm.

Location:	Highway S3 at Highway S22, Borrego Springs
Phone:	760-767-4205 Visitor Center
	800-559-5524 Chamber of Commerce
Website:	www.borregosprings.org

HOW TO GET THERE

Exit I-5 or I-15 at Highway 78 and proceed east past Ramona to Highway S3. Turn left and proceed north into town.

Ocotillo Wells State Vehicular Area

Near Anza-Borrego Desert State Park, this 42,000-acre off-road vehicle area attracts dirt bikes, dune buggies and four-wheel drive all-terrain vehicles. The terrain varies from below sea level to 400-foot elevations with buttes, dry washes, sand dunes and a sand bowl. Camping is permitted and there are pay showers, picnic tables and fire rings, but no water. The town of Ocotillo Wells provides the nearest services.

Location:	Highway 78 at Ocotillo Wells
Hours:	Daily 24 Hours
Admission:	Free
Phone:	760-767-5391 Ranger Station
Website:	www.ohv.parks.ca/gov

HOW TO GET THERE

Exit I-5 or I-15 at Highway 78 and proceed east through Anza Borrego State Park; north of Highway 78 beyond Ocotillo Wells.

Death Valley
Inyo County

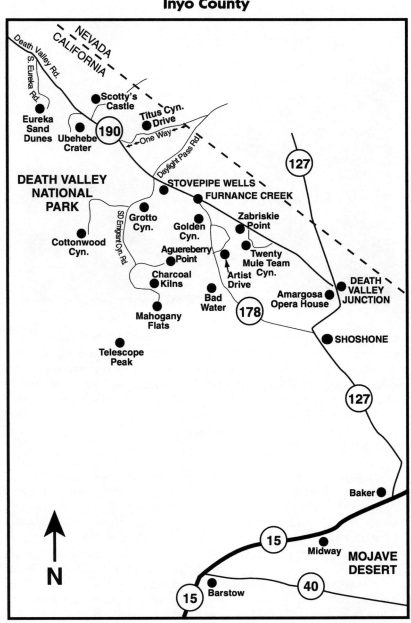

DEATH VALLEY

Amargosa Opera House & Hotel

A once-in-a-lifetime experience awaits at Marta Becket's "little opera house that could." In the middle of nowhere, a mesmerizing evening of ballet, pantomime and performance fascinates visitors who fill a converted 1923 Pacific Coast Borax Company building. The building, once known as Corkhill Hall, is part of what captivates each guest. The walls surrounding the stage are adorned with Becket's elaborate hand-painted mural showing a 16th century audience of costumed ladies and gentlemen, nuns and monks, and of course the center-stage balcony seated king and queen.

The Amargosa Opera House is the realization of Marta Becket's wild imagination and the inspiring story behind the experience is as fascinating as the experience itself. Becket, who was a Broadway performer, was camping in Death Valley recovering from a hectic ballet schedule in 1967. She woke to a flat tire one morning and was pointed to Death Valley Junction for repair. As the tire was getting fixed, she nosed around the long abandoned Pacific Coast Borax Company buildings, and happened to peek through a door hole of what was at the time a dilapidated community center with a small stage and some benches. The next day, Becket managed an agreement to rent the building from the town for $45 a month if she assumed repairs.

She cleaned the theater, renamed it and gave her first performance less than a year later. That night twelve people attended the show and over the years, audiences included locals, tourists and at times nobody. It was the latter that inspired her to paint the mural, which took four years. She spent another two years embellishing the ceiling. Some scenes are a lady dancing to the sounds of a musician playing an antique instrument, ladies of the night and gypsies, a group of royal children tended by a governess, a cloud-filled blue sky with cherubs and doves and the four winds in each corner. Over time 105 garden chairs were donated and a nine foot concert grand piano arrived as a gift from a couple in Spokane, Washington. Eventually, the opera house incorporated as a nonprofit and bought the town of Death Valley Junction, which is now listed in the National Register of Historic Places. Finally, in 1983 the Opera House was able to buy 120 theater seats to replace the well worn garden chairs.

Becket presents multiple programs of original ballet-mimes covering forty-seven different characters and multiple costume changes each performance. She has managed three performances a week for years, but now hosts her same evening schedule only during cooler months. For a list of upcoming show dates, call or visit the website and reserve early.

Location:	Highway 127, Death Valley Junction
Hours:	Doors 7:45pm, Show 8:15pm
Admission:	General-$15;
	Youth Under 12-$12; Under 5-Not admitted
Phone:	760-852-4441
Website:	www.amargosa-opera-house.com

HOW TO GET THERE
Take I-15 to Highway 127 at Baker. Proceed north on Highway 127 through Shoshone to Death Valley Junction.

Death Valley National Park

Considered the largest national park in the contiguous U.S. with over a million acres, Death Valley is truly something to marvel at. From 280 feet below sea level at Bad Water it climbs to an elevation over 11,000 feet at Telescope Peak. Bad Water can literally be the hottest place on earth, where summer temperatures typically exceed 120 degrees, while Telescope Peak can occasionally see snow. A land of spectacular contrast, the colors of the mountains and canyon walls change dramatically within the same day. Moreover, there are places in the park where nature's changes can even be heard, such as the "singing" sand at Eureka Sand Dunes and the expanding and contracting hills of Twenty Mule Team Canyon. In spite of little rain and extreme weather, more than 900 plant species, many unique to Death Valley, and several creatures somehow survive in the park.

Furnace Creek is the township within the park and home to the Visitor Center & Park Headquarters. Lodging and campgrounds reside mostly in this area. Also at Furnace Creek, the free Borax Museum relates some interesting history about Death Valley's mining past and the Twenty Mule Team. The museum is open daily 9:30am-4pm. A few miles north, Harmony Borax Works Ruins discloses more of the story. Stove Pipe Wells is another community area with some interesting trivia at Burned Wagons Point.

To observe an intense palette of colors, two notable scenic driving routes are the one-way loops through Titus Canyon, best in the morning, and Artist Drive, best in the afternoon.

Charcoal Kilns off Emigrant Canyon Road are intriguing and provide the starting point for a four mile trail hike with a 3,000 foot gain to Wildrose Peak for outstanding views of Death Valley. Popular hiking areas include Eureka Sand Dunes, which are California's highest dunes, Cottonwood Canyon, Grotto Canyon and Golden Canyon. The seven mile trail from Mahogany Flats to Telescope Peak affords incredible views. Other great views can be had at Dante's View and Zabriske Point, which are both breathtaking in the morning, and Aguereberry Point, which is best in the afternoon.

Remnants of gold, silver, copper and other mineral mines and mills can be found at Chloride City Ghost Town, Ashford Mill Ruins, Ballarat Ghost Town, Keane Wonder Mine & Mill Ruins, Skidoo Ghost Town, Echo Canyon and Hidden Valley.

Scotty's Castle is an offbeat "must see" attraction with an interesting, if not humorous, story. The castle is open daily 9am-5pm. Nearby Ubehebe Crater is the result of a major volcanic explosion.

Important things to know before visiting Death Valley include checking the weather and making lodging reservations before traveling. Visitors should bring plenty of water when hiking, pack for both extreme warm and extreme cool temperatures and know that several of the natural attractions can only be accessed by four-wheel drive or by foot.

Location:	Highway 190, Death Valley
Hours:	Daily 24 Hours
	Furnace Creek Visitor Center:
	Daily 8am-6pm. Open until 7pm during Summer
Admission:	$10/Vehicle; $5/Pedestrian. Valid for 7 days
Phone:	760-786-2331 Furnace Creek Headquarters
	760-786-2342 Stovepipe Wells Ranger
	760-786-2313 Grapevine Ranger
	702-553-2200 Beatty, Nevada, Ranger
Website:	www.deathvalley.com

HOW TO GET THERE

Take I-15 to Highway 127 in Baker to Highway 190 in Death Valley Junction and proceed to Furnace Creek.

Imperial Valley Desert
Imperial County

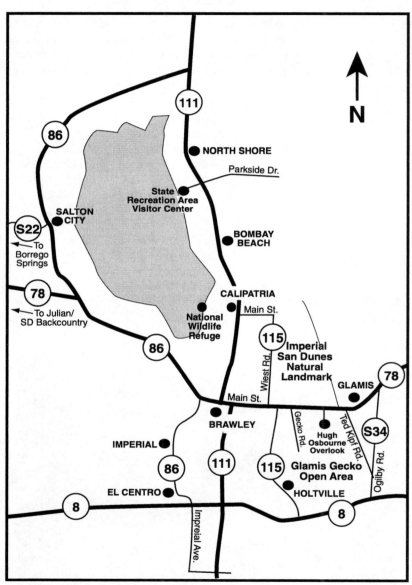

N

86

111

• NORTH SHORE

Parkside Dr.

State
Recreation Area
Visitor Center

**SALTON
CITY**

S22

← To
Borrego
Springs

**BOMBAY
BEACH**

78

← To Julian/
SD Backcountry

CALIPATRIA

Main St.

86

National
Wildlife
Refuge

115 Imperial
San Dunes
Natural
Landmark

Wiest Rd.

GLAMIS

78

Main St.

Gecko Rd.

Hugh
Osbourne
Overlook

Ted Kipf Rd.

S34

BRAWLEY

IMPERIAL •

86

111

115 Glamis Gecko
Open Area

Ogilby Rd.

EL CENTRO •

HOLTVILLE

8

8

Imperial Ave.

IMPERIAL VALLEY DESERT

Brawley Cattle Call

This agricultural town comes to life for ten festive days in November for the annual Cattle Call. The major draw is Professional Rodeo Cowboys Association's nationally sanctioned rodeo, but the Main Street parade with over 3,000 floats, bands, clowns, equestrians and entertainers is a close second. High profile rodeo cowboys and champions usually attend and perform at the event. Cook-offs, western dancing, cowboy poetry, bluegrass and mariachi music are other highlights. Street stands and shops sell western wear, souvenirs, balloons, and snacks. Reserved seating can be arranged in advance through the Brawley Chamber of Commerce.

Location:	Cattle Call Arena on Imperial Avenue, Brawley
Hours:	Event times vary
Admission:	Event prices vary
Phone:	760-344-3160 Chamber of Commerce
	760-344-5206 Rodeo Tickets
Website:	www.cattlecall.brawleychamber.com

HOW TO GET THERE

Exit I-8 at Imperial Avenue/Highway 86 and proceed north along Highway 86 to Brawley.

Exit I-5 or I-15 at Highway 78 and proceed east through Anza Borrego to Highway 86. Proceed southeast along Highway 86 to Brawley.

Salton Sea

Salton Sea is actually a lake, a big lake. In fact, it is the largest in California measuring 45 miles long and 25 miles wide at 250 feet below sea level. A sunrise or sunset over this lake is incredible. The sun reflects off the high concentration of salts painting the sky shades of red, orange and yellow. The lake is saltier than the ocean. Boating and fishing are the most popular sports, but bird watching is just as common as this lake is a nesting ground for more than 350 migratory species.

The Salton Sea State Recreation Area at the east end of the lake is popular for sailboarding, water skiing and sunbathing on the beaches. There are numerous public campgrounds in this area, as well as one to the south near the Wildlife Refuge and several private campgrounds on the western edge of the lake.

Location:	Highway S22 at Highway 86, Salton Sea
Hours:	Daily 9am-5pm October-May
Admission:	Free. Fees for various activities
Phone:	760-393-3052
Website:	www.saltonsea.ca.gov

HOW TO GET THERE

From points south, exit I-8 at Highway 86 and proceed north to the sea. From points north, exit Highway 78 east to Highway 86 and proceed to the sea.

Imperial Sand Dunes Recreation Area

Forty miles of magnificent sand dunes, some reaching 300 feet in height, have been naturally created by the wind and ancient beach sand of former Lake Cahuilla. Hugh Osborne Overlook provides a panoramic view of the sandy, patterned hills off Highway 78.

Most of the area is dedicated to off-road vehicle use, but some wilderness areas, such as Imperial Sand Dunes National Natural Landmark, are reserved for hiking and horseback only. Hikers can climb the one mile Mesquite Mine Overlook Trail to view California's second largest goldmine daily 8am-4pm. A brochure at the trailhead describes points of interests along the trail. The Cahuilla Ranger Station on Gecko Road off Highway 78 provides visitor information during peak season from October through May.

Glamis/Gecko Open Area boasts the highest dunes and is usually loaded with dirt bikes, dune buggies, ATVs and 4-wheel drive trucks. There are miles and miles of dunes to ride, stretching between Highway 78 to the north and Highway 8 to the south. Night riding is allowed, but quiet time is enforced 10pm-7am. The Glamis Beach Store at the northeast corner of the dunes off Highway 78 has basic amenities, a restaurant, a bar and a shower. Fuel and water are not available and visitors should bring plenty of both. It is advisable to check the weather before visiting the dunes. There are a few pit and portable toilets in main areas such as along Gecko Road.

Primitive camping is allowed anywhere that is at least ten feet from the road. There are some designated primitive spots with asphalt and gravel camping pads if you seek them out. These sites do not have facilities. Popular camping spots line Gecko Road. Near Highway 78, best spots include Glamis Flats, Cement Flats and Garbage Flats. Off Highway 8, Microwave Tower and Dunebuggy Flats are common camping locales. There is a weekly camping fee of $10 per non-OHV vehicle.

Location:	Highway 78 at Glamis
	Highway 8 at Ogilby Road (S34)
Hours:	Daily 24 Hours
Admission:	Free
Phone:	760-337-4400 El Centro Office - Year-round
	760-344-3919 Ranger Station - Seasonal
Website:	www.glamisonline.org

HOW TO GET THERE

From points south, exit Highway 8 at Ogilby Road and proceed north to Ted Kipf Road for dunes access.

From points north, exit Highway 78 at Gecko Road and proceed south to the Cahuilla Ranger Station & Visitor Center.

Indio & Joshua Tree
Riverside County

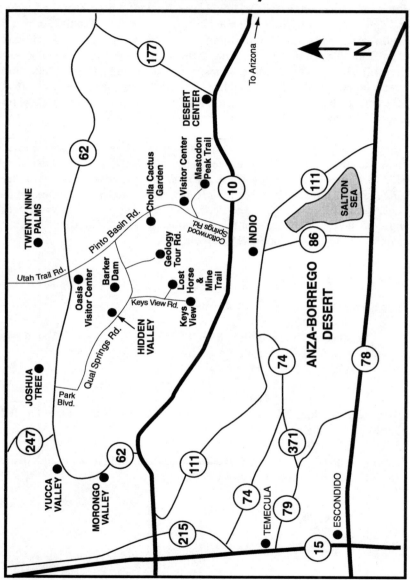

INDIO

Indio is considered the "Date Capital of the World," which explains all the palm groves that decorate the landscape. Since the 1800s, this area has grown and exported dates. To tour a date garden and sample a date shake, visit Indio Orchards at 80-521 Highway 111. Indio Orchards can be reached at 760-347-7534. Shields Date Gardens at 80-225 Highway 111 also makes date shakes. Shields can be reached at 760-347-0996. In February, the National Date Festival draws a large crowd to celebrate Coachella Valley's favorite fruit.

Riverside County Fair & National Date Festival

For ten days in mid-February, food, music, headliner entertainment and amusing competitions create a festive atmosphere in Indio.

The annual County Fair & Date Festival is known for camel and ostrich races by day and elaborate pageantry shows by night. The races are a spectator favorite due to the unpredictability of these animals. The "Arabian Nights Parade" kicks off the pageantry with colorful floats, marching bands, ornamented horses and costumed entertainers. The theme continues throughout the festival with exotic performances each night depicting stories of ancient Baghdad.

Carnival rides and competitions such as pie eating, arm wrestling and a diaper derby are constant background merriment. There are endless public exhibits competing for prizes in art, woodworking, agriculture, livestock, horticulture and a variety of other skill sets. Music runs the gamut from country western to gospel to jazz and rock. A circus, petting zoo, and free admission to Shalimar Off-Track Betting are other highlights. Food is everywhere, especially that which includes dates.

Location:	46-350 Arabia Street, Indio
Hours:	February. Call for exact dates
	Daily 10am-10pm
Admission:	General-$7; Seniors(55+)-$6;
	Youth(5-12)-$4; Under 5-Free
	Parking-$5
Phone:	760-863-8247 or 800-811-3247
Website:	www.datefest.org

HOW TO GET THERE

Take I-15 to Highway 79 in Temecula and proceed east to Highway 371 in Aguanga. Take Highway 371 northeast to Highway 74. Take Highway 74 northeast to Highway 111. Take Highway 111 east to Indio.

JOSHUA TREE

Joshua Tree National Park

The stunning and unique landscape is the magnetism of this 870-square mile playground. Huge boulders scattered helter skelter, mesmerizing fields of strange succulents and the Joshua trees make this high desert wonderland a favorite for hikers, bikers, rock climbers and photographers.

Deserted mines can be found via Lost Horse Mine Trail and Mastodon Peak Trail. Desert wildlife sightings of roadrunners, coyotes and foxes are common. Bighorn sheep and bobcats also inhabit the park, along with several birds, rabbits, squirrels and raccoons.

Hidden Valley has fantastic trails that wind through natural rock gardens and provide access to Keys View, which provides a panoramic view of the entire valley, mountains and desert at an elevation of 5,000 feet. Cholla Cactus Garden in the low desert of Pinto Basin is a startling sea of yellow-green bushes that shimmer in the sun. Barker Dam and the self-guided Geology Tour Road are other park highlights.

Day Outings From San Diego

There are several year-round campgrounds for tent and RV campers. Each campground has a picnic table and fire ring. Some sites have water and nearby restrooms. Headquarters for the park is at Oasis Visitor Center, which is located at Highway 62 and Utah Trail. It is open daily 8am-6pm for information. Black Rock Canyon Ranger Station is at the north entry to the park along Highway 62 and Cottonwood Visitor Center is at the south entry of the park along Interstate 10.

Location:	Between I-10 & Highway 62, near Palm Springs
Hours:	Daily 24 Hours
Admission:	$10/Vehicle; $5/Pedestrian. Valid 7 days
	Annual Pass-$15
Phone:	760-367-5500
	760-365-9585
Website:	www.joshua.tree.national-park.com

HOW TO GET THERE
Take I-15 to I-215 and proceed north. Connect to I-10 and proceed east.

South entrance to the park is accessed by proceeding east on I-10 through Thousand Palms and Indio and turning north onto Cottonwood Springs Road.

North entrance to the park is accessed by exiting I-10 at Highway 62 and proceeding north through Morongo and Yucca Valley. Turn onto Park Boulevard to reach the park.

MOJAVE DESERT

Calico Ghost Town Regional Park

To truly understand what life was like in old west mining towns one should visit this authentic ghost town. With the generosity of Walter Knott's of Knott's Berry Farm, Calico was meticulously preserved and restored to resemble the town during its reigning period between 1881 and 1907. A third of the county park is original. It is one of only a few original old west mining camps in the country.

It was silver rather than gold that created the rush to Calico. One of the largest silver strikes in California history led to over five hundred mines, about fifty of which ultimately produced 15-20 million ounces of silver. The most famous of those mines were Silver King, Oriental Bismarck, Odessa and Maggie's. It was one of the richest mining districts in the state creating "boomtown" status. Calico boasted 22 saloons, China Town and a "red light district" all supported by 4,000 newly rich miners and 1,200 residents. More than thirty miles of tunnels and shafts were built, but when silver prices plummeted and borax mining stopped in the area, Calico became a ghost town.

Adventuresome visitors may enter an underground mine, while the less eager can search for small cave-like openings in the mountain faces from a narrow gauge railroad car and imagine the mines and houses behind these "doorways." When occupancy in houses and dugouts along Main Street maxed out, eager miners would makeshift wooden bridges and gangplanks to cross gullies and dig out places to live in the canyonsides. Free 45-minute walking tours with historians relate the lifestyle of miners, the famous Twenty Mule Team and a popular U.S. postal mail dog named Dorsey at 10am, 12pm and 2pm daily. The Mystery Shack is a favorite park attraction. There are only six of these mystery spots left in the western U.S. These six rarities are defined as showcasing some strange natural phenomenon. In the case of the Mystery Shack, water runs uphill. Spontaneous gunfight stunt shows are common and endless entertainment, shopping and eateries surround the park.

While several festivals are held year-round, two mainstays are Spring Festival held Mother's Day weekend and Calico Days held Columbus Day weekend. Spring Festival is an old time music festival with several games and contests, including a chili and stew cook-off. Calico Days is a mining festival with a national gunfight exhibition, burro run, parade and several games and contests. Admission prices are a few dollars more during festival periods. A full-service, twenty-four hour campground is located in the canyons below town and there are numerous accommodations in nearby Barstow.

Location:	Ghost Town Road at I-15, Yermo
Hours:	Daily 8am-Dusk
	Attractions: Daily 9am-5pm. Closed Dec 25
Admission:	General-$6; Youth(6-15)-$3; Under 6-Free
	Camping: $18-28/Night. Includes Admission
Phone:	800-862-2542 or 760-254-2122
Website:	www.calicotown.com

HOW TO GET THERE

Take I-15 north to Barstow. Proceed ten miles past Barstow and exit I-15 at Ghost Town Road. Follow signs to the park, which is located 3 miles off I-15 on Ghost Town Road.

Mojave National Preserve

This vast and desolate 1.4 million-acre preserve is a lesson in geology and solitude. There is plenty of hiking and nature exploration throughout this desert sanctuary.

Providence Mountains State Recreation Area is home to Mitchell Caverns and two high peaks, Colorful Fountain at just under 7,000 feet and Edgar Peak at just over 7,000 feet. Over the course of twelve million years, amazing stalactites, stalagmites, helictites, flowstone, cave shields and rare coral pipes were formed by seismic and volcanic activity, creating cavernous rooms that visitors can tour with a guide. Anthropologists, archaeologists and geologists all share an interest in the caves for a variety of reasons.

Cima Dome, which is blanketed in Joshua trees, is a favorite roadside attraction and hiking area with its nearly perfect symmetrical shape. Camp Rock Springs is a historical point-of-interest. Camping can be found at Mid Hills and Hole-in-the-Wall where there is a Visitor Center. Be fuel-conscious in this area as services are not readily available. Also be aware that many of the main roads in the preserve are not paved.

Location:	Between I-15 & I-40, near Baker
Hours:	Daily 24 Hours
	Tues-Sun 8am-4pm Information Center
Admission:	Free
Phone:	760-326-6322 Information Center
	760-733-4040
Website:	www.nps.gov/moja

HOW TO GET THERE

Take I-15 North and exit south at Kelbaker Road or Cima Road to enter the preserve from its northern edges. To enter the park from its south southern edge, take I-15 northbound and connect to I-40 eastbound. Proceed east on I-40 and exit north at Kelbaker Road or Essex Road.

Mojave Desert
San Bernardino County

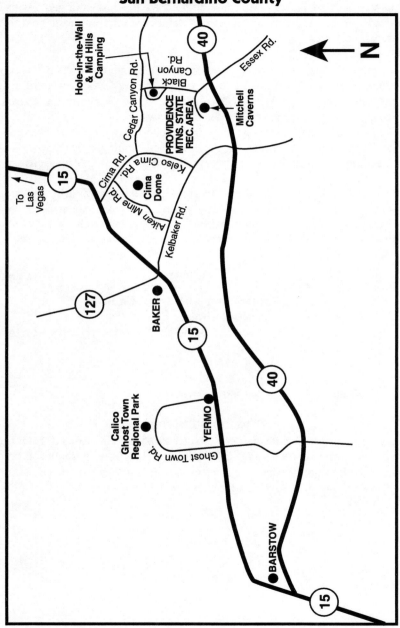

PALM SPRINGS

As the desert's premier resort town, Palm Springs is loaded with entertainment for all personalities. From Hollywood fanatics and sun lovers to golfers and spa goers to campers and nature lovers, this desert mecca has something for everyone. Architecture fans will appreciate the midcentury modern structures that lend the area its unique character.

The first Friday of each month, the Palm Springs Heritage Galleries and Antique District stay open late so that visitors can peruse the shops and galleries until 9pm while enjoying live entertainment and area restaurants. Call 760-325-8979 or 760-778-8415 for details. On Thursday evenings, a Farmer's Market & Village Fest takes place 6pm-10pm with arts and craft vendors, food and live entertainment on North Palm Canyon Drive at Baristo Road. During summer months, the event starts at 7pm. There is no fair on holidays. Call 760-320-3781 for details.

Just north of Palm Springs is Desert Hot Springs, a resort town known for its curative hot mineral water. The crystal clear water has no odor or taste and can be enjoyed at dozens of spas and accommodations in the area. Call 760-329-6403 for details on the pools and lodging.

Agua Caliente Indian Reservation

Only a few miles from downtown Palm Springs, this nearby reservation features the lush Indian Canyons and Agua Caliente Resort Casino & Spa.

Indian Canyons features Palm Canyon, Andreas Canyon, Murray Canyon and Tahquitz Canyon with a 60-foot waterfall. These palm-filled valleys offer great hiking and horseback riding opportunities along well-marked trails. A visit to Tahquitz Canyon, the location for Frank Capra's 1937 film *Lost Horizon*, is only allowed via a two-hour guided walking tour. The tour is $10 per adult and $5 per child. Reservations are recommended.

The casino features nearly 50 gaming tables, a high-limit gaming area, over 1,000 slots and video poker machines and a players club. Entertainment, restaurants and a lounge, luxury rooms and a variety of fitness and spa services are available.

Location:	South Palm Canyon Drive, Palm Springs
Hours:	Daily 8am-5pm
Admission:	General-$6; Seniors(62+)-$4.50
	Students & Military (with ID)-$4.50
	Youth(6-12)-$2; Under 6-Free;
	Equestrians-$10
Phone:	760-325-5673 Reservation Info
	760-325-3400 or 800-790-3398 Canyons
	760-321-2000 Casino
Website:	www.aguacaliente.org
	www.indian-canyons.com

HOW TO GET THERE

Exit Highway 111 at Palm Canyon Drive and proceed south to the reservation entrance.

Palm Springs Aerial Tramway

A fifteen minute breathtaking ride carries visitors up nearly 6,000 feet aboard one of two 80-passenger rotating tramcars. Lunch and dinner are served at a restaurant at the top of the mountain. Winter months attract those that like to cross-country ski, snowshoe and snowtube. The trams run every fifteen to thirty minutes. The last tram up the mountain departs at 8pm and the last tram down the mountain departs at 9:45 pm.

Location:	Highway 111 at Tramway Road, Palm Springs
Hours:	Daily 10am-10pm. Open at 8am weekends
Admission:	General-$20.80; Seniors(60+)-$18.80;
	Youth(3-12)-$13.80; Under 3-Free
Phone:	760-325-1391 or 760-325-1449
Website:	www.pstramway.com

HOW TO GET THERE

Exit Highway 111 at Tramway Road and proceed up the hill 3.5 miles to the entrance.

Palm Springs Desert Museum

This museum attracts top touring exhibitions and is home to a quality permanent collection along with galleries, sculpture gardens and the intimate state-of-the-art Annenberg Theater. The first Friday of each month admission is free. There is a nice café on site.

Location:	101 Museum Drive, Palm Springs
Hours:	Tues-Sat 10am-5pm, Sun 12am-5pm
Admission:	General $7.50; Senior(62+)-$6.50; Youth-$3.50
Phone:	760-325-0189 Recorded Info
	760-325-7186
Website:	www.psmuseum.org

HOW TO GET THERE

Follow Highway 111 to Palm Canyon Drive in town. From Palm Canyon Drive, turn west at Tahquitz Canyon Way. Turn right at Museum Drive.

Plaza Theater's Palm Springs Follies & Walk of Stars

Since 1936, the historic Plaza Theatre has been hosting gala events, radio broadcasts and live performances for huge stars and celebrities such as Jack Benny, Bob Hope and Frank Sinatra. Outside the Spanish-style film house begins the Palm Springs Walk of Stars, a spin-off of Hollywood's Walk of Fame. Today the theater hosts the Fabulous Palm Springs Follies, a humorous variety show with a chorus line of costumed ladies ages 50 and older.

Location:	128 S. Palm Canyon Drive, Palm Springs
Hours:	Performances 1:30pm & 7pm
Admission:	Prices vary. Expect $37-$75/Person
Phone:	760-327-0225 Theater/Follie's
	760-322-1563 Walk of Stars
Website:	www.psfollies.com

HOW TO GET THERE

Follow Highway 111 to Palm Canyon Drive in town. The theater is on Palm Canyon Drive between Tahquitz Canyon Way and Arenas Road.

Knott's Soak City U.S.A.

This water park has something for everyone. *Tidal Wave Tower* features two high-speed slides that drop seven stories. *Sea Snake* is a 50-foot dark tube slide. *Pipeline Point* has three 70-foot tall body slides called *Pipeline*, *Wipeout* and *Undertow*. *Rip Tide Reef* is an 800,000-gallon wave pool. Families with young children appreciate the lazy river ride called *Sunset River* and *Gremmie Lagoon* with two cautious yet fun slides. Private cabanas can be rented for up to eight people.

Location:	1500 S. Gene Autry Trail, Palm Springs
Hours:	Daily 10am-6pm March-September
Admission:	General-$22.95, After 3pm-$13.95;
	Youth(3-11)-$16.95, After 3pm-$9.95;
	Parking-$6
Phone:	760-327-0499
Website:	www.soakcityusa.com

HOW TO GET THERE

Follow Highway 111 to Gene Autry Trail. The water park is on the east side of Gene Autry Trail/Highway111.

Village Green Heritage Center

The Village Green Heritage Center in the middle of town houses several museum buildings.

The Palm Springs Historical Society runs the 1885 McCallum Adobe and 1893 Cornelia White House. The McCallum Adobe features the society's collections while the Cornelia White House showcases pioneer memorabilia. From mid-October through May, these two buildings are open Wednesday and Sunday 12pm-3pm and Thursday-Saturday 10am-4pm.

Ruddy's 1930s General Store Museum is reminiscent of an old-fashioned general store with authentic products and displays. October through June, the museum is open Thursday-Sunday 10am-4pm and on weekends 10am-4pm the remainder of the year.

Agua Caliente Cultural Museum relates the history and culture of the Cahuilla Indians with traditional basketry, artifacts and a full-size kish Cahuilla dwelling. September through May, the museum is open Monday-Saturday 10am-4pm and Sunday 12pm-4pm. It is open on weekends the remainder of the year.

Location:	219-223 S. Palm Canyon Drive, Palm Springs
Hours:	Hours vary. See above
Admission:	Each Museum-50¢/Person
	Agua Caliente-Free
Phone:	760-323-8297 Historical Society
	760-327-2156 Rudy's General Store
	760-323-0151 Agua Caliente Museum
Website:	www.palmsprings.com/history

HOW TO GET THERE

Follow Highway 111 to Palm Canyon Drive in town. The center is on Palm Canyon Drive between Arenas Road and Baristo Road.

Palm Springs
Riverside County

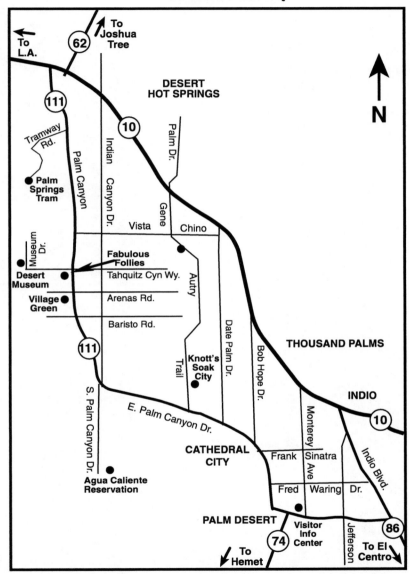

Riverside County

- **Temecula**
- **Lake Elsinore**
- **Corona**
- **Perris**
- **Hemet**
- **Idyllwild**
- **Riverside**

Temecula, Lake Elsinore, Corona, Perris, Hemet & Idyllwild

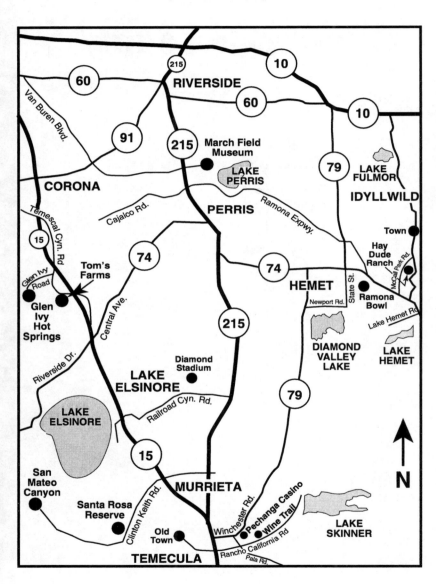

RIVERSIDE COUNTY

Riverside County is San Diego County's northern neighbor and several treasures lie along this border, such as Southern California's Temecula Wine Trail. Touring the local vineyards, tasting the many varieties and enjoying the grounds is one of the county's most popular activities. Equally popular are hot air balloon rides over Temecula wine country or Lake Elsinore. The Lake Elsinore skies are often filled with sky divers as well, while the waters are filled with swimmers, water skiers and boats. Perris often shows a similar scene with skydiving and Lake Perris activity being the main draws to the area. The county's newest and largest lake is Diamond Valley Lake near Hemet.

The county boasts several lake areas and beautiful mountains for camping and hiking. Idyllwild is a popular mountain town with a lively artist community. The town hosts several worthwhile events annually, including the popular Art Walk & Wine Tasting. Other county events that draw crowds are the Annual Tamale Festival in Indio and the National Date Fair, which doubles as the county fair and is also held in Indio. Nearby Palm Springs draws visitors year-round for winter warmth and summer heat. The desert resort town attracts those who love architecture, shopping, art and Hollywood glamour. The Palm Springs Walk of Stars, which begins outside Plaza Theater, is a spin off of Hollywood's Walk of Fame, which begins outside Mann's Chinese Theater in Los Angeles. Just outside Palm Springs, Desert Hot Springs is appreciated for its curative hot mineral waters. Several area hotels have healing mineral pools for use by visitors. One of the county's most luxurious and well-known mineral spas is Glen Ivy Hot Springs & Spa in the town of Corona. Several outdoors pools and mud baths entice one to linger for the day. A long list of spa services such as facials, massages and body wraps are offered as well.

The city of Riverside holds an architectural treasure with an interesting history, Mission Inn. A guided tour reveals the tumultuous history of this beauty. The city doubles as a "college town" to University of California at Riverside, which has an impressive Botanical Gardens and Museum of Photography. Architectural gems are scattered throughout the downtown area.

Riverside county caters to the needs of many with both beautiful desert and mountain towns coupled with fresh water lakes.

TEMECULA

Temecula is best known for its **Southern California Wine Trail**. But the wine country is rivaled by more than a handful of championship golf courses, countryside hot air ballooning, outdoor recreation, a casino and a charming Old Town district.

Old Town is loaded with antique stores, boutique shopping and restaurants designed in the old-west style complete with wooden boardwalks and sidewalk benches. Even the trash bins are old oak barrels. Horse carriage rides through Old Town add ambiance to any visit. This quaint area, which runs along sections of Front Street and Main Street, hosts several annual events including Western Days in April and Frontier Days Rodeo in May, as well as a weekly Farmer's Market on Saturdays. A Rod Run is hosted in February and October for car lovers and an International Film & Music Festival takes place each September. Barrel tastings and art festivals are other common events. **Temecula Valley Museum** is located in Old Town at 28314 Mercedes Street in Sam Hick's Monument Park. The museum is open Tuesday-Saturday 10am-5pm and Sunday 1pm-5pm.

Lake Skinner hosts the annual Balloon & Wine Festival each year in September. The festival draws hundreds for food, wine tasting, hot air ballooning and entertainment. Call 909-676-6713 for more festival information. Throughout the year, Lake Skinner welcomes those seeking to boat, fish, hike, horseback ride, picnic or camp. The lake has developed campsites, many with full hookups for Rvs and some tailored for equestrians. There is even a swimming pool at the lake open from Memorial Day through

late September. Day use is $2 per vehicle and $5 per boat launch. Camping is $12-18 per night. The park opens at 6am and closes at 7:30pm in the summer and at dusk the remainder of the year. Lake Skinner is located east of town off of Rancho California Road at 37701 Warren Road. Call 909-926-1541 for more information.

D&D Ballooning operates morning hot air balloon rides from Wilson Creek Winery. Call 909-303-0448 or 800-510-9000 to make reservations. Further details can be found at www.hotairadventures.com. Several hot air balloon outfitters in San Diego County operate rides over Temecula as well. Refer to the Coastal chapter for descriptions of those companies.

The Pechanga Band of Luiseno Indians operate the **Pechanga Resort & Casino**, which features 86 table games, 2,000 slots and a 450-seat Bingo Hall. There are six restaurants, a buffet, two bars, two lounges and a hotel at the resort. Opened in 2002, the **Pechanga Performing Arts Center** features a season line up of Broadway musicals such as Amadeus, Moulin Rouge, and Miss Saigon. Call 909-885-5152 or 909-885-6322 for tickets or information. Pechanga is located just east of I-15 off the Highway 79/Indio exit at 45000 Pala Road. Call 877-711-2946 or visit www.pechanga.com for more information.

The Wine Trail

For those seeking to enjoy the wine country, but unable to bring along a designated driver, there is the tour company alternative. Make reservations for these services at least twenty-four hours before your desired tour date. Most companies include an Old Town Temecula tour, wine tasting at three or four vineyards and a picnic lunch. Prices vary from $34-64 per person. The Grapeline operates tours from Old Town Temecula and Destination Temecula operates tours from downtown San Diego. To reach The Grapeline, call 888-894-6379 or visit www.gogrape.com. To reach Destination Temecula, call 877-305-0501 or visit www.destem.com. These companies offer private tours as well, some in luxury limousines. Call for details.

Location:	Rancho California Road, east of I-15, Temecula
Hours:	Hours vary from 9:30am-5pm
Admission:	Free. Expect tasting fees of $2-9/Person
Phone:	800-801-9463 Winegrowers Association
Website:	www.temeculawines.org

Here is a list of several wineries along Temecula's wine trail:

Baily Vineyard & Winery Open daily 10am-5pm. Tastings: $5-10/Person. 33440 La Serena Way at Rancho California Road. 909-676-9463. www.baily.com.

Callaway Vineyard & Winery Open daily 10:30am-5pm. Closed major holidays. Tastings: $5/Person for 4 wines and a keepsake glass. 32720 Rancho California Road. 800-472-2377 or 909-676-4001. www.callawaycoastal.com.

Churon Winery Open daily 10am-5pm. Tastings: $5/Person for 6 wines and a keepsake glass. There is a large bed and breakfast onsite. 33233 Rancho California Road. 909-694-9071.

Cilurzo Vineyard & Winery Open daily 10am-5pm. Tastings: $2/Person for 8 wines. 41220 Calle Contento. 909-676-5250. www.cilurzowine.com.

Falkner Winery Open daily 10am-5pm. Tastings: $5/Person for 5 regular selections, $6/Person for 3 reserve selections, $10/Person for both the regular and reserve tastings. 40620 Calle Contento. 909-676-8231. www.falknerwinery.com.

Filsinger Vineyard & Winery Open Friday 10:30am-4:30pm, Saturday & Sunday 10am-5pm. Tastings: $2/Person for 5 wines. 39050 De Portola Road (Turn off Rancho California Road at Anza Road. Turn left at De Portola Road). 909-302-6363. www.filsingerwinery.com.

Hart Winery Open daily 9am-4:30pm. Tastings: $5/Person for 6 wines and a keepsake glass. 41300 Avenida Biona. 909-676-6300.

Keyways Vineyard & Winery Open daily 10am-5pm. Tastings: $5/Person for 7 wines and a keepsake glass. 37338 De Portola Road (Turn off Rancho California Road at Anza Road. Turn left at De Portola Road). 909-302-7888. www.keywayswinery.com.

Maurice Carrie Winery Open daily 10am-5pm. Tastings are free. 34225 Rancho California Road. 909-676-1711.

Miramonte Open daily 10am-4:45pm. Tastings: $4/Person for 4 wines and a keepsake glass. Return with the glass on future visits for free tastings. 33410 Rancho California Road. 909-506-5500. www.miramontewinery.com.

Mount Palomar Winery Open daily 10am-5pm. Tastings: $5/Person for 6 wines. 33820 Rancho California Road. 909-676-5047 or 800-854-5177. www.mountpalomar.com.

Ponte Family Estate Winery & Smokehouse Cafe Open daily 10am-5pm. Tastings: $6/Person for 6 wines and a keepsake glass. 33530 Rancho California Road. 909-694-8855.

Santa Margarita Open Saturday & Sunday 11am-4:30pm. Tastings are free. 33490 Madera de Playa. 909-676-4431.

Stuart Cellars Open daily 10am-5pm. Tastings: $8/Person for 5 wines and a keepsake glass. 33515 Rancho California Road. 909-676-6414. www.stuartcellars.com.

Thorton Winery/Culbertson Open daily 10am-5pm. Tastings: $9/Person for 3 wines or $12/Person for 3 champagnes. The tasting is served with bread and cheese and each tasting is a 1/3-filled glass. 32575 Rancho California Road. 909-699-0099. www.thortonwine.com.

Van Roekel Vineyard & Winery Open daily 10am-5pm. Tastings: $5/Person for 5 wines and a keepsake glass. 34567 Rancho California Road. 909-699-6961.

Wilson Creek Winery Open daily 10am-5pm. Tastings: $5/Person for 5 wines and a keepsake glass. 35960 Rancho California Road. 909-699-9463. www.wilsoncreekwinery.com.

HOW TO GET THERE

Exit I-15 at Rancho California Road and proceed east. The wineries line both sides of the road and some are along side streets accessed via Rancho California Road. Look for signs.

LAKE ELSINORE

Lake Elsinore is nestled in the foothills of the Ortega Mountains and home to Southern California's largest natural lake, drawing visitors for boating and beach activity. A visit to Lake Elsinore may be complemented by a hike in the mountains, a visit to historic downtown, a baseball game or some outlet shopping. The truly brave may want to make a reservation with Skydive Elsinore or visit the Motocross Park.

Hiking, nature walks and biking are enjoyed at **Santa Rosa Plateau Ecological Reserve**, which is open daily from sunrise to sunset. Call 909-677-6951 for details. Exit I-15 at Clinton Keith Road at Murrieta and proceed west four miles to the Visitor Center. Dogs are not allowed. Day use is $2 per adult and $1 per child ages two through twelve. A few miles further along Clinton Keith Road, outdoor lovers can access **San Mateo Canyon** by turning right on Tenaja Road. The 9-mile canyon offers fantastic primitive hiking trails, picnic areas and a seasonal waterfall with swimming holes. The Tenaja Creek, which drains into the ocean at San Onofre State Beach, rushes during the wet months. Popular routes are the San Mateo Trail and Bluewater Trail. Trailheads are accessed from the Tenaja Road parking area and off Cleveland Forest Road. Day use is $5 per vehicle. Call 909-736-1811 for more details.

Diamond Stadium is home to the **Lake Elsinore Storm** professional baseball team. The minor league season runs April to August and games are typically at 7pm, except on Sundays when games are played at 2pm or 6pm. The team is affiliated with the San Diego Padres. The Storm is part of the Single A Southern Division along with four other teams affiliated with the Arizona Diamondbacks, Anaheim Angels, Seattle Mariners and Milwaukee Brewers. The Single A Northern Division has five teams affiliated with the San Francisco Giants, Oakland A's, Cincinnati Reds, Colorado Rockies and Tampa Bay Devil Rays. The modern stadium seats over 6,000 fans and a grass berm accommodates another 8,000 fans. Exit I-15 at Diamond Drive/Railroad Canyon Road and proceed east to Diamond Drive and the stadium. Call 909-245-4487 or visit www.stormbaseball.com for more information. Dirt bike fans will appreciate the **Lake Elsinore Motocross Park** at 31919 Cereal Street. Call 909-496-4880 for details. **Skydive Elsinore** is a popular thrill. The company has been helping adrenaline-seekers jump since 1959 and is the longest running skydiving operation in North America. Call 909-245-9939 or visit www.skydiveelsinore.com for more information.

Downtown Elsinore hosts an open air market the first Sunday of each month and a Classic Car Show the fourth Saturday of each month along Main Street. Call 909-245-3977 for details. The **Lake Elsinore Historical Society** runs a museum at 106 S. Main Street that is open to the public on weekends. Call 909-245-4986 for more information. For bargain shopping, the **Lake Elsinore Outlets** will suffice with over 100 brand name stores. The outlets open at 10am and close at 8pm Monday through Saturday and at 7pm on Sunday. Exit I-15 at Nichols Road and follow signs to 17600 Collier Avenue. Call 866-306-7467 or visit www.lakeelsinoreoutlet.com for details.

Lake Elsinore State Recreation Area

At 3,300 acres, Lake Elsinore is the largest natural freshwater lake in Southern California. This popular lake is open year-round for boating, fishing, water skiing, wakeboarding, jet skiing, windsurfing, swimming, overnight camping, and beach use. It is common to see several hot air balloons floating above the lake affording birds eye views of the water and surrounding mountains. Boat launch fees vary, but are approximately $7.

Location:	32040 Riverside Drive, Lake Elsinore
Hours:	Daily Sunrise-Sunset
Admission:	Day Use $5/Person; Under 13-Free
Phone:	909-674-3124 (Press 6)

HOW TO GET THERE

Exit I-15 at Central Avenue/Highway 74. Turn left at Central Avenue. Turn right at Collier Avenue. Turn left at Riverside Drive.

CORONA

Just north of Lake Elsinore, the community of Corona holds a few treasures, the most luxurious of which is **Glen Ivy Hot Springs & Spa**.

Nearby, weary travelers often stop at the popular **Tom's Farms** along

 Interstate 15 to feed ducks at the pond, grab a meal, load up on road trip snacks or buy all sorts of items on sale at several specialty shops. Tom's is open daily 8am-8pm and can be reached at 909-277-9992. Exit I-15 at Temescal Canyon Road and follow signs.

Downtown's Main Street welcomed the opening of the **Fender Museum of Music and the Arts** in July 2002. The museum doubles as an educational facility with a 48-track digital recording studio, an outdoor amphitheater and classrooms. The museum also has a Visual Arts Gallery and a gift shop. Under the Kids Rock Free program, children ages 7 to 17 are offered free piano, guitar, drums and bass classes. Hundreds of children take advantage of the opportunity weekly. The museum is open Fridays 11am-4pm and Saturdays 2pm-5pm. Call 909-735-2440 for more details.

Glen Ivy Hot Springs & Spa

Set in a secluded canyon of the Santa Ana Mountains, this beautifully landscaped spa is an oasis with centuries-old natural mineral hot springs. The 5-acre resort was named one of the "24 Best Spas in America" by National Geographic Traveler Magazine.

In addition to the mineral springs, Glen Ivy boasts 17 pools and 50 treatment rooms for massages, facials, manicures, pedicures and other pampering services. The spa is reserved for guests 16 years and older, but three "Family Days" are open to all ages on Memorial Day, July 4th and Labor Day. Admission includes use of towels, a locker and all pools, saunas, steam rooms, Roman Baths, mud baths, the Vista Spa and the Salt Water Spa. Guests should bring swimsuits, sunscreen and an extra towel. Note that some treatments feature red clay that stains some fabrics.

Location:	25000 Glen Ivy Road, Corona
Hours:	Daily 9:30am-5pm.
	Open until 6pm during Daylight Savings
	Closed Jan 1, Thanksgiving & Dec 25
Admission:	Fri-Sun & Holidays-$42/Person
	Mon-Thurs-$30/Person
Phone:	888-258-2683 or 909-277-3529
Website:	www.glenivy.com

HOW TO GET THERE

Exit I-15 at Indian Truck Trail. Turn right at Indian Truck Trail. Turn left at Temescal Canyon Road. Turn left at Glen Ivy Road.

PERRIS

The main draw to Perris is the lake. However, there are a few other destinations and experiences worth noting when in the area. Each October, the **Farmer's Fair** is held at the **Lake Perris Fairgrounds**. Visit www.farmersfair.com or call 909-657-4221 for details. The fairgrounds is also home to satellite horse race wagering in the Lake Perris Sports Pavilion and a 100,000 square-foot skate park featuring a foam pit for those with bikes, inline skates, skateboards and scooters.

Perris Auto Speedway and **Perris Valley Skydiving** are popular attractions. The speedway features super stock, street stock, champ truck, dwarf and cruiser racing. Visit www.perrisautospeedway.com or call 800-976-7223 for details. Perris Valley Skydiving is open daily and offers tandem jumps at $199-239 per person and Accelerated Freefall jumps at $165-309 per person. There are discounts for repeat jumps within thirty days. Experienced certified divers can jump for $16-20 per person. The company has been in business for over 25 years and is the largest skydiving center in North America. Visit www.skydiveperris.com or call 800-832-8818 for details.

There are three museums in the area. The most widely recognized museum is the **Orange Empire Railway Museum** at 2201 South A Street open daily 9am-5pm. This museum features a large collection of various international transportation vehicles powered by steam, electric and diesel engines dating from the 1870s. The museum is free, but there are fees to ride the railway trains. Visit www.oerm.org or call 909-657-2605 or 909-943-3020 for further details. The **Ya' Heki' Regional Indian Museum**, meaning "Home of the Wind," is located at 17801 Lake Perris Drive and can be reached at 909-657-0676 and the **Dora Nelson African American Museum** is located at 316 East 7th Street and can be reached at 909-657-6032.

Lake Perris State Recreation Area

This 8,800-acre park and lake formed by Perris Dam offers endless outdoor recreation activity, even scuba diving! Yes, a section of the lake is actually reserved for divers. The vast remainder of the lake is filled with water enthusiast who swim, water ski, windsurf, sail, boat and fish from the shore and boats. Trout, catfish and bass fill the waters. There are several boat launches and boat rentals. Some recreational water craft such as wave runners may also be available. There are several green belt areas for picnics as well as miles of hiking, biking and equestrian trails circling the lake. Rock climbing is featured in an area south of the dam. There are over 400 different campsites, a well-stocked marina store with groceries and a coffee shop. Restrooms and showers make for comfortable primitive camping. Tent camping is $14 per night and hookups are $20 per night. Reservations are recommended.

Location:	17801 Lake Perris Drive, Perris
Admission:	$5/Vehicle
Hours:	Daily 6am-8pm. Open until 10pm Apr-Oct
Phone:	909-940-5600 District Office
	909-940-5603 Camping
	800-444-7275 Camping Reservations
Website:	www.cal-parks.ca.gov

HOW TO GET THERE

Exit I-15 at I-215 and proceed north to Perris. Exit I-215 at the Ramona Expressway and proceed east. Turn left at Lake Perris Drive.

HEMET

The major draw to Hemet has been **The Ramona Pageant** each spring for years, but the newly constructed **Diamond Valley Lake** is sure to attract visitors year-round. Another recreational highlight in the area is hot air ballooning with **Great American Balloon Company**. Call 909-927-2593 or 888-688-8738 for more information on ballooning in Hemet.

Hemet has several small museums, each one unique and distinct. **Hemet Museum** is located in the historic Hemet Depot and relates the area's history. Call 909-929-4409 for details. **KidZone Museum** is the local children's museum with several interactive exhibits tailored to entertain and teach youth. Call 909-765-1223 for further information. **Ryan Field Museum** features memorabilia about the 10,200 WWII pilots that were trained in the area. Call the museum at 909-658-2716 for details. The free **Patterson House Museum** is dedicated to history of the Winchester community and can be reached at 909-926-4039.

Diamond Valley Lake

The opening of Diamond Valley Lake in October 2003, marked the creation of Southern California's largest fresh water lake. The 4,500-acre lake will link to Temecula's Lake Skinner by an open space area, creating a 2,000-acre natural recreation zone for fishing, picnicking, hiking, biking and horseback riding. Because the lake is intended to provide drinking water, personal watercraft and swimming are not allowed. A Visitor's Center showcases the construction of the dam and local history with a focus on area water issues and paleontological discoveries. There is also an overlook called Clayton Record Jr. Viewpoint off Winchester and Construction Road. The overlook is open Friday through Monday 8:30am-4pm. Call before visiting as hours sometimes change due to weather and other restrictions.

Location:	300 E. Newport Road, south of Hemet
Hours:	Fri-Mon 10am-4:30pm
Admission:	$7/Vehicle; $6/Boat
Phone:	909-765-2612 or 800-211-9863

HOW TO GET THERE

Exit I-15 at Winchester Road/Highway 79 in Temecula and proceed east along Winchester Road. Turn right at Newport Road.

The Ramona Pageant

Since 1923, The Ramona Pageant has been staged by local residents to relate the dramatic true story of the area's ill-fated lovers Allesandro and Ramona. The production is based on an 1884 novel written by Helen Hunt Jackson. The story reveals the tension between the Hemet-San Jacinto area Native American Indians and the new American settlers through the story of these two lovers, one a full-blooded Indian, the other a half-blood. Each year more than 400 actors, singers, dancers and horses stage the show at the Ramona Bowl in late April and early May with brightly colored costumes and traditional Indian and Mexican music. February through May, the Ramona Bowl Museum is open.

Location:	27400 Ramona Bowl Road, Hemet
Hours:	Show times vary
	Box Office: Mon-Fri 9:30am-4:30pm
Admission:	General-$20-25; Seniors(62+)-$18-25;
	Youth(Under 12)-$18-25
Phone:	800-645-4465 or 909-658-3111
Website:	www.ramonapageant.com

HOW TO GET THERE

Exit I-15 at Winchester Road in Temecula and proceed east along Winchester Road to its end at Florida Avenue in Hemet. Turn right at Girard Street. Turn right at Ramona Bowl Road.

IDYLLWILD

This beautiful town, nestled among endless acres of aromatic pines at 5,200 feet above sea level, coins itself a "small alpine village, big art town". Well put. The outdoor inclined community embraces its artisans and their many galleries. Most local events and shows are either sporting activities or artistic festivals. The friendly laid back mountain town is a perfect place to camp, rent a cabin or stay at a bed and breakfast to escape urban life in exchange for simpler ways. There are several lodging options. Town center runs along North Circle Drive which is lined with numerous individually owned and operated specialty shops, antique stores and restaurants. One could window shop for hours. The trademark totem pole in the center of town is the chain saw creation of Jonathan A. Benne, who transformed the 300-year-old, 65-foot ponderosa pine into a piece of art when the road department condemned the tree.

Nature-lovers will cherish Idyllwild's hiking, biking and equestrian trails. The **Idyllwild Visitor's Center** just north of town, on Route 243, can provide trail information and camping details. Call the information center at 909-659-3850. Trout fishermen and picnickers should head to **Lake Fulmor** northwest of town or **Lake Hemet** southeast of town. The lakes are twenty minutes in either direction. Fishin' Eddies' at 54445 N. Circle Drive can provide the inside scoop on area fishing or discuss poles, tackle, bait, permits and lessons. Call them at 909-659-6233. Experienced rock climbers will appreciate **Suicide Rock** and **Tahquitz Rock** a.k.a. Lily Rock. Nomad Ventures at 54415 N. Circle Drive can "talk rock" and offers lessons. Call them at 909-659-4853.

Riverside County

Jazz in the Pines is a wildly popular two day event held each August. Visit www.idyllwildjazz.com or call 909-659-3774 for details. The Art Alliance of Idyllwild and the renowned Idyllwild Arts Academy host dozens of events year-round. A show is likely the first Saturday of each month March through December. The annual Art Walk and Wine Tasting is one of the most worthwhile events. Messiah by the Master Chorale is another annual music event as is a summer concerts series. Visit www.artinidyllwild.com and www.artsacademy.org for current offerings.

To reach Idyllwild, exit I-15 in Temecula at Winchester Road/Highway 79 South and proceed to Highway 371. Take 371 northbound to connect to Highway 74.

Hay Dude Ranch

This full service horseback riding operation offers guided trail rides and pack trips. They also operate the horse drawn trolley that occasionally runs through downtown Idyllwild. Their horses are moved among three area locales based on the season. During the summer, the horses are just five miles below Idyllwild in Mountain Center. Guides take riders through the tall pines of the San Jacinto Mountains with vista and meadow openings. Pony rides are offered for children younger than seven years at $10 per child. Reservations are accepted during the week and group discounts are available.

Location:	Highway 74 at the 58 Mile Marker/McCall Park, Mountain Center
Hours:	Summer: Daily 9am-5pm
Admission:	Half-Hour Rides-$20/Person
	Hour Rides-$30/Person
Phone:	909-763-2473 or 909-659-0383
Website:	www.hayduderanch.com

HOW TO GET THERE

Exit I-15 at Winchester Road/Highway 79 South and proceed to Highway 371. Proceed north on Highway 371 and connect to Highway 74. Take Highway 74 to the 58 Mile Marker and turn left into McCall Park. Follow "Horse Camping Only"/Hay Dude Ranch signs.

Idyllwild Area Lakes

Two area lakes offer mostly trout fishing, although there are some largemouth bass and catfish.

Lake Fulmor is relatively small at two surface acres, but perfect for picnics with tables, barbecues and restrooms. The lake features a fully accessible wooden fishing pier. Float tubes and kayaks are permitted. Swimming is allowed, but not recommended.

Location:	Highway 243, north of Idyllwild
Hours:	Daily 6am-10pm
Admission:	$5/Vehicle
Phone:	909-659-2117

HOW TO GET THERE
Exit I-15 at Winchester Road/Highway 79 and proceed east through Hemet to Highway 371. Take Highway 371 and proceed north to Highway 74. Turn left at Highway 74 and proceed to Highway 243. Proceed north on Highway 243 through Idyllwild. The lake is on the east side on Highway 243.

Lake Hemet is a privately owned lake open year-round for kayaking, boating, fishing and camping. Swimming is not allowed. Shore fishing is limited. There is a boat launch ramp and a store that carries permits, tackle and supplies. The boat launch fee is $4. Boats rentals run $15-40 and campsites are $15-$19 per night.

Location:	56570 Highway 74, south of Idyllwild
Hours:	April-Sept: Daily 6am-10pm,
	Oct-Mar: Daily 7am-8pm
Admission:	$8/Person
Phone:	909-659-2680 Campground

HOW TO GET THERE
Exit I-15 at Winchester Road/Highway 79 and proceed east through Hemet to Highway 371. Take Highway 371 and proceed north to Highway 74. Turn left at Highway 74 and continue 9 miles to the lake.

RIVERSIDE

Riverside is a Southern California-style university town loaded with historical landmarks and interesting architecture, most notably the **Mission Inn**. To get in the spirit of Riverside's architecture and ambiance, bike or stroll along the seven mile tree-lined **Victoria Avenue** where the landscaping of palms, eucalyptus trees and romantic rose bushes have been the same since 1892. **Buena Vista Drive & Park** is another favorite pedestrian path with its 1931 granite bridge. Climb to the top of **Mount Rubidoux** for an overview of the city and to watch vintage planes take off and land at Flabob Airport. Mount Rubidoux is a popular recreation site for mountain bikers, rock climbers, hikers, picnickers and dogs. The Father Serra Cross and World Peace Tower decorate the 1,300-foot summit, which can be accessed via a pedestrian road that twists and turns from its entrance at 9th Street and Mount Rubidoux Drive. Call 909-683-3436 for further information regarding the mount.

Each fall and spring, Riverside Film Festival showcases art films from around the world. A series of ten films is shown every other Thursday at the historic 1929 **Fox Theater**, which was the first theater to screen *Gone With The Wind* in 1939. Fox Theater is at 3801 Mission Inn Avenue. Food and entertainment abound during the annual Riverside Orange Blossom Festival each April. On Magnolia Avenue at Arlington Avenue, pause to marvel at the **Parent Navel Orange Tree**, one of two navel orange trees sent to Washington D.C. around 1875 from Brazil. From these parent trees, the navel orange flourished as a preferred table variety world-wide. The parent tree still bears fruit today.

The **Riverside Art Museum** at 3425 Mission Inn Avenue mounts more than a dozen major exhibitions each year in three different galleries. Call 909-684-7111 or visit www.riversideartmuseum.com for details. The **University of California at Riverside** operates an impressive 39-acre **Botanical Gardens** and a downtown **Museum of Photography**. Contact the gardens at 909-787-4650 and the photography museum at 909-787-4787. Other places of interest in the area include **March Field Air Museum** with an extensive military aircraft display off Interstate 215 at Van Buren Boulevard. Call 909-697-6600 for further information. Historic **Jensen-Alvarado Ranch**, located at 4350 Briggs Street, features animals and a rural atmosphere of groves, orchards and vineyards. Call 909-369-6055 for details. **Jurupa Mountain Cultural Center** is an earth science museum open Tuesday through Saturday at 7621 Granite Hill Drive. Call 909-685-5818 for hours and further information.

Mission Inn & Downtown Architecture

A mix of various Victorian-era and Spanish-style architecture make for a city with its own unique ambiance. The Chamber of Commerce at 4261 Main Street provides free historic sites maps. The Chamber can be reached at 909-683-7100.

Mission Inn is among the most famous and most impressive of the city's architecturally stunning buildings. The inn covers an entire city block and has a fascinating history. Mission Inn Foundation docents lead 75-minute tours at four times on weekdays and every half hour on weekends beginning at the Mission Inn Museum. During the Festival of Lights, the grounds are illuminated with over a million lights. The festival runs from Thanksgiving through the New Year.

The Riverside Main Street Mall borders the hotel between 6th and 10th Street with boutique shopping, antique stores and casual dining along a tree-lined pedestrian walkway.

Location:	3649 Mission Inn Avenue at Main Street, Riverside
Hours:	Museum Daily 9:30am-4pm
	Hotel Daily 24 Hours
Admission:	Free
Phone:	909-781-8241 Mission Inn Museum
	909-784-0300 Mission Inn Hotel
Website:	www.missioninn.com

Other places of architectural interest near Mission Inn:

One block east of Mission Inn, the 1920s Moorish-Mission Revival architecture at **Riverside Municipal Auditorium** is complemented by a sunken garden and cloistered walk. A wide variety of concerts and events are hosted in this 1928 building at 3485 Mission Inn Avenue.

Two churches along Mission Inn Avenue represent different architectural styles. **First Congregational Church** at 3504 Mission Inn Avenue reflects Spanish Renaissance Revival architecture. The church was completed in 1913, however the carillon was not added to the bell tower until 1989. The 1891 **Universalist-Unitarian Church** at 3525 Mission Inn Avenue is built in Gothic Revival style reminiscent of medieval England complete with detailed stained glass windows.

Built in 1904, the **Riverside County Courthouse** at 3050 Main Street replicates the facade of the 1900 Paris Exposition's Grand Palace of Fine Arts in beau arts style.

Benedict Castle at 5445 Chicago Avenue was built in two stages between 1922 and 1931 in Spanish-Moorish architecture.

Heritage House at 8193 Magnolia Avenue is an 1892 Queen Anne-style Victorian home. Visitors are welcome inside when the restored house is open. Call 909-689-1333 for tour information.

HOW TO GET THERE
Exit I-15 at Highway 215 and proceed north to Riverside. Take the 91 Freeway (towards Beaches) and exit at Mission Inn Avenue. Turn right and the inn will be on the right side after Orange Street.

Riverside County
8 - 23ment>

Downtown Riverside

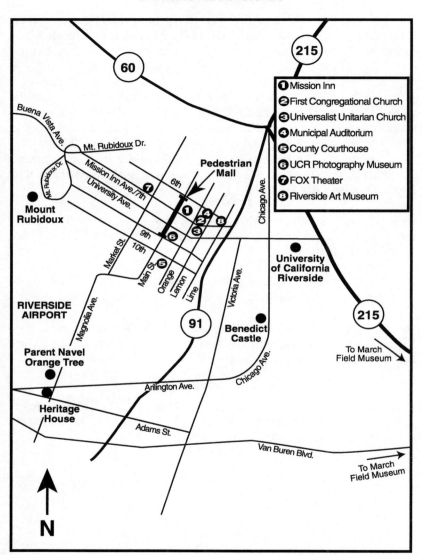

Orange County

- **Anaheim**
- **Buena Park**
- **Coastal Orange County**
- **Irvine**
- **San Juan Capistrano**

ORANGE COUNTY

Orange County

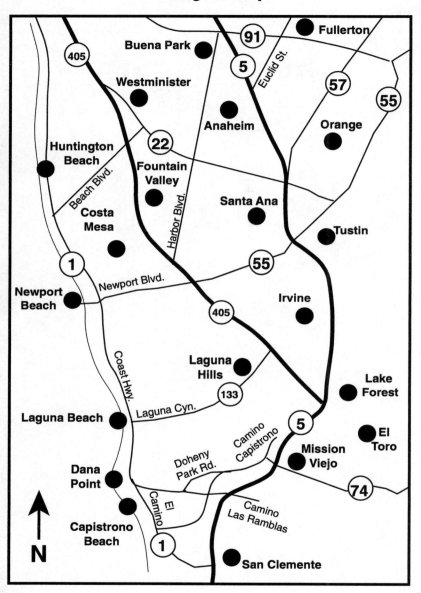

ORANGE COUNTY

While best known for its major theme parks, Orange County has several worthwhile museums among its many cities, the "jewel of the California missions" and miles of beautiful beach towns that line the historic Pacific Coast Highway (PCH). Anaheim, Buena Park and Irvine boast the theme parks that attract thousands each year. At the coastal town of San Clemente, there is access to the historic Highway 1 for a beautiful scenic route north through the cities of Dana Point, Laguna Beach, Newport Beach and Huntington Beach with several charming, sleepy beach towns in between.

ANAHEIM

Disneyland Resort is *the* attraction in Anaheim.

Before Disneyland, Anaheim was an agricultural town. For an interesting history lesson about the county's transition from grape vineyards to orange groves to theme parks, visit **Anaheim Museum** at 241 S. Anaheim Boulevard. Most impressive are the vintage photographs on display in this 1908 historic building. Call 714-778-3301 for details.

Beyond Disneyland, two smaller themed destinations attract visitors. **Hobby City Doll & Toy Museum** at 1238 S. Beach Boulevard features over 4,000 thousand domestic and foreign dolls including more than 500 Barbies housed in a half scale model of the White House. An assortment of toys, teddy bears and toy soldiers round out the collection. The museum is open daily 10am-6pm but closed major holidays. Call 714-527-2323 for details. Adjacent to the doll and toy museum, **Adventure City** is a 10-acre kid-focused "little city" with nine rides, including a roller coaster and carousel, an arcade with prizes, face painting, live shows and a petting zoo. The theme park is generally open 10am–9pm daily. Visit www.adventurecity.com or call 714-236-9300 to confirm hours before visiting. To reach the Hobby City Complex, exit I-5 at Beach Boulevard and proceed west.

Disneyland, Disney California Adventure & Downtown Disney

California's Disney experience includes two theme parks, a shopping and entertainment district called Downtown Disney and three Disney hotels. The entrances to the two theme-parks, Disneyland and Disney California Adventure, are directly across from each other. The two parks are connected by the Esplanade, where visitors can purchase tickets to both parks and catch trams to and from the parking lots.

Southern California residents can buy a special Annual Passport good at both theme parks on 205 pre-selected days of the year for $105 per person. The Annual Passport also provides discounts and benefits at restaurants, hotels and more. Other annual passes cost between $165 and $225 per person.

Both parks offer a fantastic free service called FASTPASS for the most popular attractions. At the attraction present your park ticket to get a FASTPASS, which will list a time for you to return to the attraction and board without waiting in line. In addition to the rides and attractions, the parks offer shopping, dining and free entertainment.

Disneyland & Disney California Adventure

Disneyland, the original theme-park coined "the happiest place on earth", is the classic enchanted kingdom experience full of fantasy and imagination. Disneyland encompasses eight themed lands: Main Street USA, Tomorrowland, Frontierland, Fantasyland, Adventureland, Critter Country, New Orleans Square and Toon Town.

The most popular attractions, which feature FASTPASS, are Autopia, Big Thunder Mountain Railroad, Haunted Mansion, Indiana Jones Adventure, Pirates of the Caribbean, Space Mountain, Splash Mountain, Star Tours, Roger Rabbit's Car Toon Spin and The Many Adventures of Winnie the Pooh.

There is a monorail that travels around the Disneyland park, starting and ending at the Disneyland Hotel.

Disney California Adventure, a whimsical action-packed park, pays tribute to the state's incredibly diverse culture with four unique areas of discovery: Sunshine Plaza, Golden State, Paradise Pier and Hollywood Pictures Backlot. This newer theme-park also features the classic and timeless Electric Parade, which was a Disneyland mainstay for decades. The parade features half a million colored light bulbs which work in synch with a memorable soundtrack and showcases favorite Disney characters along with fireworks.

The most popular attractions, which feature FASTPASS, are California Screamin', Grizzly River Run, It's Tough to Be a Bug! based on the hit movie A Bug's Life, Mulholland Madness, Jim Henson's Muppet Vision 3D, Soarin' Over California and Who Wants To Be a Millionaire.

Location:	1313 S. Harbor Boulevard, Anaheim
Hours:	Daily 8am-12am
	Call ahead. Hours vary by season
Admission:	Single Day Ticket Good at 1 Park:
	General-$47; Youth(3-9)-$37; Under 3-Free
	Call for multi-day and multi-park ticket prices, special offers and vacation packages
Phone:	714-781-4400 Tickets
	714-781-4565 Recorded Info
	714-956-6425 Disneyland Hotels
Website:	www.disney.com

Downtown Disney

This free shopping, dining and entertainment district allows visitors to experience Disney without the need to purchase a theme-park ticket. The monorail carries visitors between the parks and Downtown Disney, which is a popular nightlife spot that caters to singles, couples and families.

Live music, dancing and shows abound. Two popular music venues are House of Blues and Jazz Kitchen. With 175 TV screens, ESPN Zone is a popular gathering place to watch big sports games, as well as to dine and participate in interactive games. A movie theater plays several current feature films.

Location:	1500 block, S. Disneyland Drive, Anaheim
Hours:	Daily. Call ahead. Hours vary by season
Admission:	Free. Parking: 3 Hours Free; $6/Additional Hour
Phone:	714-781-7290 Guest Relations
	714-781-3463 Dining Reservations
	714-778-2583 House of Blues Tickets
Website:	www.disney.com

HOW TO GET THERE
Exit I-5 at Katella Avenue or Harbour Boulevard and follow directional signs to the area of the Disney Resort you plan to visit.

BUENA PARK

Buena Park's Beach Boulevard and its surrounding area are called the "E-Zone", meaning Entertainment Zone as it is filled with major tourist attractions. Knott's parks are the most famous of these attractions but two dinner theater shows and two entertainment museums draw thousands as well.

The two long-running, incredibly popular dinner theater shows are Medieval Times and Wild Bill's. **Medieval Times** at 7662 Beach Boulevard is a reenactment of an eleventh century banquet and tournament complete with magic and pageantry set in a castle. Decorated knights on horseback compete in dramatic jousting matches as guests feast with their hands on a four-course meal. Castle highlights include the Hall of Banners and Flags, Museum of Torture and Knight Club filled with authentic armor. Shows run Monday-Thursday at 7pm, Friday at 6:30pm and 8:45pm, Saturday at 6pm and 8:15pm and Sunday at 5pm and 7:15pm. The cost is $34.95 per person. Children 12 and younger are $22.95. Seniors and military get a 10% discount. Reservations are required. Visit www.medievaltimes.com or call 714-521-4740 or 800-899-6600 for further details. **Wild Bill's Western Dinner Extravaganza** at 7600 Beach Boulevard provides a two hour Americana experience that includes a generous four-course meal. Entertaining staged numbers of daring skill and performance are accompanied by western music and singing, sparkling costumes and audience participation. Shows run Sunday-Thursday at 7pm, Friday at 7:30pm and Saturday at 5pm and 8pm. The cost is $41.95 per person. Children ages 3 through 11 are $26.95. Seniors get a $4 discount. Reservations are recommended. Call 714-522-6414 or 800-883-1546 for further details. To reach either attraction, exit the 91 Freeway at Beach Boulevard and turn left.

Movieland Wax Museum at 7711 Beach Boulevard and **Ripley's Believe It or Not! Museum** at 7850 Beach Boulevard are neighboring attractions. Visitors to both museums save $5 by purchasing a combination ticket. Movieland Wax Museum reproduces movie sets complete with sound effects, animation, Kleig lights and clap boards utilizing an extensive collection of authentic costumes and props often donated by the stars and studios themselves. Special effects and illusions are glorified in the Chamber of Horrors scary films gallery. Movie and television memorabilia abound, including autographs, hand and footprints of Hollywood greats. Lifelike wax replicas of famous people make for great photo opportunities. Visit www.movielandwaxmuseum.com or call 714-522-1154 for more information. Inspired by Robert Ripley's personal collection, Ripley's Museum exhibits worldly oddities ranging from the humorous to the downright bizarre. Visit www.ripleys.com or call 714-522-7045 for more details.

Knott's Berry Farm & Knott's Soak City U.S.A.

Knott's Berry Farm has an old west charm to it, covering 160 acres with six different themed areas filled with more than 160 rides, attractions and shows.

The areas are Ghost Town, The Boardwalk, Camp Snoopy, Fiesta Village, Wild Water Wilderness and Indian Trails. Supreme Scream, Boomerang, Montezuma's Revenge and the wooden rollercoaster GhostRider are favorite thrillers. Knott's is famous for its chicken dinners, berry deserts and preserves. The original 1920 Knott's Chicken Dinner Restaurant still stands. Special events and concerts are held throughout the year.

Knott's Soak City U.S.A. is a separate 13-acre water park next door to the theme park with 21 rides, including slides, wave pools and a calm river. The park is reminiscent of 1950s coastal California. The water park is open daily Memorial Day through Labor Day and weekends in May and September.

Location:	8039 Beach Boulevard, Buena Park
Hours:	Daily 9am-12am
	Call ahead. Hours vary by season
Admission:	Theme Park: General-$42; Seniors(60+)-$32;
	Youth(3-11)-$32; Under 3-Free
	$10 Discount for Southern California residents
	Discount prices after 4pm
	Water Park: General-$22.95; Youth(3-11)-$15.95;
	Under 3-Free
	Discount prices after 3pm
	Parking: $8/Car; $12/RV
Phone:	714-220-5200 Recorded Information
	800-742-6427
Website:	www.knotts.com

HOW TO GET THERE

Take I-5 to the 91 Freeway. Exit Freeway 91 at Beach Boulevard. Turn left and proceed straight to the parking lot.

Anaheim & Buena Park

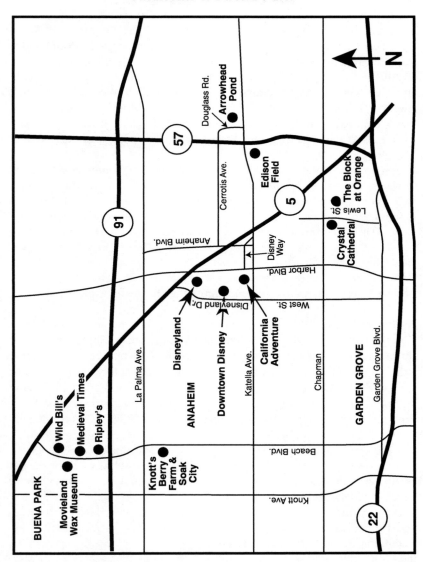

COASTAL ORANGE COUNTY- PCH

A drive north along Highway 1, known as **Pacific Coast Highway (PCH)**, is a Southern California coastal treasure. En route along Interstate 5, **San Onofre State Beach** boasts 3,000 cliff-side acres that overlook the Pacific. Overnight camping is offered and daytime use includes surfing and fishing opportunities. At **San Clemente**, one can wind through town to catch Highway 1 or continue along I-5 for a more direct turnoff near Dana Point. San Clemente's sandy beach is graced with sunbathers, swimmers, surfers and an active pier. **San Clemente State Beach** south of town offers camping.

Sixty-two acre **Doheny State Beach** and picturesque **Dana Point** are the southern stops along Orange County's PCH, accommodating sailing, swimming, cycling and other outdoor activities as well as boutique-style shopping and dining. There are several restaurants, some with outstanding views. The bluff-top Chart House is a favorite at 34442 Green Lantern. Call 949-493-1183 for reservations. Doheny Beach offers camping with beach-level sites, showers, barbecues and tables at 25300 Dana Point Harbor Drive. Call 949-496-6171 for details. At the underwater **Doheny State Marine Life Refuge**, a 400-gallon tide pool tank offers hands-on exploration.

A promenade hugs the Dana Point harbor, which is home to the **Orange County Marine Institute** at 24200 Dana Point Harbor. This free nonprofit educational center is open to the public 10am-4:30pm on weekends. Marine artifacts, the Whale Room and a hands-on touch tank of local tide specimens are highlights. Unique cruises including the Killer Dana Harbor Cruise, the Marine Wildlife Cruise, the Catalina Island Snorkeling Cruise and the Night Bioluminescence Cruise also draw interest. Call 949-496-2274 for details.

Outside the Institute, visitors can experience a real tide pool and tour the Pilgrim on Sundays 10am-2:30pm. **The Pilgrim**, which is used for special excursions and as a classroom, is a replica of Richard Henry Dana's boat, which would maneuver the tricky point to pick up precious hides from the nearby mission and ranches. According to his "Two Years Before the Mast", recollecting a time around 1834, long boats could only approach at high tide. Strong men called droughers heaved doubled-over hides down to sailors 400 feet below. Set-

tlers impressed with the tale named the city after Dana and today a giant bronze sculpture of a drougher overlooks the harbor.

Further North, charming **Laguna Beach** offers quality swimming beaches and coves popular for tide pool exploration. North Laguna is good for snorkeling and diving. Whale watching is a seasonal draw. Year-round this quaint town attracts visitors to its lovely promenades, numerous restaurants and, of course, its art scene. In 1917, the community established an artist colony giving birth to California Impressionism. Art lovers appreciate **Gallery Row**, **Laguna Art Museum** and North Laguna's **Heritage Homes and Cottages**. The first Thursday of each month an evening gallery art walk is held. During July and August, the **Sawdust Art Festival** at 935 Laguna

Canyon Road features nearly 200 artists and craftsmen with entertainment and workshops a mile from the ocean in Laguna Canyon. For further details, call 949-494-3030 or visit www.sawdustartfestival.org. Coinciding with this event is the annual **Festival of Arts-Pageant of the Masters** at 650 Laguna Canyon Road in the Irvine Bowl Park. Festival exhibits are open daily 10am-11:30pm and the world-famous pageant is staged nightly. At 8:30pm in a tree-lined amphitheater, live models recreate famous paintings, sculptures artifacts and artworks. Live narration and a full pit orchestra enhance the spectacular visual production which is widely accepted as the finest presentation of living pictures, *tableaux vivants*, anywhere. The theater has 232 seats and tickets cost $10-$50 per person. Festival tickets cost $5. Students and seniors receive a $2 discount. Call 800-487-3378 or 949-464-4282 or visit www.foapom.org for further details. The Laguna Beach Visitors Bureau can be reached at 800-877-1115.

Continuing north, the seaside village of **Corona Del Mar** has a Lookout Point that provides gorgeous views of the ocean and harbor. **Sherman Library & Garden** at

2647 E. Coast Highway is a two-acre treasure where lunch can be enjoyed at
Café Jardin. Call 949-673-2261 or visit www.slgardens.org for details. Head
towards the water on Marguerite Avenue to access **Big Corona Beach** and
Little Corona Beach for swimming, volleyball, snorkeling, tide pools and
beach fire rings.

North of Corona Del Mar, along the southern **Newport Beach** waterfront, is
the peninsula **Balboa Village**. The beautiful Balboa pier and boardwalk are
launch pads for shopping, dining, harbor cruises, boating and beach-going. A
beach path suitable for biking and rollerblading connects the **Balboa Pier**
with the Newport Pier. At the **Newport Pier**, the Dory Fishing Fleet is one of
the last beach-side fishing co-ops of its kind in the country with a sunrise
open air fish market. The **Balboa Ferry** provides a short ride across the
Newport Bay connecting **Balboa Island** with Newport Beach and Balboa
Village. A visit to Balboa Island is best enjoyed along Marine Avenue. Where
the peninsula and mainland meet, a cobblestone pedestrian zone coined **Lido
Village** offers boutiques and cafes.

Balboa Pavilion, as well as Mariner's Mile further north along PCH,
provide access to harbor cruises, whale watching tours, Catalina Island trips
and private charters. Every half hour from 11am-7pm, the **Fun Zone Boat
Company** operates 45-, 60- and 90-minute cruises for $6-$8 per person and
only $1 per child. Call 949-673-0240 for details. There are endless water-
recreation opportunities such as parasailing, water biking, boating and
personal watercraft use along the bay.

The **Upper Newport Bay Ecological Reserve** is Southern California's
largest saltwater marsh ecosystem and estuary of its kind. Kayaking the
reserve is popular. Newport Dunes Resort at 1131 Back Bay Drive offers a
2-hour guided kayak tour Sundays at 10am for $20 per person. Call 800-
585-0747 or 949-729-1150 for details. Ten miles of hiking and biking trails
wind through the reserve. Just inland from the reserve is Newport Center.
The **Orange County Museum of Art**, which is located in Newport Center,
is dedicated to presenting the works of 20th century California artists. Call
the museum at 949-759-1122 for further details.

At the north end of Orange County's PCH coastline, **Huntington Beach** is
"Surf City U.S.A." with a promenade featuring a **Surfers Walk of Fame** and
an **International Surf Museum** at 411 Olive Street. Call 714-960-3483 for
museum details. Main Street becomes the lively **Huntington Beach Pier**
featuring a 1950s-style diner at its end. **Huntington City Beach**,
Huntington State Beach and **Bolsa Chica State Beach** provide surfing,

swimming and fire rings for visitors. **Bolsa Chica State Ecological Reserve** is a bird-inhabited salt-marsh with a 1.5-mile loop trail. Inland, **Huntington Central Park** at Talbert Avenue and Golden West Street draws visitors with two lakes, an 18-hole Frisbee golf course, a nature center, the central library and an equestrian center.

Coastal Orange County

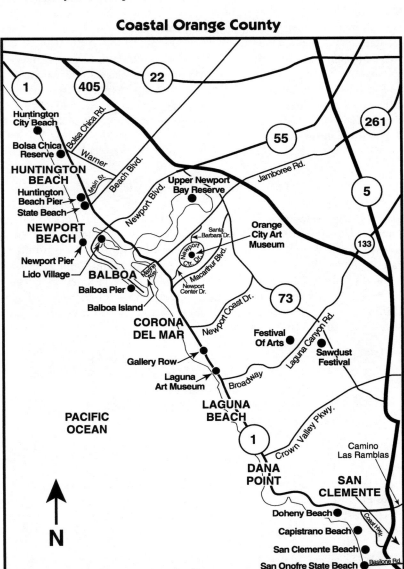

IRVINE

Irvine is most widely known for the **University of California at Irvine** and Wild Rivers Water Park, but the city has some lesser known attractions. **Irvine Museum** houses a collection of 1880-1930 California Impressionism at 18881 Von Karman Avenue. Call 949-476-0294 for details. The **Irvine Fine Arts Center** showcases contemporary art exhibitions at 14321 Yale Avenue. Call 949-724-6880 for more information. **UCI Arboretum** houses exotic and endangered flora near the corner of Jamboree Road and Campus Drive. Call 949-824-5833 for further details. **Flightline Flight Simulation Center** is a military jet simulation center open to the general public at 17831 Sky Park Circle. Call 949-253-9538 or visit www.fightertown.com for details. **Irvine Spectrum Center** is an entertainment complex featuring an IMAX theater as well as trendy restaurants and shops. Call 949-789-0014 for details.

Wild Rivers Water Park

This 200-acre water park is divided into three areas: Wild Rivers Mountain, Thunder Cove and Explorer's Island. Each area is distinct in the style of rides and pools it features. Wild Rivers Mountain is best-suited for daredevils desiring rushing water and steep drops while Thunder Cove is tailored to surfers and swimmers seeking wave pools. Explorer's Island is for relaxation-seekers with wade pools, lazy inner tube floats and spas. Dozens of rides and attractions are included in the price of admission. Food, beverages and lockers are available.

Location:	8770 Irvine Center Drive, Irvine
Admission:	Over 47"-$26/Person; Under 48"-$18/Person; Under 3-Free
Hours:	May-September: Daily 10am-8pm
Phone:	949-788-0808
Website:	www.wildrivers.com

HOW TO GET THERE

Exit I-405 at Irvine Center Drive and proceed south to the park. Exit I-5 at Bake Parkway and proceed west to Irvine Center Drive. Proceed north one block.

SAN JUAN CAPISTRANO

Two dozen charming historic buildings and sites comprise a downtown architectural walking tour of San Juan Capistrano. A map brochure is available at city hall and in dispensers mounted on downtown directional signs. Call the city at 949-493-1171 for further details. **Los Rios Historic District**, near the **Capistrano Depot**, contains dozens of adobe homes built as early as 1794. Within the district, Ramos House Café is famous county-wide for its breakfasts. The 1870s **O'Neill Museum** at 31831 Los Rios Street and **Jones Family Mini Farm** at 31791 Los Rios Street are favorite highlights. Call the museum at 949-493-8444 and the farm at 949-831-6550.

Mission San Juan Capistrano

The 10-acre mission site is a beautiful respite with gardens, fountains and walkways. The mission chapel, California's oldest building, is still in use. The impressive chapel altar, which came from Spain, is made of cherry wood and decorated with carved gold-leaf angels. Only ruins of the mission's three original 1776 churches remain. Within the walls of the ruins are mud nests left by the now-famous swallows that until recently would arrive annually around March 19th and depart around October 25th. The coming and going of the swallows, which flew about 6,000 miles from Argentina annually to rear their offspring, was recorded each year since 1777. The mission hosts a Swallows Day Festival, *Fiesta de las Golondrinas*, each March in remembrance.

Location:	Interstate 5 at Highway 74, San Juan Capistrano
Admission:	General-$6; Senior(54+)-$5; Youth(3-11)-$4
Hours:	Daily 8:30am-5pm
	Closed Good Friday, Thanksgiving & Dec 25
Phone:	949-234-1300
Website:	www.missionsjc.com

HOW TO GET THERE

Exit I-5 at Highway 74 (the Ortega Freeway) and proceed west two blocks to the mission.

Inland Orange County

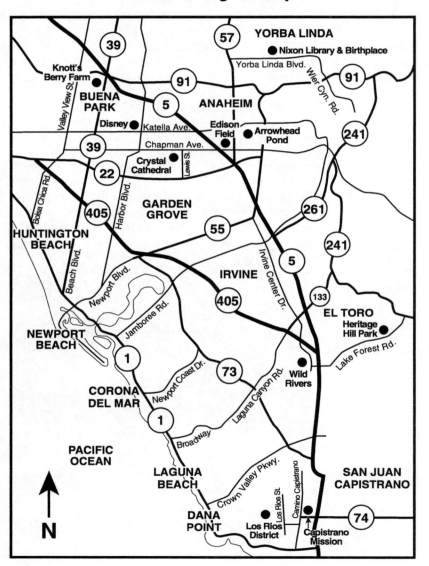

Los Angeles County

- **Central L.A. & Downtown**
- **Beverly Hills & Hollywood**
- **Griffith Park**
- **West L.A.**
- **Burbank & Universal City**
- **Pasadena**
- **San Fernando Valley**
- **Coastal L.A.**
- **Long Beach & South Bay**
- **Catalina Island**

LOS ANGELES COUNTY

Los Angeles County

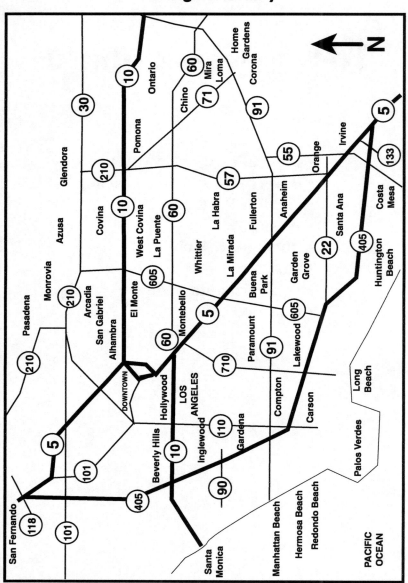

LOS ANGELES COUNTY

Hollywood may have made Los Angeles famous worldwide, but it is the city's diversity that gives it staying power. Los Angeles is a place of many cultures where businessmen and beach bums are equally regarded. It is a place where movie stars are born and where trends are set. It is a place with a character unmistakably its own. It is "L.A."

L.A. is the largest Mexican city outside of Mexico, the largest Korean city outside of Korea, and one of the largest Chinese cities outside of China. In downtown Los Angeles one can explore many ethnicities and cultures in China Town, Little Tokyo and El Pueblo de Los Angeles Historic District.

To explore the beach cultures of Los Angeles, look no further than Venice Beach, Santa Monica and Malibu. In Venice Beach, Ocean Front Walk is a people-watcher's paradise. Bronzed bodybuilders in muscle shirts compete for your attention with bikini-clad Rollerbladers and politically-charged orators. Santa Monica's Third Street Promenade pedestrian mall is a bit more tame. This is where the local beach-goers meet up to grab a meal and shop. A few steps west and you are graced by the charming 1906 Santa Monica Pier with its ferris wheel and carnival attractions. A walk along Santa Monica's palm-lined Palisades Park offers beautiful ocean views. A drive north along Highway 101 will lead to beautiful Malibu, where visitors can spot surfers and sand volleyball games or catch glimpses of beach-front mansions.

For movie star glitz and glamour, there are a few choices for visitors, but Hollywood and Beverly Hills remain the mainstays. Hollywood can be disappointing for visitors expecting celebrity studded sidewalks. Nevertheless, the pink marble stars decorating the Hollywood Walk of Fame coupled with a visit to the footprinted Mann's Chinese Theatre courtyard is entertaining. A drive along Sunset Boulevard also evokes the larger than life spirit of Hollywood. A more eclectic choice is Melrose Avenue with its bohemian-style shops, tatoo parlors and fashion statements. Hollywood diehards should opt for a studio tour. One is more likely to truly spot a famous name in Beverly Hills than Hollywood. Along three upscale blocks of Rodeo Drive one can shop like the stars at Tiffany, Versace, Gucci and other fine boutiques.

Despite its reputation for smog and horrific traffic, which do in fact both exist, there are beautiful places to escape the congestion within city limits. Griffith Park is well worth a visit, providing trees and greenbelts, good hiking and great views of Los Angeles and that famous Hollywood sign.

CENTRAL L.A. & DOWNTOWN

The diversity of Los Angeles is highlighted downtown with China Town, Little Tokyo and Olvera Street within blocks of each other celebrating the Chinese-, Japanese- and Mexican-American cultures. Other draws to downtown include Exposition Park (especially when the L.A. Lakers are playing basketball), the Los Angeles Music Center and several museums.

China Town is at the 900 block of N. Broadway and **Little Tokyo** fills several blocks bordered by East 1st Street, Alameda Street, East 3rd Street and Los Angeles Street. The **Japanese American National Museum** is housed in a restored Buddhist Temple at 369 East 1st Street. Other popular downtown museums include the **Museum of Contemporary Art** at 250 S. Grand Avenue, its sister museum **Geffen Contemporary at MOCA** at 152 N. Central Avenue and the **Children's Museum** at 310 N. Main Street. **Exposition Park** is home to the **California African American Museum** at 600 State Drive, the **California Science Center** at 700 State Drive and the **Natural History Museum** at 900 Exposition Boulevard. Other draws to Exposition Park are the IMAX Theater, **Memorial Coliseum**, and the **Staples Center Sports Arena**. The park's seven-acre rose garden with nearly 200 varieties smells marvelous when in bloom. **University of Southern California** is just north of the park.

Olvera Street lies within **El Pueblo de Los Angeles Historic District**. The district's 27 historic buildings relate the origin of Los Angeles beginning in 1781. A Visitor Center at the 1887 Sepulveda House on Olvera Street provides walking tour brochures. Across from Olvera Street is one of America's finest train depots, **Los Angeles Union Station** at 800 N. Alameda Street. Among tall palm trees, the romantic 1939 building has mosaic marble floors, wood-beamed ceilings and mission-style archways. Trains depart often for San Diego and Santa Barbara and places in between.

Olvera Street

Merchants haggle with buyers over Mexican clothing, authentic wares, silver jewelry and miscellaneous treasures at this festive open air market-place. Restaurants with homemade tortillas and traditional dishes are among the shops and stalls that line both sides of the street. On many weekends and holidays, especially Cinco de Mayo, mariachi bands and traditional dancers provide street entertainment.

Location:	Area within North Alameda Street, Arcadia Street, North Spring Street and Chavez Avenue
Admission:	Free
Hours:	Park: Daily 10am-7pm
	Visitor's Center: Daily 10am-3pm
Phone:	213-628-1274
Website:	www.olvera-street.com

HOW TO GET THERE

Exit I-5 at the 101 Freeway and proceed north on Freeway 101. Exit Freeway 101 at Aliso Street and proceed straight on Arcadia Street to Main Street. Turn right at Main Street for parking.

Downtown Los Angeles

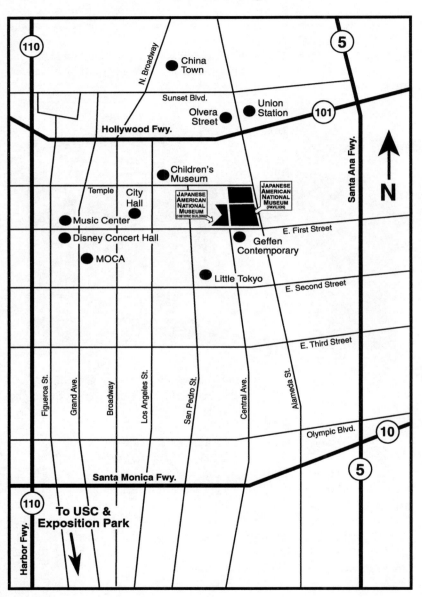

BEVERLY HILLS & HOLLYWOOD

Los Angeles is well known for its famous Beverly Hills zip code and, of course, for Hollywood.

Beverly Hills' **Rodeo Drive** and the "Golden Triangle" area, which is bound by Cresent Drive, Wilshire Boulevard and Santa Monica Boulevard, are best explored on foot. The draw is usually trendy restaurants, upscale boutiques such as Gucci, Tiffany & Co. and Cartier and star gazing at celebrities. Near Rodeo Drive, the impressive **Museum of Television & Radio**, contains a collection of more than 90,000 television and radio programs as well as commercials at 465 N. Beverly Drive. "**Star Maps**," which are mostly sold along Sunset Boulevard, detail who has lived in which Beverly Hills mansions since the 1920s. However, it is equally fun to simply drive through the palm-lined streets and appreciate the opulence from a car window. The **Beverly Wilshire Hotel** is another notable neighborhood landmark at 9500 Wilshire Boulevard. The hotel can be reached at 310-275-5280.

Hollywood is not nearly as glamorous as one might expect, however, it is the birthplace of the west coast film industry and where movie stars are born. Most notably, it is home to several major studios, **Mann's Chinese Theatre** at 6925 Hollywood Boulevard and the **Hollywood**  **Walk of Fame**. Movies are still screened in the historic theater known for years as "Grauman's." At the theater's entrance, visitors can place their hands and feet in the cement imprints of several cinematic greats and then walk in either direction to follow the famous bronze and pink marble stars that decorate the sidewalks of Hollywood Boulevard. **The Hollywood Entertainment Museum** at 7021 Hollywood Boulevard showcases several entertainment industry exhibits and is home to the sets of *Cheers* and *Star Trek: The Next Generation*. The new **Kodak Theater** at Hollywood and Highland is home to the annual Oscar Awards Ceremony. The surrounding entertainment complex offers shopping and dining year-round.

GRIFFITH PARK

Griffith Park is L.A.'s 4,000-acre backyard with hiking and equestrian trails, golf courses, playgrounds and picnic areas. Anyone can enjoy horse back riding by renting from any of the stables outside the park near Riverside Drive. There are pony rides for children near the Los Feliz Boulevard entrance. Children and adults alike appreciate the 1926 vintage carousel with its painted wooden horses. Locomotive and automotive buffs value the

free vintage displays at **Travel Town Museum** and Live Steamers along Zoo Drive. Summer concerts are often held at the outdoor **Greek Theatre** at 2700 Vermont Street. Call 323-665-1927 for concert details. Park headquarters is at 4730 Crystal Springs Drive for further information.

Griffith Observatory & Planetarium is a major draw to the park with its fantastic view of the city at 2800 E. Observatory Road. The 1935 art-deco observatory hosts laserium shows set to music in the copper-domed planetarium. Educational astronomy displays decorate the Hall of Science complete with a Foucault pendulum. Visit www.griffithobs.org or call 323-664-1191 for further information. The **Autry Museum of Western Heritage** at 4700 Western Heritage Way and the **Los Angeles Zoo** at 5333 Zoo Drive are other major attractions within the park. Call the museum at 323-667-2000 and zoo at 323-644-4200. Visit www.lazoo.org for further information.

That famous **Hollywood Sign** can be seen from Griffith Park. Exit Los Feliz Boulevard at any of the park entrances and connect to Mount Hollywood Drive. From Mount Hollywood Drive, follow the road that leads to the summit of Mount Hollywood. The Hollywood sign is to the west, just south of Cahuenga Peak and Mount Lee.

WEST L.A.

Just inland from the beach and west of Hollywood, this desirable neighborhood is loaded with museums, graced with the beautiful **University of California at Los Angeles** campus and near the foothills of the Santa Monica Mountains. The Miracle Mile along Wilshire Boulevard is a major draw for visitors with several restaurants, the La Brea Tar Pits and the three block Museum Row.

Just east of Fairfax Avenue, **Museum Row** features the **Los Angeles County Museum of Art (LACMA)** at 5905 Wilshire Boulevard, the **Craft & Folk Art Museum** at 5814 Wilshire Boulevard, the **Peterson Automotive Museum** at 6060 Wilshire Boulevard and the **Museum of Miniatures** at 5900 Wilshire Boulevard. The powerful **Museum of Tolerance** is nearby at 9786 West Pico Boulevard.

The **La Brea Tar Pits** at 5801 Wilshire Boulevard feature what can best be described as 40,000-year-old bubbling asphalt ponds that attracted thousands of Ice Age animals who were trapped in the sticky black tar. Today, paleontologists continue to excavate the large collection of Pleistocene fossils from the tar pits. The museum displays the reconstructed fossil skeletons. Call 323-934-7243 for further information.

Will Rogers State Historic Park at 14253 Sunset Boulevard in the Santa Monica foothills is a popular destination for picnics and mountain hikes. The 180-acre estate was once the actor's home. The 31-room house is open to visitors curious to see the original furnishings as well as career memorabilia of the cowboy humorist. Call 310-454-8212 for details.

In Culver City, the 2-hour walking **Sony Pictures Studio Tour** highlights the Hollywood glory days on the former site of MGM Studios. The working studio allows visitors to get a sneak peek at television and movie programs while in production and highlights high-tech movie innovations. Tour reservations are required. The studio is at 10202 W. Washington Boulevard. Call 323-520-8687 for details.

The Getty Center

There are several reasons to visit "the Getty." The hilltop location with stunning views, the striking architecture of white marble and shiny metal, the gardens and, of course, the art name a few. Seven pavilions, each dedicated to a specific art history period, comprise the museum. Everything from Greek statuary to 20th-century photographs to Impressionist paintings decorate the walls. Among the most popular attraction is Van Gogh's "Irises". A café with outdoor seating and several porches offer ocean views.

Location: 1200 Getty Center Drive, Los Angeles
Admission: Free. Parking reservations must be made in
            advance for $5/Vehicle
Hours: Tues-Wed 11am-7pm. Thurs-Fri 11am-9pm.
            Sat-Sun 10am-6pm
Phone: 310-440-7300
Website: www.getty.edu

HOW TO GET THERE

Exit the 405 Freeway at Getty Center Drive (north of Sunset Boulevard) and proceed to the parking lot. A five minute tram ride from the parking lot delivers visitors to the museum.

West Los Angeles

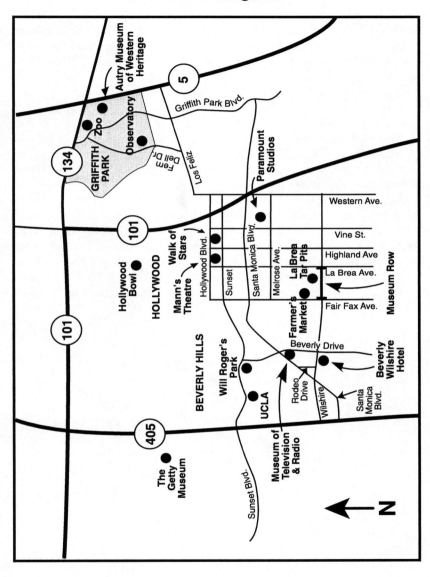

BURBANK & UNIVERSAL CITY

Burbank's best known attraction is Universal Studios & Citywalk, however Warner Brothers and NBC also offer public studio tours. Burbank is the headquarters address for many entertainment giants, including Disney. As such, there is a good chance of running into an entertainment powerhouse or recognizable star doing business in Burbank.

NBC Studios Tour is a 75-minute guided tour that departs on the hour Monday through Friday 9am-3pm on a first-come, first-serve basis at 3000 W. Alameda Avenue. Call 818-840-3537 for details. For a chance to be part of the "Tonight Show with Jay Leno" audience, call 818-840-3537 for tickets. **Warner Brothers Studios V.I.P. Tour** is a 2-hour driving and walking tour through the 1925 studio's backlot street sets. Reservations are required for the tour, which depart on the half-hour Monday through Friday 9am-3pm at 4210 W. Olive Avenue. Call 818-972-8687 for details. **Audiences Unlimited, Inc.** and **Television Tickets** distribute free tickets for TV tapings produced by ABC, CBS, NBC, Fox, UPN, WB and Nickelodeon. Tickets are typically distributed starting 30 days prior to the show date. Call Audiences Unlimited at 818-753-3470 and Television Tickets at 323-467-4697.

Universal Studios & Citywalk

At 420 acres, Universal Studios movie-based theme park is a day in itself. A tram carries visitors across an enormous backlot and rides recreate movie experiences such as E.T. Adventure, Jurassic Park The Ride and Backdraft. Live-action shows like Waterworld and Terminator 2:3D are other highlights.

Universal Citywalk is a free entertainment complex popular for nightlife with restaurants, shops, night clubs and a movie theater. Vintage neon signs, magicians, comedians, and lively streets create a festive spirit. Citywalk is open daily 11am-9pm and until 11pm on Friday and Saturday.

Location:	100 Universal City Plaza, Universal City
Admission:	General-$36; Seniors(59+)-$29;
	Youth(3-11)-$26; Parking-$6/Vehicle
Hours:	Summer: Daily 8am-10pm
	Rest of Year: Daily 9am-7pm
	Closed Thanksgiving & Dec 25
Phone:	818-622-3801
Website:	www.universalstudios.com

HOW TO GET THERE
Exit Interstate 5 at Freeway 101 and proceed north. Exit Freeway 101 at Universal Center Drive and turn right to the park.

PASADENA

Famous for the annual **Tournament of Roses Parade** and **Rose Bowl** on New Year's Day, Pasadena is well-known. The city is graced with a quaint **Old Town** district with trendy eateries, endless shopping and a thriving nightlife. A drive through Pasadena's many neighborhoods reveals stunning architecture and large, beautiful old trees. **Gamble House** is one of the city's architectural treasures designed by the famous Pasadena architects known as Greene & Greene. The 1908 house showcases detailed carved wood  mouldings, hand-worked beams, custom-designed furniture and Tiffany glass windows at 4 Westmoreland Place. Call 626-793-3334 for details.

The **Norton Simon Museum** boasts pieces by several masters including Degas, Monet, Rembrant, Renoir, Picasso, Van Gogh and Diego Rivera. The museum gardens are graced by sculptures from Henry Moore and Auguste Rodin. The museum is at 411 W. Colorado Boulevard. Call 626-449-6840 or visit www.nortonsimon.org for more information.

Los Angeles County

Huntington Library, Art Collections & Botanical Gardens

What makes this cultural attraction so fantastic is the combination of its treasures. The 207-acre estate was built by railroad tycoon Henry Huntington and housed his impressive book and art collection. There are twelve magnificent gardens that cover 140 acres. The fragrant Rose Garden and the Japanese Garden are favorites, however the Desert Garden and Shakespearean Garden are equally impressive. The art collection is primarily 18th century English and French art, including the famous "Blue Boy" by Gainsborough and "Pinkie" by Lawrence. Next door to the art collection are incredible rare and valuable manuscripts from nine centuries of literature. A Gutenberg Bible, original printings of Shakespeare's plays and a folio edition of Audubon's "Birds of America" are highlights. Moreover, handwritten letters by George Washington and Thomas Jefferson are accompanied by a handwritten autobiography by Benjamin Franklin. The historical significance of the collection is remarkable. A very nice high tea is offered in the afternoon.

Location: 1151 Oxford Road, San Marino
Admission: General-$8.50; Seniors(65+)-$7;
Students (with ID)-$4;Under 13-Free
Free 1st Thursday every month
Hours: Tues-Fri 12pm-4:30pm, Sat-Sun 10:30am-4:30pm
Phone: 626-405-2141
Website: www.huntington.org

HOW TO GET THERE
Take I-15 North to I-10 East to the 210 Freeway and proceed north. Exit the 210 at Hill Avenue and proceed south. Turn left at California Boulevard. Turn right at Allen Avenue and proceed to the entrance.

SAN FERNANDO VALLEY

"The Valley" lies just north of Los Angeles surrounded by the Santa Monica and Santa Susana Mountains. Most people access the valley for outdoor recreation. Several historic buildings relate the areas past, such as **Los Encinos State Historic Park** at 16756 Moorpark Street, which can be reached at 818-784-4849, **Mission San Fernando Rey De Espana** at 15151 San Fernando Mission Boulevard, which can be reached at 818-361-0186 and **Orcutt Ranch Horticultural Center** at 23600 Roscoe Boulevard, which can be reached at 818-883-6641.

Paramount Ranch

The very beginning of Hollywood is preserved by the National Park Service at Paramount Ranch. Remains of old movie sets can be seen at the site where some of the earliest westerns were shot, including *Wells Fargo*, *The Adventures of Marco Polo*, *The Cisco Kid*, *Have Gun Will Travel* and *Bat Masterson*.

In the early twenties, Paramount Pictures bought 4,000 acres of ranch land with rolling hills, streams, oak trees and a real working ranch to produce programs with realistic settings. Due to the distance from the studio, the ranch became a city unto itself. Bunkhouses and a commissary were built to accommodate over 500 workers, actors, cameramen and technicians. Paramount sold the ranch in 1948. The present 326 acre site was purchased by the park service in 1980 and opened to the public in 1981.

Location:	Cornell Road, east of Kanan Road, Agoura
Admission:	Free
Hours:	Daily Dawn-Dusk
Phone:	805-370-2301 National Park Service

HOW TO GET THERE

Exit I-5 at Freeway 101 and proceed north. Exit the 101 Freeway at Kanan Road and proceed south . Turn left at the sign reading Cornell Way/Sideway and veer right onto Cornell Road. Continue south to the park entrance on the right.

Los Angeles County

Six Flags Magic Mountain
& Hurricane Harbor

Roller coaster enthusiast and adrenaline seekers get hyped over a visit to
Magic Mountain. The park has over 100 rides
with the most popular thrills being the Viper
coaster, the Tidal Wave, the Goliath coaster and
the Ninja coaster. The park boasts fifteen
extreme roller coasters for true daredevils.
Some rides reach speeds of 85 miles per hour,
many have tight banked turns, and some
involve free falls and dives of 255 feet.

Adjacent to Magic Mountain, Hurricane
Harbor is a 12-acre water park open May
through September. The park features 22 speed
slides and other water adventures.

A combination ticket is available for admission
to both parks.

Location:	26101 Magic Mountain Parkway, Valencia
Admission:	Magic Mountain:
	Over 47"-$39.99; Under 48"-$19.99;
	Seniors(55+)-$19.99; Under 2-Free
	Hurricane Harbor:
	Over 47"-$19.99; Under 48"-$12.99;
	Seniors(55+)-$12.99; Under 2-Free
	Combination Ticket-$49.99
	Parking-$7/Vehicle
Hours:	Magic Mountain: Daily 10am. Closing times vary
	Hurricane Harbor: Daily 10am-9pm during
	Summer. Weekends rest of year
Phone:	661-225-4111
Website:	www.sixflags.com

HOW TO GET THERE

Exit I-5 in Valencia at Magic Mountain Parkway and turn left at the light.
Proceed to the park.

Burbank, Pasadena & San Fernando Valley

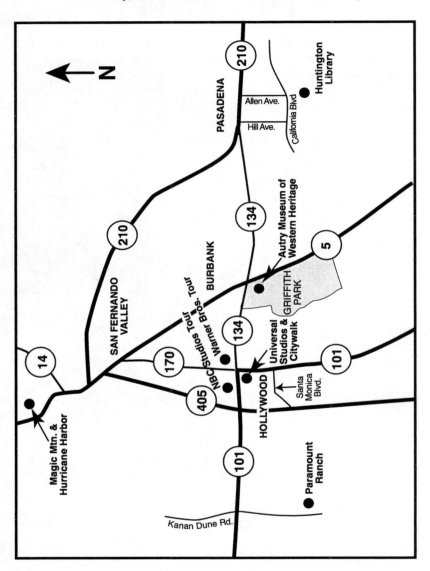

COASTAL L.A.

Malibu offers a cherished section of the Pacific Coast Highway winding between side-by-side beaches and mountains. A drive south from Malibu to Santa Monica provides clear views of the curving coastline speckled with charming beach shacks and desirable mansions along 27 narrow miles.

Several beaches line Malibu's coast including **Las Tunas**, **Topanga** and **Will Rogers** state beaches, **Zuma Beach** and **Surfrider Beach** near **Malibu Pier**. The **Santa Monica Mountains Recreation Area** preserves some of the best natural areas for outdoor enthusiasts. **Point Magu State Park** encompasses three beaches and more than fifty miles of hiking trails, including Overlook Trail with its incredible ocean views. To reach the park, exit PCH at Sycamore Canyon Road. **Charmalee County Natural Area** also provides ocean views from the bluff top Ocean Vista Trail. To reach Charmalee, exit PCH at Encinal Canyon Road. **Malibu Lagoon House & Historic Adamson House** at 23200 Pacific Coast Highway is a worthwhile stop to learn Malibu's history from its Chumash Indian roots to its celebrity status today. Call 310-456-8432 for details.

Santa Monica is graced with beautiful palm-lined, bluff-top **Palisades Park** overlooking the ocean, a wooden pier noted for its giant Ferris wheel, wide sandy beaches and the popular **Third Street Promenade** pedestrian mall. A 22-mile cement path coined the **South Bay Bicycle Trail** connects the pier to the city of Torrance.

Venice offers a more eclectic and bohemian atmosphere than L.A.'s other beach communities. Nowhere is this more evident than along the "anything goes" **Ocean Front Walk** packed with colorful characters in everything from bikinis to costumes. Biking or roller blading the famed beach boardwalk is a favorite local pastime.

More than 10,000 boats are docked in **Marina Del Rey's** yacht harbor. The area is tailored to sailing, boating and fishing. **Fisherman's Village** offers restaurants, specialty shops and waterfront walkways with New-England ambiance.

Smaller, more residential beach communities lie south of Marina del Rey. **Manhattan Beach**, **Hermosa Beach** and **Redondo Beach** all offer miles of sand and sea, as well as friendly restaurants and sidewalk shops worth exploring.

Coastal Los Angeles

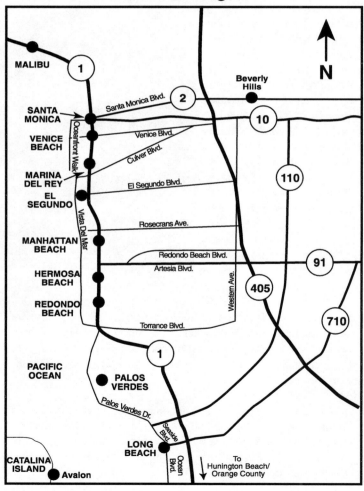

Los Angeles County

LONG BEACH & SOUTH BAY

Five miles of white-sand beaches give this waterfront playground its name. Long Beach is a popular destination for sailing, windsurfing, jet skiing and sea kayaking. It is also the primary launching point for the 22-mile jaunt across the ocean to **Catalina Island**, famous for buffalo burgers and glass bottom boats. The city's largest harbor attraction is the **Queen Mary**. Other draws are the grassy parks, the long bike path, the museums and aquarium and the quaint shops and restaurants at Shoreline Village.

The best beaches can be found just south of downtown at **Belmont Shores Peninsula**. Further south along Ocean Boulevard, **Alamitos Bay State Park** is a bayside beach option near the town of Seal Beach. **Ocean Boulevard** is a main thoroughfare with endless attractions and entertainment. On Fridays, a popular outdoor Farmers Market runs from 10am-4pm at the **Downtown Promenade**.

Just south of the busy Los Angeles Harbor, three major attractions draw visitors: the Queen Mary, Aquarium of the Pacific and Long Beach Museum of Art. The **Queen Mary** is an impressive spectacle with a 365-room hotel on board, several fine restaurants that require reservations and even a wedding chapel. Visitors are welcome to take a self-guided tour, but a guided

tour is worthwhile for behind-the-scenes access. The boat is docked at 1126 Queens Highway. Call 562-435-3511 for details. Nearby, off Shoreline Drive, **Aquarium of the Pacific** is one the country's largest marine exhibits with more than 10,000 varieties of sea life in several gigantic multilevel tanks at 100 Aquarium Way. For further information and details, visit www.aquariumofpacific.org or call 562-590-3100. A seawall and 2-story esplanade outside the aquarium has dozens of shops and restaurants. The **Long Beach Museum of Art**

is located on a bluff-top site overlooking the Pacific Ocean and Long Beach harbor. The museum galleries are complemented by oceanview gardens, historic building, a museum store and a cafe. The museum is open Tuesday through Sunday. Call 562-439-2119 or visit www.lbma.org for details.

For those seeking a unique experience, visit the area in mid-April when the city streets are converted into a race track for the **Long Beach Grand Prix** or indulge in **The Gondola Getaway** any day of the year. The romantic Gondola Getaway offers authentic rides through the Naples Island canals in Italian-style gondolas, complete with gondoliers and Italian classical music. The adventure starts at 5437 East Ocean Boulevard. Call 562-433-9595 for details.

Just north of Long Beach, the Los Angeles Harbor is the busiest import/export port in the United States. Watching the port in action, it is hard to believe it was man-made in the 1880s. Fantastic views of the port, as well as Catalina Island and the coastline can be had at the 64-acre grassy hill top **Angeles Gate Park**. Along the water, the harbor activity can be watched from **Ports O'Call Village** with its 19th century seaport ambiance and cobblestone streets. The village features restaurants and specialty shops. Several educational marine and military museums near the port are open to the public. **Los Angeles Maritime Museum** located on Berth 84 at 6th Street can be reached at 310-548-7618. **Cabrillo Marine Aquarium** at 3720 Stephen White Drive can be reached at 310-548-7562. **Fort MacArthur Military Museum** at 3601 S. Gaffey Street can be reached at 310-548-2631 and the **Marine Mammal Care Center** at 3601 S. Gaffey Street can be reached at 310-548-5677.

North of San Pedro and the Los Angeles Harbor, the exclusive **Palos Verdes Peninsula** draws visitors for dramatic views of the ocean, especially January to April when the Pacific gray whales migrate south to Baja, Mexico. A favorite viewing point is the **Point Vincente Lighthouse & Interpretive Center** at 31501 Palos Verdes Drive West. Call 310-377-5370 for lighthouse information. Other area attractions include **South Coast Botanic Gardens** at 26300 Crenshaw Boulevard and **Wayfarer's Chapel** built of glass, stone and redwood beams by Frank Lloyd Wright's son at 5755 Palos Verdes Drive South. The gardens can be reached at 310-544-6815 and the chapel can be reached at 310-377-1650.

Catalina Island

The friendly, single-town island of Santa Catalina off the Southern California coast is home to only 3,000 year-round residents. William Wrigley, Jr., famous for Wrigley's chewing gum, owned the island and developed it into the resort town it is today. Visitors can take a self-guided tour of the Wrigley Memorial & Botanical Gardens.

The island has several interesting bits of trivia. For instance, the Chicago Cubs used the island as a spring training facility at one time. More commonly known is the fact that the famous circular Casino in Avalon roared during the 1930s and 1940s when the Avalon Ballroom hosted Big Band dances. Today, guided tours of the casino provide a good overview of the island's history.

There are endless tours to choose from catering to the various interests of visitors. Catalina Adventure Tours offers day and night glass bottom boat excursions, harbor cruises and an "Inland Motor Tour" on buses that wind through the island's mountainous interior. Call them at 310-510-2888.

Discovery Tours also offers glass bottom boat tours day or night and a nightly "Flying Fish Boat Trip" that uses searchlights to spot fish using their wings to glide hundreds of feet. They also offer a semi-submersible submarine tour called the "Undersea Catalina Adventure". Call them at 310-510-2500.

Catalina Kayak Adventures and Catalina Island Expeditions offer guided kayak tours. Catalina Ocean Rafting uses 24-foot inflatable rafts to provide high speed trips to isolated coves for snorkeling. This outfitter also offers the "Inland Motor Tour." Call Kayak Adventures at 310-510-2229, Island Expeditions at 310-510-1226 and Ocean Rafting at 800-990-7238.

Along the shore, visitors sunbathe on the beach and partake in sailing, kayaking, scuba, snorkeling, boating, deep sea and pier fishing. A trail system wraps through the island, offering hikers, bikers and equestrians plenty of space to explore.

The island can accommodate a perfect day trip or a few nights stay. There are less than 20 hotels on the island and some small cottages for rent, so it is advisable to plan ahead for overnight stays. Transportation rentals are limited to bikes and golf carts. To reach the island, you must make a reservation with one of several cruise companies for the one to two hour trip or reserve a zippy 14 minute ride with Island Express Helicopter Service at 310-510-2525. The ride costs $66 one-way or $121 round-trip. Boat trips range in price from $27-$38 round-trip for adults and seniors, while children prices are generally $20-$28.50 and infants $1-$2. Catalina Cruises which can be reached at 800-228-2546 and Catalina Express which can be reached at 800-805-9201 depart out of Long Beach. Catalina Express offers a one-way fare as well and also provides service out of San Pedro. Catalina Explorer which can be reached at 949-492-5308 departs out of Orange County's Dana Point and Catalina Passenger Service which can be reached at 949-673-5245 makes one crossing daily out of Newport Beach's Balboa Pavilion in Orange County.

Phone:	310-510-1520 Visitors Bureau
	310-510-2595 Hiking & Camping Permits
Website:	www.catalina.com
	www.visitcatalina.com

San Bernardino County

- Big Bear
- Lake Arrowhead

San Bernardino County

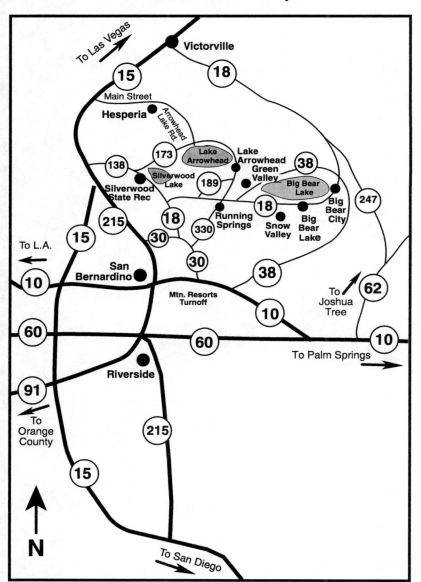

San Bernardino Area
11 - 2

SAN BERNARDINO COUNTY

Much of San Bernardino County is covered by the beautiful San Bernardino National Forest, making the area an alpine wonderland catering to the outdoor enthusiast. The towns of Big Bear and Lake Arrowhead are favorite destinations. These two resort communities lie within 30 miles of each other connected by windy, picturesque mountain roads.

BIG BEAR

While best-known as a Southern California ski resort, Big Bear offers plenty of outdoor recreation year-round with wildflowers in the Spring, warm thunderstorms in the Summer, changing colors in the Fall and snow in the Winter. The lake provides water sport opportunities and the mountains provide plenty of camping, mountain biking, hiking, skiing and snowboarding opportunities.

The Village is where visitors linger in coffee shops, grab a meal or shop. This is also the best place to seek out nightlife, enjoy live entertainment, go bowling or see a movie. The area is usually buzzing with special activities, contests and entertainment. Annual events include **Old Miners Days** western celebration in mid-June and **Oktoberfest** in late October. The Visitors Center in the Village at 630 Bartlett Road can provide more information on area activities and accommodations. They can be reached by calling 800-424-4232 or via their website at www.bigbearinfo.com.

San Bernardino Area
11 - 3

During warm seasons, **Big Bear Lake** is busy with those fishing, sailing, water skiing, wakeboarding, parasailing, canoeing and kayaking. Pine Knot Landing is a good resource for boating details and can be reached at 909-866-2628. There are a number of private boat rental marinas around the lake and two public boat launches. Afternoon lake tours are offered aboard the **Big Bear Queen** out of Big Bear Marina and aboard the **Time Bandit Pirate Ship** out of Holloway Marina. Both tours run an hour and a half. Call 909-866-3218 to reach Big Bear Marina and 909-878-4040 to reach Holloway Marina.

Other warm weather activities include horseback riding, golfing, hiking, biking and camping. **Baldwin Lake Stables** can be reached at 909-585-6482 to arrange horseback rides. Year-round **Victoria Park Carriages** offer nostalgic horse-drawn carriage rides. They can be reached at 909-584-2277. **Bear Mountain Golf Course** has a 9-hole course, pro-shop, driving range, practice green and The Bear Trap Restaurant. It also offers lessons. Call 909-585-8002 to arrange a tee time. The **Big Bear Discovery Center** is knowledgeable about area hiking and camping details. They can be reached at 909-866-3437. At one of Big Bear's three ski resorts, Snow Summit, visitors can take a 15 minute ride on the **Scenic Sky Chair** to the 8,200-foot mountain summit and bike or hike down to the base at 7,000 feet. There are more than 40 miles of trails to explore. Visitors are welcome to take the chairlift roundtrip and simply enjoy the breathtaking views and photo opportunities. Call 909-866-5766 for further details. **Bear Valley Bikes** is located just west of the Village and rents mountain bikes. They can be reached at 909-866-8000.

During winter months, downhill and cross-country skiing, snowboarding and snowshoeing are the activities of choice. There are several area resorts to choose from. Those seeking lessons before braving the mountains, can contact **Ski School** at 909-866-4546. It is always a good idea to have chains when visiting the resorts during snow season. For Big Bear area road conditions, call 909-866-7623. The National Weather Service also provides weather condition reports via phone at 213-554-1212.

HOW TO GET THERE

Take I-15 North to I-215 North. Exit I-215 at I-10 East. Exit I-10 East at Highway 30 labeled "Mountain Resorts/Running Springs" and proceed north. Exit Highway 30 at Highway 330 and proceed east. Highway 330 turns into Highway 18. Proceed east along Highway 18 up the mountain to the Big Bear area.

Area Ski Resorts

Bear Mountain

At a base elevation of 7,140 feet, Bear Mountain mostly caters to the mid-level skier with half of the trails labeled as blue runs. The remaining half is equally divided between green runs for beginners and black diamond runs for advanced skiers. There are nine chair lifts and 195 skiable acres with off-trail terrain as well. Geronimo is the longest run at 1.89 miles.

Location:	4310 Goldmine Drive, Big Bear Lake
Admission:	Prices vary. Holiday rates are slightly higher
	Regular season pricing is roughly:
	General-$48; Youth(13-21)-$36; Youth(7-12)-$15;
	Under 7-Free
Hours:	Daily 8:30am-4pm
Phone:	909-585-2519
Website:	www.bigbearmountainresorts.com

HOW TO GET THERE

Take I-15 North to I-215 North. Exit I-215 at I-10 East. Exit I-10 East at Highway 30 labeled "Mountain Resorts/Running Springs" and proceed north. Exit Highway 30 at Highway 330 and proceed east. Highway 330 turns into Highway 18. Proceed east along Highway 18 up the mountain to the Big Bear area. Turn right at the dam and proceed into town along Big Bear Boulevard. Turn right at Moonridge Road. Stay to the right and follow signs to Bear Mountain.

Snow Summit

Snow Summit has 31 runs catering mostly to mid-level blue run skiers and advanced black diamond skiers. The 230 skiable acres start at a base elevation of 7,000 feet. There are 11 chair lifts and Westridge is the longest run at 1.25 miles. Steep drops are accessible via the Olympic, The Wall and Side Chute runs. Beginners will appreciate Skyline Creek, Mainstream and

Summit. Night skiing is offered 3pm-9:30pm on Friday, Saturday and holidays.

Location:	880 Summit Boulevard, Big Bear Lake
Admission:	Prices vary. Holiday rates are slightly higher Regular season pricing is roughly: General-$48; Youth(13-21)-$36; Youth(7-12)-$15; Under 7-Free
Hours:	Mon-Fri 8:30am-4:30pm; Sat-Sun & Holidays 7:30am-6pm
Phone:	909-866-5766
Website:	www.bigbearmountainresorts.com

HOW TO GET THERE
Take I-15 North to I-215 North. Exit I-215 at I-10 East. Exit I-10 East at Highway 30 labeled "Mountain Resorts/Running Springs" and proceed north. Exit Highway 30 at Highway 330 and proceed east. Highway 330 turns into Highway 18. Proceed east along Highway 18 to Big Bear. Turn right at the dam and proceed into town along Big Bear Boulevard. Turn right at Summit Boulevard and proceed to the resort.

Snow Valley
Snow Valley features 240 skiable acres at a base elevation of 6,800 feet. There are 11 chair lifts and 30 runs catering to all levels of skiing and snowboarding. The longest run is 1.25 miles. The mountain features an all-terrain board park and two winter terrain half pipes. Half days start at noon. When night skiing is available, the slopes remain open until 9pm. There are bars and restaurants at the mountain base.

Location:	35100 Highway 18, Running Springs
Admission:	Prices vary. Holiday rates are slightly higher Regular season pricing is roughly: General-$42; Youth(6-12)-$15; Under 6-Free; Seniors(65+)-$30; Over 69-Free
Hours:	Daily 8am-4pm
Phone:	909-867-2751 800-680-7669 Snow Report
Website:	www.snow-valley.com

HOW TO GET THERE
Take I-15 North to I-215 North. Exit I-215 at I-10 East. Exit I-10 East at Highway 30 labeled "Mountain Resorts/Running Springs" and proceed north. Highway 30 turns into Highway 18. Snow Valley is located 5 miles east of Running Springs on Highway 18.

San Bernardino Area

Rim Nordic & Green Valley Nordic

Rim Nordic & Green Valley Nordic ski areas provide cross country and snowshoeing trails. There are onsite rentals of skis, boots, poles and snowshoes. Half day starts at 12:30pm. Lessons are offered on weekends at 10:30am and 1pm.

Location:	Highway 18, 5 miles east of Running Springs
Admission:	General-$15; Youth-$10; Under 11-Free
Hours:	Daily 9am-4pm
Phone:	909-867-2600
Website:	www.rimnordic.com

HOW TO GET THERE

Take I-15 North to I-215 North. Exit I-215 at I-10 East. Exit I-10 East at Highway 30 labeled "Mountain Resorts/Running Springs" and proceed north. Highway 30 turns into Highway 18. Rim Nordic & Green Valley Nordic is located 5 miles east of Running Springs on Highway 18 near Snow Valley.

Mountain High

Northwest of the Big Bear area, Mountain High is another nearby ski resort at 6,600 feet. Two mountains, East Resort and West Resort, comprise the ski area. Both mountain summits reach 8,000 feet. There are 220 skiable acres with 46 trails and ten lifts. Seventy-five percent of the mountain is groomed for intermediate and advanced skiers, while the remaining twenty-five percent caters to beginners. Lessons are offered at the mountain. The mountain is generally open early November to late April. The resorts have ski shops, rentals and restaurants. The mountain lodge keeps the same hours as the slopes. Night skiing is available 5pm-10pm and costs much less than the 4- and 8-hour flex tickets offered for day skiing.

Location:	24510 Highway 2, Wrightwood
Admission:	General-$40-45; Youth-$17; Under 7-Free; Over 69-Free
Hours:	Daily 8:30am-10pm
Phone:	760-249-5808 888-754-7878 Snow Report
Website:	www.mthigh.com

HOW TO GET THERE

Exit I-15 North at Highway 138 West. Turn left at Highway 2 and proceed three miles past Wrightwood.

San Bernardino Area

Day Outings From San Diego

LAKE ARROWHEAD

Lake Arrowhead's close proximity to several cities makes it a favorite weekend escape or day trip destination. With clean air and mountain scenery, most visitors make the journey for the area's outdoor recreational activities. There is endless hiking, biking and camping. The lake that gives the area its name is privately owned by Arrowhead Woods residents so lake use is very limited. However, Lake Arrowhead Village features a marina and swimming beach on the lake. At the marina, visitors can rent canoes, bumper boats, motorboats and water skis for lake use. There is also plenty of stream fishing in the area. The marina can be reached at 909-337-2553.

Lake Arrowhead Village has several shops, restaurants and attractions. During summer months, the popular **Arrowhead Queen Boat Tour** carries up to sixty passengers on a 50-minute cruise aboard the sternwheeler from 11am-5pm. On weekends there is an additional departure at 10am. Call 909-336-6992 for further details. A train ride around the peninsula, an antique carousel and **Lake Arrowhead Children's Museum** are other popular Village attractions. The museum, which features hands-on learning exhibits, can be reached at 909-336-3093. Music concerts and special events are common to the Village, especially during holidays. The Village is generally open 10am-5:30pm Sunday through Thursday and until 8pm on Friday and Saturday. The Visitor Center & Chamber of Commerce are located in the Village and can be reached at 909-337-3715.

Adventurous spirits can indulge in an alpine paragliding adventure with **Paragliding Adventures**. Call 909-338-4099 or visit www.flyaglider.com for inquiries about tandem flights or to make a reservation. **Above & Beyond Sports** rents mountain bikes at 26898 Highway 189 in Agua Fria and can be reached by calling 909-336-3732.

HOW TO GET THERE

Take I-15 North to I-215 North. Exit I-215 at I-10 East. Exit I-10 East at Highway 30 labeled "Mountain Resorts/Running Springs" and proceed north. Exit Highway 30 at Waterman Avenue North and follow signs to Lake Arrowhead.

San Bernardino Area

11 - 8

Silverwood Lake State Recreation Area

This outdoor wonderland situated at 3,350 feet is graced by a beautiful reservoir lake created by Cedar Springs Dam. The lake is a wonderful place to fish, boat, water-ski, windsurf or swim. Picnic locations are scattered throughout the park, including three areas accessed only by boat. The lake is stocked with trout, large-mouth bass, catfish and bluegill. There is a marina and floating dock with rentals and a convenience store.

There are heavily forested primitive areas perfect for camping, hiking and mountain biking. The impressive Pacific Crest Trail, which spans the western United States from Mexico to Canada, runs through the Silverwood Lake area. The Visitor Center can provide trail details. Campsites accommodate up to eight people in either tents or RVs up to thirty-four feet. Licensed dogs are allowed free of charge, but must be on a leash at all times.

Location:	14651 Cedra Circle, Hesperia
Admission:	Day Use-$5/Vehicle
	Camping-$13/Night
Hours:	Office: Mon-Fri 8am-4:30pm
	Recreation Area: Summer 6am-9pm;
	Winter 7am-7pm
Phone:	760-389-2303
	800-444-7275 Camping Reservations
Website:	www.parks.ca.gov

HOW TO GET THERE
Take I-15 and exit at Route 138 (about 35 miles north of San Bernardino). Proceed east on Route 138 for roughly 11 miles to the lake.

Baja California, MEXICO

- **Ensenada**
- **Rosarito**
- **Tecate**
- **Tijuana**

BAJA CALIFORNIA, MEXICO

Just a short drive or trolley ride from downtown San Diego is a whole new world waiting to be explored. Well, a whole new country. The San Diego-Mexico border is the busiest in the world. Tourists visit Tijuana to shop, Rosarito to relax at the beach, Ensenada to sample the libations of Mexico's wine country and Tecate to tour one very famous brewery known for inspiring a twist of lime with a Mexican beer.

Baja California offers endless activities and destinations for those that enjoy the sun and the sand. Most visitors travel along Baja's Gold Coast stopping in towns that line the Pacific Ocean. However, more secluded beaches and less developed towns hug the gulf side of Baja along the Sea of Cortes. For further details on the peninsula, visit www.discoverbajacalifornia.com.

Trips of three days or less do not require a passport or tourist card. However, it is important to carry a photo I.D. at all times. It is advisable to obtain a tourist card when traveling south of Ensenada. Anyone taking a car across the border should purchase automobile insurance from AAA or another reputable agent. Mexican officials do not recognize U.S. liability insurance. There are several companies that provide tours of Tijuana and Baja from San Diego for those unsure about driving in Mexico. One such outfitter is San Diego Scenic Tours. Visit www.sandiegoscenictours.com or call 858-273-8687 for details.

The trolley is another option for trips to Tijuana. The Blue Line has a stop in San Ysidro at the Mexican border. Call 619-231-8549 or 619-233-3004 for further information. When calling Mexico, remember to dial the 011 international access code and then Mexico's country code, 52. Then dial the area code/city code and phone number.

Northern Baja, California

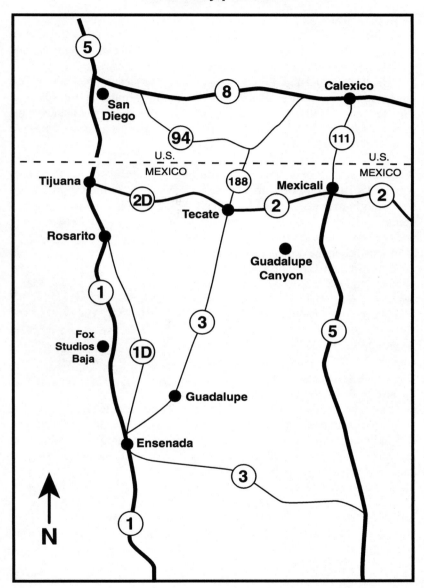

ENSENADA

Ensenada is a well-established port city often decorated by large cruise ships hauling in visitors anxious to shop along **Avenida Lopez Mateos** and indulge in authentic fish tacos. A walk along the waterfront promenade to historic **Riviera del Pacifico** is worthwhile. The beautiful buildings that now comprise a cultural center were originally a hotel and casino that attracted many Hollywood greats. Boxer Jack Dempsey even managed the casino at one time. The architecture and surrounding gardens make it a favored destination today.

A few miles south of downtown, **Punta Banda** peninsula boasts the wildly popular **La Bufadora** blowhole, loosely meaning "the buffalo snort." When the ocean is rough, foam and water spit through the headlands to create a dramatic display of powerful waves. Equally luring is nearby **El Mirador**, a well-known overlook with incredible views of Ensenada and the ocean. Punta Banda is a good destination for snorkeling and scuba diving. Along the piers, local outfitters offer organized sportsfishing trips and seasonal whale watching adventures.

Ensenada is the heart of Mexico's wine country. While most vineyards are in nearby Guadalupe Valley, the well-known **Bodegas de Santo Tomas** winery offers tours and tastings downtown at 666 Avenida Miramar. Thirty minute tours are offered daily at certain times between 10am-3pm. Tours cost roughly $3.00 per person and include four tastings. The winery produces chardonnay, pinot noir and cabernet. For a few dollars more, visitors can take home a souvenir glass and enjoy triple the tastings. Call (011)(52)(6)178-3333 or (011)(52)(6)178-2509 to reach the winery.

Ensenada comes alive each February for its popular **Carnaval** festival and hosts the finish-line party for the Rosarito-Ensenada bicycle rides each April and September. Visit www.enjoyensenada.com for further details.

Guadalupe Valley Wineries

Ninety percent of Mexico's wine is produced in Ensenada and its surrounding valleys. The climate makes it a perfect place to produce several red and white varieties, as well as port, sherry, sparkling wine and brandies. Typically, visitors may purchase up to two bottles duty-free. Purchases of three or more bottles will be charged a 3-10% duty. Every August a wine harvest festival called Fiesta de La Vendimia is held with food, tastings, tours and music at several wineries. In Mexico, wine is properly called *vino de uva* rather than vino, which refers to all alcoholic beverages.

L.A. Cetto

The winery provides tours that relate the region's history and winemaking process. Guests are welcome to sample the winery's various vintages. L.A. Cetto wine prices are between $9 and $20 per bottle. Purchases are cash only. There is also a Tijuana branch that offers tours and tasting for $2 per person.

Location:	Km 73 on Highway 3, near Guadalupe
Admission:	Free
Hours:	Daily 9am-5pm
Phone:	(011)(52)(6)685-3031
Website:	www.lacetto.com.mx

Domecq

This large winery actually presses grapes from all over the Baja peninsula. Tours and tastings are available.

Location:	Km 73 on Highway 3, near Guadalupe
Admission:	Free. Tastings: Roughly $2/Person
Hours:	Weekdays 10am-4pm; Sat 10am-1:30pm
Phone:	(011)(52)(646)155-2249

HOW TO GET THERE

Take I-5 south to the San Ysidro border crossing or take Route 94 west to Route 188 and follow Route 188 south to the Tecate border crossing. The wineries of Guadalupe Valley are along Highway 3 between Ensenada and Tecate. L.A. Cetto and Domecq Winery are near the Km 73 mile marker in the Calafia Wine Valley.

ROSARITO

This friendly coastal town attracts endless visitors with its wide, sandy beaches only 30 minutes from the border. Ocean water sports include everything from surfing and sailing to fishing and kayaking. Horseback riding on the beach is a popular pastime. Horses are usually for hire outside the well-known **Rosarito Beach Hotel**. On weekends and holidays, Rosarito hosts a serious party with endless music, dancing, drinking and even an occasional mechanical bull. Hotels, restaurants and bars are typically packed. Visit www.rosarito.org for further details.

Each September, Rosarito is the starting place for one of North America's largest bike rides, the **Rosarito Ensenada 50 Mile Fun Ride**. Thousands of riders gather in front of the Rosarito Beach Hotel at 10am to begin the ride south to Ensenada where the Finish Line Fiesta takes place. The fiesta starts at 12:30pm and runs till dusk with live music, entertainment, alcohol and food. The ride begins with twelve scenic coastal miles and then two inland miles before reaching the hill with an 800-foot incline and 7.5% grade. Many bikers push their bikes over the two mile hill. The stretch across the hilltop mesa, the descent to the ocean and the final leg south measure eight miles each. For more information on the event, including costs and where to find entry forms, call Bicycling West, Inc. at 619-583-3001 or visit www.rosaritoensenada.com.

Baja California, Mexico

Fox Studios Baja
Foxploration

Fox Studios chose the site of Popotla, three miles south of Rosarito, as the temporary site for the filming of the 1997 James Cameron film *Titanic*. Over the course of filming, the site evolved into a permanent studio. Today, the 40-acre oceanfront studio houses some of Hollywood's largest stages and water tanks for filming. While the stages, dressing rooms and studio offices are separate from Foxploration, visitors have access to an extensive collection of wardrobe, props and sets. Other blockbuster hits filmed at Fox Studios Baja include *Pearl Harbor* and *Tomorrow Never Dies*.

Highlights include a set called Canal Street, reminiscent of a vintage Manhattan city street, and Titanic Expo, a guided tour of the sets, costumes, props and artifacts from the Oscar winning movie. The ship replica has been dismantled. A special effects exhibit called Cinemagico provides insight into the world of sound and animatronics.

Location:	Km 33 on Highway 1, Poptola
Admission:	General-$6
Hours:	Weekends 10am-6pm
Phone:	866-369-2252 U.S. Toll Free
	(011)(52)(661)614-9444 Direct
Website:	www.foxploration.com

HOW TO GET THERE

Take I-5 south to the San Ysidro border crossing or take Route 94 west to Route 188 and follow Route 188 south to the Tecate border crossing. Follow the Ensenada Scenic Road signs along Calle Internacional, which is a toll road. The toll should not exceed $2.50. Continue along Mexico 1D for nearly ten miles to Rosarito. Immediately before the second toll gate, take the fourth and last exit for Rosarito labeled La Paloma, Popotla, Calafia, Las Rocas. Exit to the right and connect to the free Highway 1 and proceed south. Foxploration is before the white arch of Popotla at Km 32.8.

TECATE

Tecate sits right on the U. S. Mexico border, about 34 miles east of Tijuana with its own border crossing open 6am-midnight. However, compared to Tijuana, Tecate is a mild border town with only 50,000 residents compared to Tijuana's millions. It is more reminiscent of a true inland Mexican pueblo. Town activities usually unfold in the tree-lined central plaza known as **Parque Hidalgo**. Visitors often park on the U.S. side and walk across the border to the plaza. Tecate is a favorite town for artisan Mexican crafts, most notably pottery, and bakeries with traditional Mexican pastries. During the second week of August, Tecate hosts **Pamplonada**, a festival celebrating the running of the bulls as done in Pamplona, Spain. In May, thousands visit Tecate for the annual bike race to Ensenada. The Office of Tourism is open weekdays at 1305 Callejon Libertad. Call the Office of Tourism at 619-654-1095 or visit www.tecatemexico.com.mx for further details.

The San Diego Railroad Museum in Campo runs tours to Tecate aboard historic trains on select dates throughout the year. Refer to the East County/ Campo section of the book for details.

Tecate Brewery Tour

The 1944 Cerveceria Cuauhtemoc-Moctezuma brewery churns out up to 1,500 cans per minute of both Tecate and Carta Blanca beer. Many argue Tecate started the slice of lime with a Mexican beer tradition. On some Saturday mornings tours are offered and at times enough coaxing by visitors leads to impromptu tours. Tours are only guaranteed by reservation and groups of at least ten people are preferred. Jardin Cerveza, the beer garden, is typically open Tuesday through Saturday 10am-5pm. In October, the Tecate Brewery Festival brings a parade, tours, food booths and horse races to town.

Location: Avenida Hidalgo between
              De La Huerta and Obregon, Tecate
Admission: Free
Hours: By reservation
Phone: (6)654-1111

HOW TO GET THERE
Take Route 94 west to Route 188. Follow Route 188 south to Tecate.

TIJUANA

This world-renown border-town is Mexico's third largest city and tourism remains its primary source of income. Bearing in mind that Tijuana is the world's busiest border and North America's most visited city, border crossings can last hours. To avoid the hassles involved with bringing a car into Mexico, such as traffic, parking, insurance and violations, many visitors park their car on the U.S. side of the San Ysidro crossing, walk into Mexico and buy an all day TJ Trolley ticket. The **Tijuana Trolley** stops at several tourists destinations, including Avenida Revolucion, Mexitlan, Plaza Fiesta, Agua Caliente Racetrack, Grand Hotel Tijuana and the Tijuana Cultural Center. The bus to Las Playas carries passengers to Tijuana's beaches.

It is a long-held tradition to get a picture taken in sombreros and serapes on a zebra striped mule. Visitors seeking duty-free shopping usually cover the seven-block section of **Avenida Revolucion** lined with shops selling everything from leather goods and crystal crafted silver to sombrero hats and sarape shawls. This area also features night clubs, discotheques, curio shops and several restaurants. **Plaza Fiesta** also has sidewalk cafes, bakeries and shops.

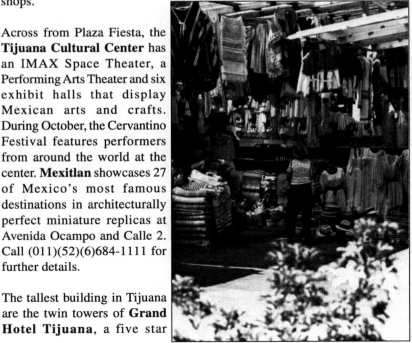

Across from Plaza Fiesta, the **Tijuana Cultural Center** has an IMAX Space Theater, a Performing Arts Theater and six exhibit halls that display Mexican arts and crafts. During October, the Cervantino Festival features performers from around the world at the center. **Mexitlan** showcases 27 of Mexico's most famous destinations in architecturally perfect miniature replicas at Avenida Ocampo and Calle 2. Call (011)(52)(6)684-1111 for further details.

The tallest building in Tijuana are the twin towers of **Grand Hotel Tijuana**, a five star

accommodation with several fine restaurants, trendy boutiques and specialty shops. Call 800-472-6385 for reservations or inquiries.

Greyhound racing at **Agua Caliente Race Track** and bullfights at **El Toro Downtown Bullring** and **Plaza Monumental Bullring-by-the-Sea** are other attractions. The dogs race daily at 7:45pm and on weekends at 2pm. Admission is free. The bullfights take place on Sunday at 4pm in May and July through September. The ticket desk in the Grand Hotel sells bullfight tickets. Rodeos usually take place around town on Sunday afternoons, May through September.

The **Tijuana Tourism & Convention Bureau** can provide further details on the area at 619-298-4105 or 800-522-1516. A good resource for information on the area is www.seetijuana.com. U.S. citizens planning to stay longer than three days or planning to travel farther than 75 miles need proof of citizenship and a Mexican tourist card. U.S auto insurance is not valid in Mexico. It is advisable to purchase Mexico auto liability insurance from an agent on the U.S. side.

HOW TO GET THERE

Take I-5 south to the San Ysidro border through Mexican Customs. Cross the river and turn onto 3rd Street to Avenida Revolucion, the center of the shopping district in Downtown Tijuana.

Tijuana, Mexico

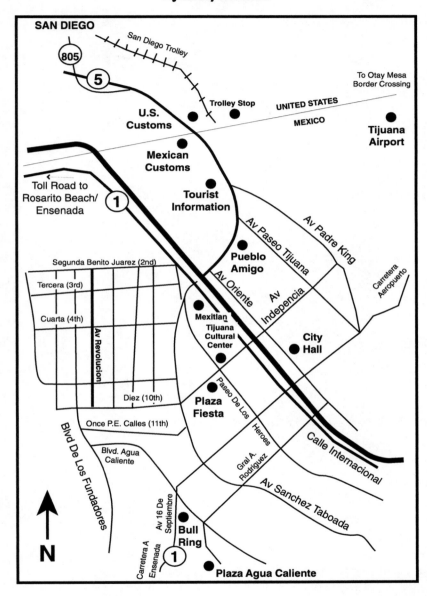

Index by Subject

Animals & Marine Life

Bicycling Scenic Areas

Beaches

Camping/RVing

Hiking & Walking Scenic Areas

Kid's Outings

Missions

Museums & Historical Places

Music, Television & Theatre

Observatories

Skiing & Snow Fun

Theme Parks

Shopping & Eating

More Explore Books Offered by Premier Publishing

Tel: 858.586.7692 • Fax: 858.586.7389
dayoutings@earthlink.net • www.dayoutings.com

Name: _____

Address: _____

City/State/Zip:_____

Phone: _____

Email: _____

Qty	Title	Unit	Price
_____	**Day Outings From SAN DIEGO**	$19.95	$_____
_____	**Day Outings From LOS ANGELES**	$16.95	$_____
_____	**Day Outings From PHOENIX**	$18.95	$_____
_____	**So. California Garden Getaways**	$18.95	$_____
_____	**San Diego: Home Base For Freedom**	$12.95	$_____
_____	**Outdoors San Diego:** **Hiking, Biking & Camping**	$19.95	$_____
_____	**Hidden History: Day Tours in San Diego**	$16.95	$_____
_____	**Beach Walking in San Diego County**	$10.00	$_____
_____	**Street Walking in San Diego County**	$10.00	$_____
	CA Sales Tax (.0775)		$_____
	Shipping & Handling		$____5.00
	TOTAL:		$_____

Make check payable to: Premier Publishing
15721 Bernardo Heights Parkway • Suite B, Box 17 • San Diego, CA 92128